THE PAST AND FUTURE OF INFORMATION SYSTEMS: 1976-2006 AND BEYOND

IFIP – The International Federation for Information Processing

IFIP was founded in 1960 under the auspices of UNESCO, following the First World Computer Congress held in Paris the previous year. An umbrella organization for societies working in information processing, IFIP's aim is two-fold: to support information processing within its member countries and to encourage technology transfer to developing nations. As its mission statement clearly states,

> *IFIP's mission is to be the leading, truly international, apolitical organization which encourages and assists in the development, exploitation and application of information technology for the benefit of all people.*

IFIP is a non-profitmaking organization, run almost solely by 2500 volunteers. It operates through a number of technical committees, which organize events and publications. IFIP's events range from an international congress to local seminars, but the most important are:

• The IFIP World Computer Congress, held every second year;
• Open conferences;
• Working conferences.

The flagship event is the IFIP World Computer Congress, at which both invited and contributed papers are presented. Contributed papers are rigorously refereed and the rejection rate is high.

As with the Congress, participation in the open conferences is open to all and papers may be invited or submitted. Again, submitted papers are stringently refereed.

The working conferences are structured differently. They are usually run by a working group and attendance is small and by invitation only. Their purpose is to create an atmosphere conducive to innovation and development. Refereeing is less rigorous and papers are subjected to extensive group discussion.

Publications arising from IFIP events vary. The papers presented at the IFIP World Computer Congress and at open conferences are published as conference proceedings, while the results of the working conferences are often published as collections of selected and edited papers.

Any national society whose primary activity is in information may apply to become a full member of IFIP, although full membership is restricted to one society per country. Full members are entitled to vote at the annual General Assembly, National societies preferring a less committed involvement may apply for associate or corresponding membership. Associate members enjoy the same benefits as full members, but without voting rights. Corresponding members are not represented in IFIP bodies. Affiliated membership is open to non-national societies, and individual and honorary membership schemes are also offered.

THE PAST AND FUTURE OF INFORMATION SYSTEMS: 1976-2006 AND BEYOND

IFIP 19th World Computer Congress, TC-8,
Information System Stream, August 21-23, 2006,
Santiago, Chile

Edited by

David Avison
Essec Business School, Cergy-Pontoise, France

Steve Elliot
School of Business, University of Sydney, Australia

John Krogstie
Norwegian University of Science and Technology and SINTEF
Trondheim, Norway

Jan Pries-Heje
IT University, Copenhagen, Denmark

 Springer

The Past and Future of Information Systems: 1976-2006 and Beyond

Edited by D. Avison, S. Elliot, J. Krogstie, and J. Pries-Heje

p. cm. (IFIP International Federation for Information Processing, a Springer Series in Computer Science)

ISSN: 1571-5736 / 1861-2288 (Internet)

eISBN: 10: 0-387-34732-1
Printed on acid-free paper

ISBN: 13: 978-1-4419-4183-1   e-ISBN: 978-0-387-34732-5

9 8 7 6 5 4 3 2 1
springer.com

Preface

The International Federation for Information Processing (IFIP) is a non-profit umbrella organization for national societies working in the field of information processing. It was founded in 1960 under the auspices of UNESCO. It is organized into several technical committees. This book represents the proceedings of the 2006 conference of technical committee 8 (TC8), which covers the field of information systems. This conference formed part of IFIP's World Computer Congress in Chile. The occasion celebrated the 30th anniversary of IFIP TC8 by looking at the past, present and future of information systems. The proceedings reflect not only the breadth and depth of the work of TC8, but also the international nature of the group, with authors from 18 countries being represented in the 21 papers (including two invited papers) and 2 panels. All submissions were rigorously refereed by at least two reviewers and an associate editor and following the review and resubmission process nearly 50% of submissions were accepted. This paper introduces the papers and panels presented at the conference and published in this volume. It is never straightforward to classify a set of papers but we have made an attempt and this classification is also reflected in the sessions of the conference itself. The classification for the papers is as follows: the world of information systems – early pioneers; developing improved information systems; information systems in their domains of application; the discipline of information systems; issues of production; IT impacts on the organization; tools and modeling and new directions.

1   The world of information systems: Early pioneers

The world of information systems is well represented in this book, because for 30 years Technical Committee 8 of IFIP has been working in this field. Some of the early history of this group is beautifully captured in T. William Olle's paper 'IFIP TC8 Information Systems – Conception, birth and early years'. Bill has every right to be seen as the 'organizational knowledge' of the group as he was an early pioneer as well as a consistent contributor to the group's work over the years. Another of his contributions has been to one of the 'working groups' of IFIP TC8 on the design and evaluation of information systems (Working Group (WG) 8.1). The work on information systems development methodologies has been very influential, and this is seen particularly in the Comparative Review of Information Systems (CRIS) conferences of the 1980s represented in Olle et al. [1-3]. In his paper Bill Olle describes the early work of IFIP itself (it was already 16 years' old when TC8 was established) but concentrates on the early years of TC8. This is indeed a 'warts and all' account of its difficulties as well as contributions. It also highlights some of the actors who were important in these early years.

It will not surprise anyone that we chose Gordon B. Davis as one of our two invited keynote speakers. For some years Gordon was chair of TC8. This committee meets once a year in the main to agree the programs of the WGs, which consist mostly of working conferences, workshops and affiliated meetings, and also to agree a strategy for TC8. Gordon's work is known by all those interested in information systems, indeed, he is one of the principal founders and intellectual architects of the academic field of information systems. His book [4], originally published in 1974, is recognized as a foundational classic in the field.

In his paper 'Information Systems as an Academic Discipline: Looking Back, Looking Forward, and Ensuring the Future', Gordon stresses the fact that organization systems enabled by information and communications technology (ICT) are vital to every organization. In the backlash following the sadly influential but half-baked article by Carr [5] this needs to be said again and again, otherwise management complacency will lead to failures and disasters as Avison et al. clearly demonstrate in [6]. Davis parallels the development of the organizational function with the academic discipline it reflects, both developing and maturing over a period of 55 years. As is well shown in the paper, the result has been a revolution in our time. New capabilities and new affordances have been applied to the activities of organizations. This period of rapid innovation in organizations has resulted in successes, challenges, failures, and surprises. The paper also looks at the present and towards the future: this is a critical juncture with both negative and positive forces in evidence.

2   Developing improved information systems

A major theme of TC8 throughout its 30 years (and the discipline and practice of information systems) concerns information systems development. The focus of WG 8.1 is the 'Design and Evaluation of Information Systems' and, as mentioned above, it has made many contributions. David Avison and Guy Fitzgerald have been researching and teaching in this area since 1980 [7]. The former was chair of WG 8.2 and has also been influenced by the themes of that group, essentially, the organizational and societal (human) impacts of information systems. Thus their paper 'Methodologies for Developing Information Systems: An Historical Perspective' looks at the different perspectives of information systems development: systemic, strategic, participative, agile and contingency, for example, along with the more conventional approaches such as structured, data, prototyping and engineered. They suggest four 'eras' in the study and practice of information systems development. Interestingly they see the present era as one of consolidation and stability, perhaps suggesting some maturity in practice.

One of the fundamental principles of IFIP as a whole, and certainly TC8, relates to ensuring that we have technical systems which impact positively on individual people, society as a whole and organizations. We have for some time emphasized the importance of user satisfaction in successful systems. More recently, we have widened our view about these people and organizational impacts. The paper of Luciana Bellejos and Jorge Montagna 'Stakeholders Selection for Interorganizational Systems: A Systematic Approach' recognizes the importance of identifying all stakeholders in any application. Identifying and satisfying these stakeholders make a successful IS project much more likely. The paper suggests a methodology for identifying all people, groups and organizations whose interests and needs are affected by the information systems in all the involved environments, which may include geographically dispersed and multiple organizations reflecting different cultures. The authors use the very ambitious UK National Health Service IT initiative to demonstrate their approach, and this reflects another working group of TC8, that is WG 8.5 concerned with Information Systems in Public Administration.

The issue of quality is obviously of key importance to successful information systems but, as Carlo Batini and Barbara Pernici point out in their paper 'Data Quality Management and Evolution of Information Systems', it is becoming even increasingly important due to the complexity of network/service-based systems and the ubiquity, diversity and uncontrolled nature of today's information systems. Barbara Pernici is presently chair of WG 8.1 and the paper again reflects some of the concerns of that group. The paper explores the main dimensions of data quality, types of information, types of information systems and application areas. Using these types and characteristics, the authors build up methodologies for information quality measurement and improvement. One of these provides an information product approach to data quality emphasising process-based methods and a second considers self-healing systems where faults are identified and repair-actions are suggested through the use of tools.

In the first panel 'OASIS in the Mirror: Reflections on the Impacts and Research of IFIP WG 8.2' Kenneth Kendall, David Avison, Gordon Davis, Julie Kendall, Frank Land and Michael Myers reflect on some of the debates and contributions of the working groups. Some of the hallmark debates include the relative merits of qualitative versus quantitative research; the question of rigor versus relevance; and whether technical or non-technical approaches are superior. It also discusses the way we accept innovative ideas, paradigms, methodologies and tools. Although centering on the work of WG 8.2, but not exclusively so, the debates are relevant to the work of TC8 as a whole.

3 Information systems in their domains of application

The first two papers of our second paper session reflect on some of the work of WG 8.5 which looks at Information Systems in Public Administration, in particular the technical, organizational and societal challenges of e-government. We begin with 'Design of the Organization of Information Services in Large Public Organizations' presented by Johan Van Wamelen. His research applied an analytical framework to twelve different programs and projects at Dutch departments of state, clustered to form three case studies, to see how they draw upon the potential of IT to innovate. These studies suggest that the IT function does not occupy a meaningful position in the organization so that its potential cannot be fulfilled. Van Wamelen argues that improvements need to be made to the organization of information services providing appropriate institutional conditions so that programs and projects are more coordinated.

Rodrigo Martin and Jorge Montagna also look at e-government in their paper 'Business Process Reengineering Role in Electronic Government'. One direction for this application domain is to implement a system that provides citizens with 'one-stop government'. But such initiatives normally imply great change and therefore it is useful to consider the potential of business process reengineering as a way to implement change more successfully, for failures in these applications are almost commonplace. Risk factors are discussed in the paper along with a suggested three-stage approach to successful implementation incorporating five different layers for e-government. An Argentine provincial state provides a useful case to illustrate the approach discussed in the paper.

The final paper of this section takes the application area from e-government to the major global treasury activity of foreign exchange trading. In their paper 'The Evolution of IS: Treasury Decision Support and Management Past, Present and Future', Alankar Karol, Mary-Anne Williams and Steve Elliot reflect on a seven year Australian–Danish research project into the impact of ICT on financial services and the development of a next generation agent-based treasury management system prototype. It is unusual and informative to see research reflecting the continuing evolution of IS in a single, core business function over such a long period. Possible future developments in IS applications are explored in terms of the capabilities of emerging technologies to address current treasury challenges. The implications for practitioners in an increasingly complex, global market are discussed and sustainable research issues, particularly for IS research, identified. The paper is relevant to a number of TC8 groups, including WG 8.3 on Decision Support Systems and not surprisingly on WG 8.4 (E-Business Information Systems: Multi-disciplinary research and practice) as Steve Elliot is presently chair of that group. Indeed it develops further work discussed in prior conferences of that group [8,9].

4   The discipline of information systems

The second panel reconsiders the status of the field of information systems within the university and in relation to industry practice (an issue first discussed in this conference in Gordon Davis' keynote address). Tor Larsen, Frank Land, Michael Myers, Robert Zmud and Linda Levine re-examine 'The Identity and Dynamics of MIS' from different points of view and stress two persistent themes. The first focuses on coherence in MIS and in framing questions such as: 'Does MIS have a core and overarching theory?' or 'Does MIS have a cumulative tradition?' and 'Are other disciplines referencing MIS?' The second theme revolves around rigor versus relevance, which is also occasionally expressed as a debate between academic and practical concerns and where a further refinement focuses on degrees of purity in the use of research methods. Further refinement on the state of coherence in MIS has examined the nature of its core and sub areas. Viewpoints expressed and topics discussed by panelists include 'myths, taboos and misconceptions in the IS domain', 'interdisciplinary identities: MIS and reference disciplines', 'intradisciplinary perspective' and 'empirics: coherence and change in the discipline'.

5 Issues of Production

In this section we look at aspects of production which have been themes in the working groups. In the first paper, Nicolás Riesco and Jaime Navón argue that although free and open source software (FOSS) is becoming more popular, most CIOs would not consider this option for their enterprise information technology needs. Their paper 'Enterprise Software: Taking the Open Source Option Seriously' suggests that there are a number of concerns about FOSS having to do with legal issues, costs, technical support, insufficient information and issues such as performance and reliability. In their paper the authors propose an initial framework for decision makers to look at FOSS in a balanced, unbiased and systematic manner that can be used for evaluation of specific scenarios from very small companies to large ones. In this way advantage may be taken from the potential of quality software with functionality and performance similar to expensive proprietary software with no license payment associated with it, whilst avoiding FOSS which may not provide these advantages to the firm.

Offshoring has become a prominent issue recently. A big gainer in offshoring over the last few years has been India, or at least some sections of that society. The industry is organized into multinational corporation (MNC) networks, whose structural, relational, and territorial dimensions are investigated in Pratyush Bharati's paper 'Understanding the Future of Global Software Production: Investigating the Network in India'. The quasi-disintegration and internationalization of MNC production activities, the commodification of services, the availability of highly skilled low cost personnel, and Indian IT services firms' links with MNCs have aided the emergence of the IT services industry in India. The research suggests that MNCs are key drivers in this complex and inter-dependent network that involve important Indian firms. This is the first study to investigate the Indian IT services industry in the context of global software production network.

John Krogstie is presently vice-chair of WG 8.1 and he reflects on an important information systems issue that has been dogging us since the beginning in his paper 'Work Distribution, Methodology and Technology for ISD and Maintenance: Trends over the last 30 Years'. His question is simple but the answer seems elusive: 'how do we support organizations with information technology in an efficient and effective way'?' He draws on material gleaned from survey investigations performed by his group in 1993, 1998, and 2003 among nearly 250 Norwegian organizations relating to how they conduct information systems development and maintenance. One interesting result is the comparatively greater time spent now on application portfolio upkeep (the functional coverage of the application system portfolio of the organization) rather than providing new services to the organization. The survey also provides some useful technical data on trends within IS practice.

6 IT impacts on the organization

Our second keynote address is given by Niels Bjørn-Andersen and entitled 'The never ending story of IT impact on the organization – the case of Ambient

Organizations'. Niels was the second president of AIS, became a LEO Fellow in 1999 and he was the Danish representative to TC8 for many years. The presentation concentrates on one of the main concerns of IS researchers almost from the introduction of the first computers, that is the almost eternal discussion of the impact of IT on organizations. It includes the early prediction of organizations turning hourglass-shaped proposed by Leavitt and Whisler in 1969, the impact studies of the 70s, the discussion of organizational change by default or by design, the new networked organizations paradigms of today, and the future challenge in this area. The key assertion of Niels Bjørn-Andersen is that today we are finally achieving such a level of sophistication in the technology that we shall see the emergence of totally new organizational forms that he labels 'ambient organizations'. This concept is described and examples of embryonic ambient elements of existing organizations are discussed. Research challenges in this area are also suggested.

TC8 as a whole is concerned with the impact of IT on organizations, though WG 8.6 focuses on the transfer and diffusion of information technology in different settings and from different perspectives. The paper of Karl Heinz Kautz and Helle Zinner Henriksen 'An Analysis of IFIP WG 8.6 – In Search of a Common Theoretical Denominator' reflects at the work of this group. In particular, it analyses the frameworks, models and theories that have been used to understand diffusion. A much cited work in the field is that of Rogers [10], initially published in 1962. But this is a somewhat positivistic study and many studies in the multi-disciplinary WG 8.6 community (Karl Heinz Kautz is chair of this group) are interpretive, being critical rather than objective (a 'myth' as seen in the eyes of these authors).

Chiara Frigerio, Federico Rajola and Alessia Santuccio also look at innovation and impact but concentrate on the related issue of organizational learning in their paper 'Promoting Learning Practices: Moving Towards Innovation'. Organizational learning, first put forward by Simon [11], is seen as fundamental in order to gain competitive advantage and survive in a turbulent environment. The two research questions explored are: (1) what are the determinants for organizational learning, depending on the firm's general approach towards information and knowledge management? and (2) How can a hierarchical organization move towards innovation through the organizational learning approach? The paper develops a particular framework in order to understand the determinants for organizational learning, depending on the firm's general approach towards information and knowledge management. Their research framework is applied to a sample of 54 Italian banks. The empirical analysis was carried out through questionnaires and interviews. Differences between banks refer to the presence of technological tools which support knowledge management, the culture, incentives used toward knowledge sharing and individual learning, informal cooperation, opportunities created dedicated to collaboration, the presence of virtual areas for long distance learning and the kind of hierarchical decisions the organizational learning approach supports. Regarding the second question under research, the need to promote new relationships between members or groups in order to change the organizational knowledge base is emphasized. Further, the importance of an initial informality in the way new activities are approached is also highlighted.

Ellen Christiaanse looks even further back than to the beginnings of TC 8, to '1.5 Million Years of Information Systems: From Gatherers-Hunters to the Domestication of the Networked Computer'. Ours is not the first information age in history nor do PCs run the first information systems. But only during the last 500 years, she argues, have we slowly moved to a single global system of information exchange with collective learning at the human species level. However, the present-day domestication of the personal, networked and increasingly mobile computer, it is argued in conclusion, will have a greater impact than any other type of domestication in the past. Although this is an unusual paper, the intention is quite serious: we need to understand present-day changes in a larger historical perspective and see how humans have communicated in the past and how this affected their social structures and lives. In that way, we may forecast the changes that information and communication technologies will bring in the future.

7 Tools and modelling

The uses of models and software tools are important to information systems research and practice as they are in other domains. In their paper 'Fulfilling the Needs of a Metadata Creator and Analyst - An Investigation of RDF Browsing and Visualization Tools', Shah Khusro, and Min Tjoa explore the use of semantic web software tools. Their research aims at creating a large triple dataset consisting of a life-long semantic repository of personal information called SemanticLife. Besides semantic web tools, they use several browsing and visualization tools for analyzing their data in this ambitious project and discuss an evaluation framework of these tools in their paper. This leads to them comparing tools and suggesting recommendations for the more effective use of tools in this domain.

The paper 'LUPA: A Workflow Engine' by Emely Arráiz, Ernesto Hernández and Roger Soler discusses a prototype of the Unified Language for Administrative Processes (LUPA) which focuses on the programming and communicating tasks associated with the transactions management needed to fulfill the business processes of an organization. It attempts to model the routes and rules that information must follow in order to comply with organizational policy using Petri nets. Essentially this reflects the workflow of business processes with a view to partial or complete automation of those workflows and business processes.

Information systems would be a much easier domain to research and practice if it were not for uncertainty: of user requirements, of organizational change, of environmental change and so on. The domain is saddled with issues of uncertainty, imprecision, vagueness, inconsistency and ambiguity. The paper 'Data Modeling Dealing with Uncertainty in Fuzzy Logic' by Angélica Urrutia, José Galindo, Leoncio Jimenéz and Mario Piattini discusses models of data description that incorporate these elements of uncertainty. They propose a fuzzy enhanced entity-relationship modeling approach rather than more conventional database techniques. They provide many examples in their paper and compare various models. They also describe the potential of their approach in two cases relating to a real estate agency and a manufacturing company.

8   New directions

In this final paper session we look at further potential new directions for information systems research. Isabel Ramos and João Álvaro Carvalho describe the concept of the self- and meta-representation capabilities of the organization, a constituent of what they call the organizational mind in their paper 'Reinventing the Future: A Study of the Organizational Mind'. They claim that these capabilities are responsible for the emergence of a collective self that is of central importance in the formation of organizational identity. These capabilities are relevant to the information systems field, as IT systems play a central role on the support of those representational capabilities. Their new research project aims at developing a framework to guide managers diagnosing identity dysfunctions resulting from impaired representational capabilities of the organization. This framework is intended to be a component of a broader one, the organizational mind framework, integrating theories and tools from different scientific disciplines to guide the study and improvement of the intelligence, learning ability, and creativity of the organization as a collective self. The objectives of this new and ambitious research project are to: define the concepts of organizational self-representation capability and organizational meta-representation capability; define the structural, socio-cultural, and technological components of these concepts in organizations; to design an architecture for the key components of the concept; to develop key performance indicators to measure the maturity of the self- and meta- representation capabilities of the organization; to define a model linking the organizational representational capabilities to the emergence of organizational identity; and finally to create a method and a prototype of a supporting computer-based tool to assist (a) the diagnosis of potential identity dysfunctions related with problems in representational capabilities of the organization, and (b) the planning of effective interventions to reduce the diagnosed dysfunctions; and finally to suggest new directions for redesigning cognitive systems in the organization so that they incorporate the aspects that the project advances as important for a healthy organizational identity.

The paper of Clarisse Sieckenius de Souza 'Semiotic Engineering – A New Paradigm for Designing Interactive Systems' is also challenging and presents a new direction for research in information systems. This paper presents a semiotic theory of human-computer interaction. The author claims that the theory integrates different design and development perspectives into a single meta-communication process that affects the user's experience and, ultimately, the success of any system via software artifacts. The approach also has the ability to frame (and design) the user's experience within increasingly broader contexts of communication – from basic user-system dialogue to contemporary user-in-cyberspace activity. By means of illustrative examples, the paper shows the kinds of effects that can be achieved with the theory, and discusses why a semiotic perspective is radically different from the prevalent cognitive ones that have inspired usability criteria to date.

In their paper 'The Benefit of Enterprise Ontology in Identifying Business Components', Antonia Albani and Jan Dietz point out that companies are more than ever participating in value networks while being confronted with an increasing need for collaboration and interoperability with their business partners. Such information systems become more and more complex because, apart from providing functionality to support intra-enterprise business tasks, they also need to provide services to external companies. The enterprise ontology presented in this paper is a powerful modeling methodology allowing a complete description of the inter-enterprise business domain. Reusable and self-contained business components with well-defined interaction points facilitate the accessing and execution of coherent packages of business functionality. While enterprise ontology is becoming an established approach for business and process modeling, the identification of business components is still a crucial factor and is strongly dependent on the appropriateness and the quality of the underlying business domain model. This paper seeks to improve the identification of business components based on an enterprise ontology, satisfying well-defined quality criteria.

References

1. Olle, T. W., Sol, H. G. and Verrijn-Stuart, A. A. (1982) Information Systems Design Methodologies: A Comparative Review¬. North Holland, Amsterdam.
2. Olle, T. W, Sol, H. G. and Verrijn-Stuart, A. A. (eds) (1986) Information Systems Design Methodologies: Improving the Practice, North Holland, Amsterdam.
3. Olle, T. W. (1988) Information Systems Methodologies: A Framework for Understanding, Addison Wesley, Harlow.
4. Davis, G. B. (1985) Management Information Systems: Conceptual Foundations, Structure, and Development, McGraw Hill, Maidenhead.
5. Carr, N. G. (2003) IT Doesn't Matter, Harvard Business Review, May.
6. Avison, D. E., Gregor, S. and Wilson, D. (2006) Managerial IT Unconsciousness, Communications of the ACM, July.
7. Avison, D. E. and Fitzgerald, G. (2006) Information Systems Development: Methodologies, Techniques and Tools, 4th edition, McGraw-Hill, Maidenhead.
8. Williams, M-A and Elliot S. (2003) An Evaluation of Intelligent Agent-based Innovation in the Wholesale Financial Services Industry, Proceedings of Second IFIP WG 8.4 Working Conference, Kluwer, 91–106.
9. Williams M-A, and Elliot S. (2004) Corporate Control of Rogue Traders: An Evaluation of Intelligent Agents for Improved eBusiness Treasury Risk Management' in Elliot S., Andersen K.V. and Trauth E. (eds) Multi-Disciplinary solutions to Industry & Governments' E-Business Challenges, Trauner, Austria.
10. Rogers, E. M. (2003). Diffusion of Innovations. Free Press, New York.
11. Simon, H. A. (1976) Administrative Behaviour, Free Press, New York.

Program Committee and Reviewers

We wish to thank the following who kindly acted as reviewers: Ayman Abuhamdieh, Richard Baskerville, Frada Burstein, João Alvaro Carvalho, Josep Domingo-Ferrer, Johann Eder, Shirley Gregor, Ola Henfridsson, Kristian Hjort-Madsen, Juhani Iivari, Muhammadou Kah, George M Kasper, Karlheinz Kautz, Ken Kendall, Banita Lal, Mauri Leppänen, Rikard Lindgren, Vasiliki Mantzana, Farouk Missi, Erich Neuhold, William Olle, Barbara Pernici, Yves Pigneur, Erik Proper, Maria Raffai, Sigi Reich, Maria-Ribera Sancho, Hans J Scholl, J.P. Shim, A Min Tjoa and Tetsuya Uchiki.

Table of Contents

IFIP TC8 Information Systems
Conception, Birth and Early Years

T.William Olle
T.William Olle Associates
Walton on Thames, Surrey, England

Abstract. The paper begins by discussing the conception and birth of IFIP TC8 in Amsterdam in 1975 and 1976, describing the roles of the main players (such as IFIP and IFIP ADP). The background in terms of the IFIP organization and its already extant technical committees is reviewed. The birth pains associated with IFIP TC8's early existence are also explained. The early meetings of TC8 and its Working Groups are discussed. From 1976 to 1986 formally planned events are discussed, with emphasis on the driving forces influencing the TC8 decision process throughout thiese years. The second half of this paper then reviews the background in the IT world (outside IFIP) as it prevailed in the period leading up to 1976. This backgound is examined in terms the of software and hardware technology of the time

1 Conception

In 1976, IFIP was 16 years old, a healthy teenager, possibly a little uncertain of its future in the world, but also brimming with confidence that the world was its oyster.

IFIP had held six major international conferences prior to 1976 including the first in 1959 in Paris. This congress took place in a UNESCO convention center. It took place before the existence of the organization then called IFIPS (International Federation for Information Processing Societies) as it was initially designated. The venues for the other five conferences prior to 1975 were 1962 Munich, 1965 New York, 1968 Edinburgh, 1971 Ljubliana and 1974 Stockholm. All of these were very successful with Edinburgh establishing a record, which is still standing, for the most attendees.

By 1976, IFIPS had already changed its name to IFIP. This change may have been motivated by an ambition in some quarters not to restrict membership to "information processing societies".

Please use the following format when citing this chapter:

Olle, T.W., 2006, in IFIP International Federation for Information Processing, Volume 214, The Past and Future of Information Systems: 1976–2006 and Beyond, eds. Avison, D., Elliot, S., Krogstie, J., Pries-Heje, J., (Boston: Springer), pp. 1–10.

IFIP had already established seven Technical Committees and it is interesting to take note of the names they had adopted (as published in the IFIP Information Bulletin for July 1975.[1]

1. TC1   Terminology
2. TC2   Programming
3. TC3   Education
4. TC4   Information Processing in Medicine
5. TC5   Computer Applications in Technology
6. TC6   Data Communication
7. TC7   Optimization

It is interesting to note that TC1 was not listed in the 1975 Information Bulletin possibly because it had completed the task it set out to do, namely to produce a definitive list of terminology [21]. TC4 subsequently parted company with IFIP and formed its own association, IMIA.

Of relevance to TC8 in the July 1975 IFIP Newsletter is the mention of TC8 in terms the appointment of its first chair Børje Langefors of Sweden, as from 1 September 1975. The entry also gives the names of National Representatives from six IFIP member nations (Australia, Bulgaria, France, United Kingdom, Brazil and West Germany). Two Working Groups and their provisional names were identified:

1. WG 8.1 Analysis of Organizational Needs for Information
2. WG 8.2 Utilization of Information within Organizations.

WG 8.1 had 11 members and WG8.2 had 14 members. The names of these two working groups were subsequently formalized

1. WG8.1 Design and Evaluation of Information Systems
2. WG8.2 Interaction of Information Systems and the Organization.

The subsequently published volume entitled "Trends in Information Systems", was an anthology [2] compiled in 1985 from earlier publications by TC8 to celebrate the 10th anniversary of TC8. It indicated the following in the first line of its Preface:

"In September 1975, on the premises of the IFIP Foundation in Amsterdam, a newly established technical committee met for the first time. To be dedicated to a field of increasing importance, the formal meeting of National Representatives of TC8 "Information Systems", lasted one hour and was attended by only five persons."

In fact both the July 1975 IFIP Newsletter and the claim in the 10th anniversary proceedings were probably pre-emptive. TC8 was not formally endorsed by the IFIP General Assembly until its meeting in 1976.

The formal attendance records [3] indeed show that the 1975 meeting was attended by only five national representatives, but by the time the more formally constituted 1976 meeting was held there were 15 national representatives present.

The organization which provided considerable support to IFIP TC8 during its period of birth was the IFIP Administrative Data Processing Group (IFIP ADP or IAG). This group had been founded in Amsterdam in 1967 with the aim of serving "the specific needs of the Administrative Data Processing community". IAG consisted of a number of partners namely "commercial and industrial computer centers, companies, national and local government organizations involved or interested in the use of computers." It also published in a journal.

When the proposal for creating an IFIP Technical Committee on "information systems" was put forward, IFIP IAG offered to host the preparatory meeting as mentioned above. Apart from providing a meeting room at their own offices in Amsterdam, they also provided a staff member, Ms. Ria Lucas, as secretary and local organizer. She served at both the 1975 and 1976 meetings of the technical committee.

Another activity which must be mentioned in connection with the early conception of TC8 is the Pergamon Journal of Information Systems. This was founded in 1964. An Editorial Board meeting had taken place in Stockholm in conjunction with the IFIP Congress. The chairman of the Editorial Board was Han Jochem-Schneider from what was then Western Germany. The same person was responsible for proposing to the IFIP Council that a technical committee on information systems should be founded.

2 Early Years

The aim of this paper is not to present and review the whole 30 years of TC8's activity, but rather to concentrated on the first ten years starting in 1976.

At the 1976 meeting, the first activity to which TC8 agreed to lend its name was a Working Conference held in The Hague in April 1977. The conference had the title "Education and large information systems". The more established Technical Committee TC3 Education was very much the main organizer and participation from the TC8 side is believed to have been minor.

The year 1977 was the year of the Toronto IFIP Congress to be held as always during the last week of August. TC8 had decided at its 1976 meeting to meet in Toronto in conjunction with the IFIP Congress. The 1977 TC8 National Representatives meeting was something of a disaster. Only nine national representatives attended. Borje Langefors resigned as TC8 Chair prior to the meeting. Fortunately, the Dutch representative, the late Alex Verrijn Stuart was willing to chair the meeting.

As already indicated, secretarial duties had been carried out at the earlier two meetings by Ms. Ria Lucas, an employee of the IFIP Administrative Data Processing Group in Amsterdam. She was unfortunately not able to attend the Toronto Congress. The present author and UK National Representative to TC8 was designated to perform the role of secretary for the meeting.

TC8 elected to hold its 1978 National Representatives' meeting in Venice. The main achievement of the Venice meeting was to set up a 1981 TC8 working conference involving both working groups to be held in Budapest. The title of this conference was "Evolutionary Information Systems" [4].

The lead time to proposing and organizing working conference was in those days much longer than is currently the case. It was not until 1979 that both of the new TC8 working groups cut their teeth. In April, WG8.1 held a working conference at Oxford University in St. Edmund's college, memorably organized by one of their graduates, Ron Stamper. The title was "Formal Models and Practical Tools for Information Systems Design"[5].

In June 1979, WG8.2 held a working conference in Bonn with the title "The Information Systems Environment" [6]. TC8 held its National Representatives meeting in Bonn in conjunction with the WG8.2 working conference. The precedent for holding a National Representatives meeting in conjunction with a working group conference was thereby established at an early stage.

However, the June 1980 National Representatives meeting was held independently of either working group meeting or IFIP Congress, namely in Jouy en Josas (near Paris).

The ambitious, but highly successful, IFIP 1980 Congress was held later in the summer in Tokyo and Melbourne. TC8 had considered both venues to be unacceptably remote for what was at that time a rather Eurocentric TC8 National Representatives meeting.

In 1981, TC8 elected to hold two National Representatives meetings, The March 1981 meeting in London was held separately from any working group conferences.

The September 1981 TC8 meeting was held in Budapest after the conference involving both working groups [4]. It was fairly well attended (the best so far) with 14 National Representatives out of the 22 appointed in attendance. The meeting was a milestone in that a third TC8 working group was formed. It had the title "WG8.3 Decision Support System". There was considerable debate about the establishment of this new working group, as members representing the two existing working groups felt that their "turf" was being threatened.

WG8.3 held its first conference in 1982 in Laxenburg, Austria with the title "Processes and tools for decision support" [7]. WG8.1 actually held two working conferences in 1982, one on each side of the Atlantic. These were in New Orleans and in Noordwijkerhout in the Netherlands. This last conference was the first of a series of so-called CRIS conferences which were collectively part of an in-depth comparative review of information systems methodologies [9]. The TC8 meeting was held in Leiden in conjunction with the WG8.1 conference in Noordwijkerhout.

In Zurich in March 1983, IFIP TC8 held its first two day National Representatives meeting. A significant part of the agenda was given over to a brain storming session reviewing the past, present and future of TC8's work.

Two working conferences were also held in 1983. In July 1983, WG8.1 held the second in the CRIS series in York in the north of England. The title was "Information Systems Design Methodologies: A feature analysis" [10]. WG8.2 held its first working conference North America in the city of Minneapolis in August 1983. The title was "Beyond Productivity: information systems development for organizational effectiveness" [11].

In September 1983, IFIP held its ninth World Computer Congress in Paris. It attracted 2300 participants from 59 countries. However, it was possibly the first congress at which one began to question why the organization of the technical program appeared to be so divorced from the Technical Committee structure.

As a result of the free standing TC8 National Representatives meeting in Zurich in 1983, the Australian National Representative, Cyril Brookes, raised the question of whether it was meaningful to travel "half way round the world" to attend a two day business meeting. He offered that, in April 1984, the Australian Computer society would organize an open conference on information systems at which selected TC8 National Representatives would give presentations [12]. The TC8 National Representatives meeting would then be held in conjunction with this conference. (This formula was successful and was repeated in Australia in 1988 and in 1993).

In 1984, a second TC8 National Representatives' meeting was held in London in September. In addition, both WG 8.3 and WG8.2 held working conferences in England that year. WG8.3 held a conference in Durham with the title "Knowledge Representation for Decision Support"[13]. This was WG8.3's second working conference.

WG8.2 held what proved to be a significant and seminal conference in Manchester with the very open title "Research Methods In information Systems" [14]. After the fact, it was agreed to have been significant in stimulating interest in the work of WG8.2, a fact which was celebrated 20 years later in 2004 with a WG8.2 conference at the same location.

For TC8, 1985 was a significant year in many ways. Again WG8.1 held two working conferences, one on each side of the Atlantic. The first was held in Sitges in Catalunia in April 1985 [14]. TC8 held its most controversial National Representatives meeting in conjunction with the Sitges working conference.

The controversy was triggered by an invitation from the South African representative, Neil Duffy, based on the success of the Australian formula, to hold a subsequent meeting in South Africa. Several representatives stated that they could loose their job if they attended. Others argued IFIP should not be concerned with internal politics of a member nation and that such politics should not dictate IFIP related decisions. The compromise decision was that TC8 would lend its name to a conference held in Johannesburg and those TC8 representatives who wished to participate were free to do so, but there would be no TC8 meeting held in conjunction with the conference. (The conference was actually held in April 1987[15].)

Another item of significance in 1985 was the creation of a fourth working group, namely WG8.4 Office Systems. The creation process was started in Sitges. WG8.4 held its inaugural working conference in Helsinki in October 1985 [16]. TC8 National Representatives held a second meeting during 1985 in Helsinki in conjunction with that conference.

The year 1985 was deemed to be the 10th anniversary of the founding of TC8. The anthology of selected papers presented at earlier working conferences was prepared with the three representatives who had so far held the position of TC8 chair designated as editors, namely Børje Langefors, Alex Verrijn-Stuart and Giampio Bracchi [3].

To complete this review of the "early years" with 1986, this was in some ways a significant year for IFIP itself. The then triennial IFIP Congress was held in Dublin Ireland in September 1986, although TC8 chose not to meet there.

The Irish Computer Society was the smallest ever to try to host an IFIP Congress. They were strongly supported by their national government and it was assumed that strong support would be forthcoming from their nearest neighbors, namely the United Kingdom. Sadly this was not the case and the Irish Computer Society sustained a significant and apparently unsustainable loss as a result of the congress.

After three successive years (1983-85), each with two National Representatives meetings, TC8 held only one meeting in 1986 and this in Vienna in June and this was an independent meeting. Each of the four TC8 working groups held a working conference during 1986. Three of these conferences were held on different dates in the Netherlands at what was then a popular venue, namely Noordwijkerhout. The exception to this was WG8.4 which held its conference in Pisa in October.

In 1986 and 1987, IFIP TC8 met each year. In 1988, there were two meetings, the first in Sydney using the Australian formula and the second in Egham in conjunction with a WG8.1 working conference. From 1989 onwards, TC8 has met on an annual basis planning its meetings in the IFIP Congress years 1989, 1992, 1998, 2000 and 2002 in conjunction with the congress and in other years in conjunction with a TC8 working group activity.

3   IT Development and its Impact on TC8

As indicated in the opening section of this paper, TC8 Information Systems came into being in the mid-seventies. The organizational aspects of its conception and the development in the early years were described in the first half of this paper. It is now appropriate to look at the wider picture of information technology as it impacted on the formation and direction of TC8.

Stored program computers had been under development and in practical use since 1948 [17]. Purpose-built computers which could perform a specific task (such as breaking enemy codes or calculating missile trajectories) were in use even earlier. Punched card equipment goes back even further in time.

The years between 1948 and 1975 had seen a significant increase in the use of computers. Such use at the time was frequently categorized as either "administrative" or "scientific". The term "administrative" was preferred, particularly by civil service representatives, as more appropriate than the earlier and possibly limiting term "business".

Scientists found it possible to get the computer to perform complex calculations, such as solving differential equations, finding the roots of polynomials or inverting matrices.

Administrative uses involved performing much simpler calculations on higher volumes of data. Applications such as payroll, stock control and various kinds of accounting may be cited.

In both cases, the emphasis was on doing a job and producing results for human perusal. The technology was limited (by today's standards). It was extremely expensive and required considerable office space.

The IBM announcement in April 1964 [18] of a range of compatible computers which could be used for either scientific or business purposes had an enormous impact on the computer   manufacturing industry and in turn on the way people thought about the uses of computers.

It is perhaps pure coincidence that, around the same time, the COBOL programming language was being increasingly accepted as some kind of lingua franca for administrative applications. COBOL (Common Business Oriented Language) was much derided for its wordiness, especially by workers in the field who were familiar with any kind of mathematical formulation of numeric variables.

Whatever its faults, COBOL introduced the programming of administrative and business applications to a wider group of people.

The early sixties turned out to be a productive time for significant developments in the computer field. The era of magnetic tape storage had long been the main means of storing large volumes of business data. When the magnetic disc made its appearance, it was inappropriately referred to as a "random access" storage medium. [19]. The faux pas was recognized and the term "direct access storage" came in to more widespread use.

Direct access storage cried out for a more effective approach to storing and processing data than had been possible with magnetic tapes. The pioneer in this respect was Charles Bachman. Bachman was the first to recognize that data could be structured on direct access storage in such a way that ways of processing the data other than the established "sequential processing" were recognized. His approach led to use of the term "network structures" which were clearly more flexible than the limiting hierarchical structures possible with magnetic tape storage.

With all this relatively new technology to be harnessed, there was a move towards computer applications which were more powerful and more flexible in several ways. Firstly, the separation between data and programs (initiated in COBOL with its Data Division and Procedure Division) became more significant. The same data could be used in different ways by different programs. It was possible to modify data without having to make otherwise unnecessary changes to the programs which used that data.

Another development was the recognition that the perception of data could and should take several forms. Since the advent of stored program computers, data had been defined in the way it was being represented in storage. However, the new kinds of uses needed to take account only of the logical view of the data and preferred not to be aware of the complexities of the representation in storage. This split was reflected in the acceptance of the terms "datalogical" and "infological" introduced by TC8's first chairman Børje Langefors [20].

It is also useful to reflect on the evolution of the term "information system". The difference between "data" and "information" is an old chestnut in the IFIP environment. TC1's epoch breaking reference book entitled "IFIP/ICC Vocabulary of Information Processing" published in 1966 [21] distinguished between the two terms. "Data" is defined as "a representation of facts or ideas capable of being communicated or manipulated by some process". "Information" is defined as "the meaning that a human assigns to the data by means of the known conventions used in its representation". For the record, the term "information system" was not defined in this vocabulary.

The term "management information system" was in use long before it was broadened to "information system". There is an item of folklore which suggests that the term "management information system" was created by an IBM salesman who was selling an IBM 1401 to client management. "This machine", he said proudly, "is a management information system"!

Evolutionary thought dictated that terms used should be as broad as possible. The "management information system", whatever it was, should not necessarily be limited to "management" (even though it provided a useful sales pitch to management). Hence, the term "information system" came into use.

However, the term was too simple and too obvious not to have been used in other contexts. For example, the proceedings of the IFIP Congress 65 held in New York City [22] contain a section heading for a special session entitled "Design of Information Systems". The four papers in that section were not what TC8 would subsequently have considered relevant to its interests.

A conference organized jointly in Rome in 1967 by IFIP and FID (Federation Internationale de la Documentation) contained a paper entitled "A system to manage an Information System" by D. Hsaio and N.S. Prywes [23]. The opening sentence reads :

"An information system, as considered in this paper, consists of a network of computers with their related information bans and of consoles that are all interconnected by communication lines."

Clearly the term "information system" was perceived in the sixties and early seventies as one which could be given a multitude of interpretations. It is probable that the interpretation which the term was being given in other natural languages such as French, Dutch, German and all three varieties of Scandinavian, was closer to the usage which was chosen by the founding fathers of TC8. Apparently, the acceptance of the name for the technical committee was criticized by IFIP General Assembly members as being too broad and too much of a "catch all".

Somehow the name has survived and there has never been an attempt to change it. This is more than can be said for the names of some of the TC8 working groups. However, the name for an IFIP Technical Committee is of necessity a capacious umbrella, under which many more specific names must be able to shelter.

4 Conclusions

In conclusion, it is useful to review TC8's thirty year history. From the ten year old of 1986, it has matured to the 30 year old of today. There are now seven working groups – numbered WG8.1 to WG8.6 and most recently WG8.8.

Subsequent to the initial decade of TC8's life discussed in the first part of this paper, TC8 approved the creation of WG8.5 "Information systems in Public Administration" in 1988 and WG8.6 "Transfer and Diffusion of Information Technology" in 1994.

TC8 created WG8.7 "Informatics in International Business Enterprises" in 1996 but had the courage of its convictions to close it down in 2000 when it realized that the group was not active in any way and not responding to any contacts from TC8 officers.

TC8 created WG8.8 "Smart Cards" in 2001. This group provides a home for an annual conference called CARDIS which focuses on smart card research and applications. This group has a broadening effect on TC8's scope of activity.

The future of TC8 seems fairly secure. Information systems after 30 years is a much changed and much broader area of interest than it was in 1976. TC8 has established a modus operandi within the overall framework of IFIP activities which seems set to ensure its survival for another 30 years!

References

1. IFIP Information Bulletin July 1975 Number 9.
2. B.Langefors, A.A.Verrijn-Stuart, and   G. Bracchi.. Trends in Information Systems. Edited. North-Holland. 1985.
3. IFIP TC 8 www. http://ifiptc8.itu.dk
4. J.Hawgood. Evolutionary Information Systems. North-Holland 1983.
5. H.-J. Schneider. Formal Models and Practical Tools for Information Systems Design. North-Holland. 1979
6. H. C. Lucas, F.F. Land, T.J. Lincoln, and K. Supper. The Information Systems Environment. Edited by North-Holland 1980
7. Decision Support Systems. North-Holland 1981.
8. H.G.Sol. Processes and tools for decision support. North-Holland 1982
9. T.W.Olle, H.G.Sol, and A.A.Verrijn-Stuart. Information Systems Design Methodologies: a Comparative Review. North-Holland. 1982
10. T.W.Olle, H.G.Sol, and C.J.Tully. Information Systems Design Methodologies: a Feature Analysis. North-Holland, 1983
11. T.M.A. Bemelmans. Beyond Productivity: Information Systems. Development for Organizational Effectiveness. North-Holland 1983
12. D. Ross Jeffrey. Joint International Symposium on Information Systems. Australian Computer Society, Sydney, Australia.. 1984
13. L.B. Methlie and R.H. Sprague. Knowledge Representation for Decision Support. Elsevier 1984
14. A. Sernadas, J.Bubenko Jr., and A.Olive. Information Systems: Theoretical and Formal Aspects.   Proceedings IFIP 8.1 Working Conference on Theoretical and Formal Aspects of Information Systems. Sitges, Barcelona. North-Holland, Amsterdam, 1985.
15. P.C.Pirow, N.M.Duffy, and J.C.Ford. Information Systems in Practice and Theory. North-Holland . 1988.
16. A.A. Verrijn-Stuart and R.A. Hirscheim. Office Systems. Elsevier. 1986
17. http://www.computer50.org/mark1/new.baby.html
18. http://www.beagle-ears.com/lars/engineer/comphist/ibm360.htm
19. http://www.cedmagic.com/history/ibm-305-ramac.html
20. B. Langefors. Theoretical Analysis of Information Systems. Studentlitteratur. 1966.

21. G.C. Toothill. IFIP/ICC Vocabulary of Information Processing. North-Holland 1966

22. W.A. Kalenich. Proceeding of IFIP Congress 65 New York City Spartan Books, Inc and Macmillan & Co. 1965

23. D. Hsaio and N.S. Prywes. A System to Manage an Information System. Proceedings on the FID-IFIP Conference on Mechanized Information Storage, Retrieval and Dissemination. Edited by K.Samuelson. North-Holland. 1967.

Information Systems as an Academic Discipline
Looking Back, Looking Forward, and Ensuring the Future

Gordon B. Davis
Honeywell Professor of Management Information Systems, Emeritus
University of Minnesota
gdavis@csom.umn.edu

1 Introduction

In an organization of any size, there is an organization function responsible for the technology, activities and personnel to support its technology-enabled work systems and the information and communication needs of the organization. There is an academic discipline that teaches those who build, acquire, operate and maintain the systems and those who use the systems. Both the organization function and the academic discipline have developed over a period of 55 years (but primarily in the last 40 years).

There have been two fundamental forces driving the formation of a new organization function and the new technology-enabled systems in organizations. One is the availability of powerful computer and communications technology; the other is the desire of organizations to use the capabilities in organization work. The result has been revolutionary as new capabilities and new affordances have been applied to the activities of organizations. A new academic discipline has emerged. This period of rapid innovation in organizations has resulted in successes, challenges, failures, and surprises.

I have been a participant and an observer of this period of change. The paper will survey key developments (from my perspective) that have brought us to the present conditions in use of information and communications technology in organizations and the current status of the academic discipline. I will note the role of IFIP TC8 (Information Systems). It has been important in several key developments, but not in all of them. I will identify some of my observations about the value added by TC8.

Please use the following format when citing this chapter:

Davis, G.B., 2006, in IFIP International Federation for Information Processing, Volume 214, The Past and Future of Information Systems: 1976–2006 and Beyond, eds. Avison, D., Elliot, S., Krogstie, J., Pries-Heje, J., (Boston: Springer), pp. 11–25.

We are perhaps at a critical juncture. There are both negative and positive forces affecting the future. The question is how to respond to them. To ensure a productive, viable future for the organization function and academic discipline, both those in the organization function and those in academia need to be proactive. In this paper, I summarize some thoughts on the future of the academic field and what it should do to ensure its future.

Many of the ideas in the paper have been formulated over the last 40 years. They are based on my experiences and discussions with a large number of colleagues. I paraphrase or reuse ideas from papers I have written that have been published in proceedings. Two of my papers that were especially significant sources in preparing this overview paper are [1,2] . Much of my experience was rooted in the MIS program at Minnesota founded by me, Gary Dickson, and Tom Hoffmann in 1968. See also [3,4]

The paper begins with some definitions, summarizes some key historical events related to the field including some comments about the delay in establishing information systems compared to establishing computer science, key factors in the emergence of an international community for information systems as an academic discipline, the role of IFIP and TC8 (Information Systems) in nourishing the new academic discipline, and thoughts about the future of the academic discipline and what needs to be done to secure its future.

2   Definitions

In organizations, the term Information System (IS) or some equivalent label refers to both:

- the systems that deliver information and communication services to an organization
- the organization function that plans, develops, operates, and manages the information systems

The IS function may be organized as a separate organization function with a high level executive with a title such as Chief Information Officer (CIO), or it may be organized as a unit under an operations or financial executive. Because of the use of information and communications technology, the function and its services is often referred to as Information Technology or IT.

There are four important parts of the organization function for information systems, and these parts are found in the research and teaching activities of the academic discipline. These can be characterized as IS management, infrastructure, systems acquisition and support, and databases.

- The management, personnel and operations of the function. This includes planning and co-alignment of information system strategy and organization strategy and the evaluation and justification of organization investment in IS.
- Planning and implementing an infrastructure of hardware, system software, and enterprise systems.

- Building or acquiring, implementing, and supporting systems. This includes tailoring enterprise software to fit user needs and individual applications for individuals, groups, and functions. It also includes ongoing support and maintenance.
- Designing, building, and maintaining internal databases and access to external sources of data.

The name for the information systems academic discipline more or less mirrors the organization use. Note that I refer to the "academic discipline" and "academic field", using the terms as equivalent. Some of the names that are used for the discipline are:

- Information Systems
- Management Information Systems
- Information Management
- Management of Information Systems
- Informatics (usually modified by organization, administration, or similar terms)

Some academics have argued for the use of Informatics instead of Information Systems as the general name for the academic discipline. It seems to be a broader term. However, it is difficult and probably unnecessary to change common usage. As a historical note, in the early 1970s, some of us proposed to use Informatics, but in the USA the name was copyrighted by a firm that threatened to prevent its use on journals, etc. The firm no longer exists.

The domain of the academic discipline of information systems seems very broad. The reason for the broad domain is the fact that support and services are being provided to different functions and activities in the organization and also to customers and suppliers. The domain of information systems can be described as:

- The core knowledge that is fundamental to information systems in organizations. This core knowledge includes modeling of organization transactions and behaviors, modeling of data and design of databases, and systems concepts (including socio-technical systems).
- Knowledge of the activities, operations and management of the information systems function. The activities assume understanding of communications and information processing technologies.
- Knowledge of the applications and services provided to individuals, groups, and functions in the organization. This domain is shared with the users of the applications and services.

Two critical features of Information Systems as an academic field today are its organizational context and its international orientation. Computers and communications may affect many fields of study within the university that do not have an organization context. Examples are medical informatics, educational technology, etc. However, information systems, as an academic discipline, is tied to the use of information and communications technology in organizations. This is true even if the discipline is positioned outside a school of organization studies. The second feature of the field is its international orientation. Most academic disciplines within the broad field of organizations, management, or economic sciences developed within the context of a country or a region. Examples are accounting, marketing, and industrial relations. They are working to be international. The academic discipline of information systems became international very quickly and has maintained that outlook.

3 Historical Development

Computing (Computer Science) developed as an academic field of research and degree programs much more quickly than information systems. It developed within the academic context of engineering or mathematics. Academic researchers developed computing devices during the 1940s for use in code breaking. In the last half of the 1940s, many university research groups were engaged in building one-of-a-kind computers to test various ideas on design. By 1951, the UNIVAC I was available as a commercial computer and the LEO computer, developed by the Lyons Tea Company and Cambridge University, became operational. Scientific organizations for computing were organized in several countries. There were enough computing organizations that IFIP was organized in 1960 as an international federation of computing societies.

Unlike computing, information systems as a separate subject took a number of years to emerge. Although many universities throughout the world had individual researchers engaged in research and teaching relative to information systems, the academic homes for these pioneers varied considerably. Three events illustrate the delay in formation of a formal field of study and research: the first professor was 1965, the first formal program was 1968, and it was not until 1976 that IFIP organized TC8, recognizing information systems as a separate field within computing.

A few dates mark some noteworthy events leading to recognition of information systems as a separate field within the broad range of computing disciplines. Any person engaged in historical research knows that it is not easy to identify the "first" person or organization that did something important. There were usually many persons or organizations working on the problem or initiating the changes, and the ones identified in the literature are among the pioneers but not necessarily "the first." Given that caveat, the following are some interesting "firsts."

- First business use of computers in UK (the LEO computer); first use by Census Bureau in USA of the UNIVAC I
- First business use of a commercial computer in USA by GE (UNIVAC I)
- First speculation of importance to business of computers in Harvard Business Review
- Forming of International Federation for Information Processing (IFIP)
- Börje Langefors appointed as professor (joint chair at the Royal Institute of Technology and the University of Stockholm) in Information Processing, with special emphasis on Administrative Data Processing.

- First formal MIS academic degree programs in the USA (M.S. and Ph.D.) at University of Minnesota.
- Establishment of organization for information system executives (CIOs); first called Society for Management Information Systems and now Society for Information Management (SIM)
- Establishment of IFIP technical committee on information systems (TC8)
- The journal MIS Quarterly started at the University of Minnesota (but not the first journal in the field)
- First International Conference on Information Systems (ICIS)
- Formation of Association for Information Systems (AIS) as an international academic organization with an international governance structure. Merger in 2001 of AIS and ICIS. AIS alliances with regional conferences in Europe, Asia, and America (ECIS, PACIS, and AMCIS).

In my view, the delay in recognition of information systems as a separate computing discipline and an important field in management and organizations was caused by three major factors: the time lag between the introduction of computers and the recognition of an interesting, important IS organization function and interesting, important IS research issues; the diverse backgrounds of academic researchers with interests in information systems and conflicting loyalties with existing academic/professional societies; and conferences and journals that accepted IS research results. These issues explain much of the delay, but strong informal networks of academic colleagues were emerging and would finally lead to a strong IS academic community.

- The time lag between the introduction of computers and the recognition of an interesting, important organization function and interesting, important IS research issues. Punched card data processing was not an interesting academic subject for teaching or research. Early use of computers focused on simple transaction processing, so it didn't look interesting. What was interesting was the possibility of improved analysis, improved managerial reporting, and improved decision making. As organizations developed and implemented computer-based data processing systems, they experienced many interesting methods problems such as requirements determination, development methodologies, implementation, design of work systems, and evaluation.
- The diverse backgrounds of academic researchers with interests in information systems and conflicting loyalties with existing academic/professional organizations. Early academic researchers came from a variety of backgrounds such as management, accounting, computer science, and management science. There was no sense of urgency to establish a new academic discipline since doctoral students in the 1960s who were interested in information systems took doctorates in these existing subjects. It was not until 1968 that the first formal doctoral program in information systems in North America was established at the University of Minnesota (along with an MIS research center).

- Conferences and journals that accepted IS research results. Given the diverse backgrounds of researchers and the diverse department affiliations, the early researchers looked to their home discipline for opportunities to present and publish their work. Several organizations formed special interest groups around the issues of information systems and sponsored conferences and IS conference tracks within their regular conferences. Because there were existing conferences and publishing outlets for IS research, there was limited urgency to establish a separate academic discipline with its own conferences and journals.

4   International Differences in the Development of an International Discipline

Even though there is today an international discipline of information systems with broad acceptance of the major research themes and research methods, there were some regional differences in emphasis in the development of academic research. All major topics related to information systems were being developed in all countries, but the level of interest and the level of activity were different

Research on the four parts of the organization function (IS management, infrastructure, systems acquisition and support, and databases) do not differ significantly across the world. However, in the early development of the IS academic discipline, there were differences in the kind of research that was most prominent in the regions.

- The early work on development methods was dominated by European researchers. In the IFIP TC8 WG8.1 series of working conferences on methods, most of the contributions were by Europeans. There were some USA researchers, especially on automated development methods (e.g., Daniel Teichroew).
- There were a variety of early studies on management of the IS function including the management of personnel and operations. These tended to come from North America with Harvard and MIT providing significant inputs. Two noteworthy examples were Nolan's stage theory for managing the function and the Harvard studies on competitive advantage through information systems.
- The most powerful and insightful early research on evaluation of technology-enabled systems was done in the UK and Scandinavia by researchers based on socio-technical concepts and organization behavior. Notable were researchers associated with WG8.2 such as Enid Mumford.
- The use of information systems to improve management was a common topic. The period of emergence of computers was also a period in which management science and operations research were applying new quantitative methods to management. Some of the strongest early research was on use of models that depended on computers and on decision support systems. This research had strong beginnings in MIT

and other North American universities. There was significant experimental research, dominated in the early stages by North American academics, into cognitive style as a basis for the design of management reports and other decision support.

- The incidence of different research methods was somewhat different by region in the early development of the discipline. Positivist methods emphasizing analysis of data were dominant in North America; interpretive methods were more accepted in Europe. Design science methods involving the building of artifacts were used more commonly in Europe.

5 Some Important Developments or Events Supporting the Emergence of an International Academic Discipline of Information Systems

In explaining how it happened, I believe there were seven critical events or developments that made it possible to have an international academic discipline for information systems. These are the development of computing devices and computer science, the use of English as the common language for computing-related disciplines, the formation of the International Federation for Information Processing and its Technical Committee 8 (Information Systems), international efforts by scholars in several countries, locating the IFIP TC8 working conferences internationally, the founding of the International Conference on Information Systems (ICIS), and the founding of the Association for Information Systems (AIS) with an international governance structure.

1. Development of computing devices and computer science

Without the development of computing devices, information systems would not have become a field of study and research. It was also necessary to have academic interest and research in the hardware and software that would be employed in information systems.

After World War II, there was interest in many universities around the world in the design and development of computing machinery. The community of researchers shared designs and experiences, so the development of computing machinery was an international effort. Very early in this period of development, Computer Science societies were established by a combination of academics and practitioners. Each country tended to have its own organization. Computer Science as an academic discipline provided for academic research and teaching in algorithms for computing, system software, software development methods, and data base methods. These were important in providing scientific support for the tools and methods needed by information systems.

2. The use of English as the common language for computing-related disciplines

A common language is very important in building an international community of scholars in a discipline. Greek, Latin, German, and French have provided such a common language for various communities at different times in history. The development of computers, although occurring in different countries, had major developments in the USA and the UK. This encouraged the use of English as the language for the computing field. As will be noted later, English was adopted as the language for the International Federation for Information Processing (IFIP). At the same time, there was a general recognition by scholars and business leaders of the value of an international language. English became the common language of international commerce and of research and education in many fields.

The common language of English has meant that international conferences on computing and information systems can be held at almost any location in the world, research is freely exchanged across boundaries, and textbooks and trade books are made available internationally.

3. The formation of the International Federation for Information Processing (IFIP) and its Technical Committee 8 (Information Systems)

In the early development of computing and its use in organizations, national organizations were forming, but there was no accepted international forum. The United Nations provided the impetus for the formation of an international information processing organization. UNESCO sponsored the first World Computer Conference in 1959 in Paris (eight years after the first commercial computer). This was followed by the organization in 1960 of the International Federation for Information Processing (IFIP) as a society of societies.

Technical work, which is the heart of IFIP's activity, is managed by a series of Technical Committees (TCs). Each member society (usually identified with a country) may appoint a representative to the governance committee for each technical committee. There are currently 12 technical committees. Each technical committee forms working groups. Individuals throughout the world may be members of a working group by demonstrating interest and continuing activity in the work of the group. In other words, the main scientific work of IFIP is accomplished by individuals without regard to country or other affiliation. The governance is organized to involve the societies that belong to IFIP (which for the most part are identified with countries).

The IFIP technical committee of interest in this view of the development of an international academic discipline is TC8 (Information Systems). It was established in 1976. Its aims are to promote and encourage the advancement of research and practice of concepts, methods, techniques, and issues related to information systems in organizations. Note that it was formed 25 years after the first use of computers in business. It currently has seven working groups.

- WG 8.1 Design and evaluation of information systems
- WG 8.2 Interaction of information systems and the organization
- WG 8.3 Decision support systems
- WG 8.4 E-business: multidisciplinary research and practice
- WG 8.5 Information systems in public administration

- WG 8.6 Transfer and diffusion of information technology
- WG 8.8 Smart cards

The working groups of TC8 reflect some fundamental IS issues (WG8.1 on design and evaluation and WG8.6 on diffusion of IT innovation), the IS context (WG8.2 on interaction with organization and WG8.5 on public administration), and significant IS application areas (WG8.3 on decision systems, WG8.4 on e-business, and WG8.8 on smart cards).

TC8 was important in helping to build an international community. Its first chairman was Börje Langefors of Sweden. It started as somewhat Europe-centric but rapidly expanded to worldwide participation. I personally observed the building of that community. I was the second United States representative to TC8 and remained in that position for 20 years. I served as Chair of TC8 for two terms.

4. International efforts by scholars in several countries

It is difficult and somewhat dangerous to start mentioning specific names of important innovators and contributors. Even a casual reading of the history of inventions shows again and again that important innovations are "in the air." Several people are working on the same problem and coming to the same solutions, but one or only a few are recognized as the inventors. In the case of information systems as an academic discipline, there are a number of people who were critical in developing the field. These pioneers worked not only in their home countries but also in international organizations. They met at international conferences, took trips to become acquainted with what was happening in other places, and hosted visitors. They were founders and builders of the international societies that nourish the discipline today. The Association for Information Systems has recognized 13 of these by giving them the LEO award for lifetime exceptional achievement in information systems and 36 of them as AIS Fellows.

5. Locating the IFIP TC8 working conferences internationally

A strong comparative advantage of TC8 is its ability to draw together academics and other researchers in information systems from different countries and diverse cultural and academic backgrounds. The working group conferences became a vehicle for building an international network of scholars, both by the subjects of the conferences and the locations.

An example of how this has worked well is Working Group 8.2 on information systems and organizations. It is the group I worked with most, so my view is biased. This group now has an equal number of European and North American members plus members from other regions. The conference venues rotate in order to involve more researchers.

A very important conference in building the international community was the IFIP WG8.2 1984 Manchester Conference on information systems research methods (E. Mumford, R. Hirschheim, G. Fitzgerald, and T. Wood-Harper, 1985).

The reason I count this conference as very important is its role in opening up the discussion of the different research paradigms. Most of the researchers in North America at that time tended to emphasize a positivist approach to research with experiments, surveys, hypothesis testing, and so forth. Many of the Europeans were doing post-positivist, interpretive research. The conference opened the minds of many of the conferees and helped open the field of information systems to a variety of research paradigms. Currently, there is reasonable, international acceptance of the following:

- Positivist, hypothesis testing, data-based research
- Interpretive research including research based on case studies
- Design science research

The IS research literature clearly defines the first two; the third is less well defined. Design science research (the term used by Smith and March) is based on the research paradigms of engineering and Computer Science. In design science, designing and building a new, novel artifact such as a computer application program, development methodology, or model is a contribution to knowledge. In general, information systems research publications have expected that an artifact will not only have been built but will also be tested to demonstrate proof of concept or value of the artifact. See [5,6]

6. The founding of the International Conference on Information Systems (ICIS)

As mentioned previously, early researchers in information systems had disciplines to which they belonged. Their conferences often provided opportunities to present information systems research. This was especially true of management science, operations research, and decision sciences. The IFIP working groups on information systems focused on information systems but tended to be around narrow topics. There was no general, well-accepted, high quality information systems conference.

The first Conference on Information Systems (later renamed as the International Conference on Information Systems or ICIS) was held in 1980. A major sponsor was the Society for Information Management, a society for CIOs. ICIS began as a North American conference but grew quickly to a high quality international conference. It was held in Copenhagen in 1990 and has been held outside the United States almost half of the time in the past 12 years. A major feature is a high quality, invitational doctoral consortium with a mix of doctoral students from different countries.

There has existed a very open attitude at ICIS to subgroups within the field. Several subgroups hold conferences immediately preceding or immediately following ICIS. Examples are the Workshop on Information System Economics (WISE), the Workshop on Information Technology Systems (WITS), IFIP WG8.2, and several others.

7. The founding in 1995 of the Association for Information Systems (AIS) with an international governance structure

From the time of the first ICIS in 1980, there had been discussion of a new international organization devoted exclusively to the academic field of information systems. A poll of those attending ICIS in 1989 showed that academics were about evenly split on the issue. It became more and more evident that the lack of a single organization resulted in a lack of a strong voice in matters affecting the field.

The Association for Information Systems was formally established in 1995. The governance structure was designed to create a truly international organization. The position of president rotates among three regions: Americas, Europe-Africa, and Asia Pacific Area. AIS has grown to include close to 50 percent of faculty members worldwide.

AIS has allowed the field to concentrate and rationalize many of its resources. There has been an amalgamation of ICIS into AIS. It has taken over responsibility for preexisting assets of the field such as the Directories of IS Faculty, the past proceedings of ICIS, doctoral dissertation lists, survey of salaries for new hires, etc. It has created chapters and special interest groups. It maintains loose ties with many conferences and organizations that existed prior to its formation. AIS provides sponsorship support and doctoral consortia support for the three regional IS conferences.

AIS has two electronic journals: Communications of the AIS (CAIS) for communications about pedagogy, curriculum, and other issues in the field and Journal of the AIS (JAIS), a high quality academic journal. AIS entered into a partnership with The MIS Quarterly to provide this well established journal electronically to its members.

Information systems as an academic discipline clearly began in the developed countries. Many in the field have been concerned about reaching out to developing countries. IFIP has sponsored conferences in developing countries. AIS has initiated programs to make conferences available and less costly to faculty from developing countries. Since the cost of journals is a major impediment to developing countries, AIS has an outreach program that provides access to its e-journals, its proceedings, and the MIS Quarterly at a very nominal cost.

The Role of IFIP and TC8 in the Development and Nourishing of an Academic Discipline of Information Systems

By its very nature, IFIP did not contemplate the development of an academic discipline of computer science, computer engineering, information systems, etc. Rather, as a society of societies, it was to encourage international interaction and working conferences that would bring together participants from across the world. IFIP had a strong advantage in encouraging international cooperation and international workshops and conferences. This advantage stemmed from its role as a society of societies not identified with any one country.

IFIP had one very important weakness. It disseminated conference proceedings through high cost books marketed through a commercial publisher. Royalties provided significant revenues to IFIP, but it made the proceedings too costly for individual purchase. Sales were very low, primarily to libraries and to conference attendees. Recently, IFIP indicated proceedings are available online without cost through Springer.Com. On April 6, 2006, I examined the website and found 37 proceedings available online without cost. This may change the dynamics of distribution and improve use of IFIP proceedings

The real work of IFIP is at the Working Group level. The Technical Committee coordinates the working groups and provides some oversight. It also sponsors some conferences. The question is the role of TC8 in encouraging the development of an academic discipline. I doubt than anyone in TC8 thought of its role in this way. They tended to think of encouraging international cooperation on important topics within the domain of information systems. They have done this very well but have tended to involve fairly small groups rather than large conferences.

Would TC8 have been a viable home for an international information systems academic society such as AIS? Probably not! IFIP was not designed to accomplish the task. The IFIP publications policy did not contemplate such an association. It would have embedded the IS group within a larger organization, and the community felt the need to be more visible and more independent.

Even though TC8 was not a suitable sponsor for an international academic society, the influence of TC8 working groups has been significant. This has been especially true of WG8.2. Its perspectives on important topics such as research methods, socio-technical systems, different views of systems, etc. have made an impact on the larger (perhaps more traditional) community.

6   The Future of Information Systems as an Organization Function

The future of information systems as an academic function is directly related to the future of the organization function. The reason for this strong connection is that a vital IS function provides employment for graduates of IS programs and provides interesting problems for research. An important organization function provides good evidence for the importance of the body of knowledge for IS academic activities. This section summarizes arguments in Davis et al., 2005. More detail can be found in that reference.

Information systems are an area of ongoing, major investment by organizations. The systems provide economic benefits and when combined with other organization systems may provide competitive advantage. Failure to employ information technology effectively may lead to significant organization risks and failures. Arguments that information systems can be outsourced may be applicable to a few activities but even if outsourced, they must be managed by an IS function. Arguments that information systems do not provide competitive advantage because technology can be easily acquired fail because the competitive advantage is not in the technology but in the technology-enabled systems as they are incorporated in the organization systems.

7   Issues about the Future of Information Systems as an Academic Discipline

Conditions for computer science and information systems education differ significantly by region and by country. In North America, there has been a dramatic drop in enrollments and faculty positions (although there are some signs that these are improving.) This downturn may be associated with unique conditions or it may signal an emerging enrollment problem everywhere.

One of the good effects of a downturn is that it causes an academic field to examine itself. The results are discussion about some critical issues that need to be resolved. Extreme pessimists may say that the outcome of the downturn will be the demise of the academic field. They make four arguments: recent drops in IS course enrollment, resistance to IS instruction for all students, resistance to IS as an academic field based on diversity or lack of coherence in research, and resistance in some universities to IS as a new academic discipline.

Drops in enrollment frequently reflect employment bubbles and changes in the employment market rather than fundamental changes in the nature of the organization function and the need for employment. The phenomenon of enrollment drops has happened in other fields, and they have stabilized after the market adjusts. The resistance to a first course for all students may reflect a need for a better course and also the ongoing pressure to reduce required courses. The remedy for a better course is in our hands; the pressure to reduce required courses can be negotiated if the course has high value. Diversity in research can be a weakness, but in the long run, it is probably a strength. It is not surprising that some established schools resist a new field, but it may not reflect on the value of the field. Innovation often comes from schools that are not comfortable and secure in their current position; schools with entrenched reputations often spurn innovation.

The future hinges externally on the vitality and importance of the information systems function. There is reason to view it optimistically. A vital, important function means employment and research opportunities for the IS academic discipline. There are opportunities to study and explain the organization, roles, duties, and operations of the IS function. All students in organization studies need to understand the IS function and its role in organization systems. This need provides a strong basis for the IS academic field. Most of the concerns about the academic field and its place in academia can be dealt with by the field itself. In the midst of concerns about the future, the IS academic faculty should keep in mind the comparative advantage of IS within the business and organization schools.

8   Comparative Advantages of IS as an Academic Discipline

In any discussion of the future and what is possible or likely, it is useful to understand not only weaknesses but also strengths and comparative advantages relative to competing fields. Within the broad academic area of organization studies, the IS academic discipline and IS faculty possesses several comparative academic advantages.

1   The IS academic field understands the IS organization function and what it does that is vital and important. Therefore, the IS field has a comparative advantage in teaching and researching the body of knowledge associated with the function.

2   The IS academic field has a comparative advantage in its depth knowledge of technology-enabled organization systems. These systems are critical in modern organizations. The body of IS knowledge includes analysis of requirements, acquiring systems, operating the technology and support systems that provide services, and making sure the systems are available and secure. The trend toward integration internally and with suppliers and customers increases the importance of these system activities.

3   The IS academic field has a comparative advantage in its level of understanding of systems and systems thinking. Faculty members in other fields know something of systems but it is generally not central to their teaching or research. Students studying for work in organizations are trained in analysis, but they have virtually no training in systems concepts and systems thinking. This may be one of the most important deficiencies in their preparation. The IS function is prepared to correct this deficiency because systems thinking and systems concepts are central to the IS field and the design, implementation, and use of technology-enabled systems.

4   The IS field has a comparative advantage in modeling organizational behavior and data. The reason for this advantage is the centrality of this modeling to the design and implementation of systems and the use of databases by organization systems.

9   Recommendations for Securing the Future

Having described some issues and concerns and the comparative advantages of IS as an academic discipline, five recommendations are proposed for actions that will make a difference. These are explained in more detail in Davis et al., 2005.

a.   Be proactive in defining our domain and articulating the importance of its parts.

b.   Be aggressive in research and teaching at the fuzzy boundaries of applications with shared responsibilities. Every new IT-enabled organization work system is an opportunity for research.

c.   Add real value to students in IS courses.

d.   Be proactive as IS faculty members in keeping current on relevant technology and practice.

e.   Be aggressive in adding value to IS practice and producing graduates prepared for a productive career.

A comment about recommendation 3 that we add real value to students in the IS courses. This appears to be difficult for non majors. In thinking about this issue, I think the answer is that these students should learn to do things that they can apply for years into the future. Examples are: defining requirements for an information system application; examining an existing system to evaluate its value and its deficiencies; evaluating quality, error-prone and error-prevention features of a system; and working with a system development project team. They need to be exposed to system concepts and socio-technical concepts. They need simple, useful frameworks for making sense of the systems they will encounter and the systems they will specify. They need to be able to understand how to think about new technologies and the affordances they offer and to envision new applications.

10 Summary and Conclusions

The purpose of this paper was to organize and present some of my thoughts, based on my experiences in developing the new IS academic discipline, with the objective of helping others to think about these issues. I often am asked why it happened the way it did. I provided the basis for my response. I am also asked what will happen in the future. I am an optimist, so my views are biased toward a favorable outcome. I explained the basis for my concerns and the basis for my optimism. I concluded with some prescriptions for things that need to be done to secure the future of the academic field.

References

1. G.B. Davis. Building an International Academic Discipline in Information Systems, in Bo Sundgren, Pär Mårtensson, Magnus Mähring and Kristina Nilsson, editors, Exploring Patterns in Information Management: Concepts and Perspectives for Understanding IT-Related Change, The Economic Research Institute (EFI), Stockholm School of Economics, Stockholm, Sweden, November 2003, pp. 273-290. Also available through the Electronic Bookstore of the Association for Information Systems.
2. G.B. Davis, A.P. Massey, and N. Bjørn-Andersen. Securing the Future of Information Systems as an Academic Discipline, in Proceedings of the International Conference on Information Systems, December 2005, pp. 979-990.
3. M. J. Culnan. The Intellectual Development of Management Information Systems, 1972-1982: A Co-Citation Analysis, Management Science 33:5, February 1986, pp. 156-172.
4. G.W. Dickson. Management Information Systems: Evolution and Status, in Advances in Computers, M. Yovits, editor, Academic Press, Vol 20, 1981, pp. 1-37.
5. A.J. Hevner, S.T. March, J. Park, and S. Ram, Design Science in Information Systems Research, MIS Quarterly, 28:1, 2004, pp. 75-105.
6. S.T. March and G.F. Smith. Design and Natural Science Research on Information Technology. Decision Support Systems, 15:4, 1995, pp. 251-266.

Methodologies for Developing Information Systems: A Historical Perspective

David Avison[1] and Guy Fitzgerald[2]

1 David Avison, ESSEC Business School, Department of Information Systems and Decision Sciences (SID), 95021 Cergy-Pontoise, France. avison@essec.fr, WWW home page: http://domservices.essec.fr/domsite/cv.nsf/WebCv/David+Avison

2 Brunel University, Department of Information Systems, Computing and Mathematics, Uxbridge, UB8 3PH, UK. guy.fitzgerald@brunel.ac.uk WWW home page: http://www.brunel.ac.uk/~csstggf

Abstract. For the past 30 years and more, Information Systems Development (ISD) has been at the heart of the study and practice of Information Systems (IS). This paper examines the history of ISD methodologies and looks at some of the trends and issues concerning ISD, and shows how these have been reflected in methodologies and how organizations use (or do not use) them. Discussion of the present state of the field is followed by a discussion of possible future directions.

1 Introduction

In this paper we celebrate the 30th anniversary of IFIP Technical Committee 8, which through its working groups (especially, but not limited to, WG 8.1 and WG 8.2) has put ISD amongst its major work and contribution. We also reflect on the coincidental publication of the 4th edition of [1], a book which has a history of merely 18 years. These reflections enable us to build on and bring up to date our short *Communications of the ACM* paper [2] to examine the history of methodologies for ISD as well as reviewing the current position and suggesting some pointers to the future.

Systems development activities have been around for as long as computers but although the development of technology has been phenomenal, the development of a generally-accepted systematic approach or approaches to utilize that technology effectively has been slower and this may have been to some extent a limiting factor on the speed of progress in the use of the technology. In some other practical domains there is a 'one correct way of doing something' – why has this not been the same for ISD?

Please use the following format when citing this chapter:

Avison, D., Fitzgerald, G., 2006, in IFIP International Federation for Information Processing, Volume 214, The Past and Future of Information Systems: 1976–2006 and Beyond, eds. Avison, D., Elliot, S., Krogstie, J., Pries-Heje, J., (Boston: Springer), pp. 27–38.

This paper examines some of the trends and issues related to ISD over time. We identify four eras: pre-methodology, early methodology, methodology and post-methodology. This could be perceived as a 'maturity model for ISD' as some organizations may be in different stages in the same countries, whereas different countries may be in general in front of or behind others. Thus it is risky, if appropriate at all, to put actual dates on the 'eras' as they are more stages of ISD practice. Nevertheless we do suggest approximate decades in which each was at the fore in North America, Europe and Australia. The current era has been one of the most difficult to deal with as it is not at all clear how it will pan out. Unlike for previous eras, we do not have the benefit of hindsight. However, it would appear that the period is perhaps surprisingly one of much greater stability - methodologies are not being invented (or reinvented) as before, many methodologies discussed in previous eras do not now have much following in practice and there is some consolidation in the field. Where development is not outsourced in some way, there is emphasis on approaches which aim at developing a product with greater speed and flexibility.

2 Pre-Methodology Era

Early computer applications, up to around the time TC8 was established, were implemented without an explicit ISD methodology. We thus characterise this as the pre-methodology era. In these early days, the emphasis of computer applications development was on programming. The needs of the users were rarely well established with the consequence that the design was frequently inappropriate to the application needs. The focus of effort was on getting something working and overcoming the limitations of the technology, such as making an application run in restricted amounts of memory. A particular problem was that the developers were technically trained but rarely good communicators. The dominant 'methodology' was rule-of-thumb and based on experience. This typically led to poor control and management of projects. For example, estimating the date on which the system would be operational was difficult, and applications were frequently delivered late and above budget. Programmers were usually overworked, and spent a large proportion of their time correcting and enhancing the few applications that were operational. These problems led to a growing appreciation of the desirability for standards and a more disciplined approach to the development of IS in organisations. Thus the first ISD methodologies were established. Although this era was common in many large European and North American organizations of the '60s, the characteristics can be seen in some companies developing applications on PCs nowadays.

3 Early Methodology Era

As a reaction to the failings of the pre-methodology era:
1. There was a growing appreciation of that part of the development of the system that concerns analysis and design and therefore of the potential role of the systems analyst.

2. There was a realisation that as organisations were growing in size and complexity, it was desirable to move away from one-off solutions to a particular problem and towards more integrated IS.
3. There was an appreciation of the desirability of an accepted methodology for the development of IS.

These reflections led to the evolution of the Systems Development Life Cycle (SDLC) or waterfall model as the approach to develop IS. This was an early methodology, although at the time it was not yet known as such. It included phases, procedures, tasks, rules, techniques, guidelines, documentation, training programs and tools. The waterfall model consisted of a number of stages of development that were expected to be followed sequentially. These stages typically consisted of feasibility study, systems investigation, analysis, design, and implementation, followed by review and maintenance, and this was the approach widely used in the 1970s and even some of the 1980s, and is still a basis for many methodologies today.

The SDLC has been well tried and tested and the use of documentation standards helps to ensure that proposals are complete and that they are communicated to users and computing staff. The approach also ensures that users are trained to use the system. There are controls and these, along with the division of the project into phases of manageable tasks with deliverables, help to avoid missed cutover dates and disappointments with regard to what is delivered. Unexpectedly high costs and lower benefits are also less likely. It enables a well-formed and standard training scheme to be given to analysts, thus ensuring continuity of standards and systems.

However, there are serious limitations to the approach along with limitations in the way it is used. Some potential criticisms are: Failure to meet the needs of management (due to the concentration on single applications at the operational level of the organization); Unambitious systems design (due to the emphasis on 'computerizing' the existing system); Instability (due to the modelling of processes which are unstable because businesses and their environments change frequently); Inflexibility (due to the output-driven orientation of the design processes which makes changes in design costly); User dissatisfaction (due to problems with the documentation and the inability for users to 'see' the system before it is operational); Problems with documentation (due to its computer rather than user orientation and the fact that it is rarely kept up-to-date); Application backlog (due to the maintenance workload as attempts are made to change the system in order to reflect user needs); and the Assumption of 'green field' development (due to the tradition of a new IS 'computerizing' manual systems, an assumption inappropriate as IS now largely replace or integrate with legacy systems).

4 Methodology Era

As a response to one or more of the above limitations or criticisms of the SDLC, a number of different approaches to IS development emerged and what we term 'the methodology era' began. Methodologies can be classified into a number of movements. The first are those methodologies designed to improve upon the traditional waterfall model. A second movement is the proposal of new methodologies that are somewhat different to the traditional waterfall model (and from each other).

Since the 1970s, there have been a number of developments in techniques and tools and many of these have been incorporated in the methodologies exemplifying the modern version of the waterfall model. The various CRIS conferences of IFIP WG8.1 were important here (see, for example [3], published following the third of these conferences and provided an excellent overview of earlier ISD and the early shoots of more sophisticated approaches). Techniques incorporated include entity-relationship modelling, normalisation, data flow diagramming, structured English, action diagrams, structure diagrams and entity life cycles. Tools include project management software, data dictionary software, systems repositories, drawing tools and, the most sophisticated, computer-assisted software (or systems) engineering (CASE) tools (now broadened in scope and more frequently referred to as toolsets). The incorporation of these developments addresses some of the criticisms discussed in section 3. The blended methodologies Merise [4], SSADM [5] and Yourdon Systems Method [6] could be said to be updated versions of the waterfall model. The later method engineering movement (see for example [7], a collaboration of IFIP WG 8.1 and WG 8.2) developed the practice of blending methods and techniques further. Although these improvements have brought the basic model more up to date, many users have argued that the inflexibility of the life cycle remains and inhibits most effective use of computer IS.

It is possible to classify alternative approaches that developed during the 1980s and beyond within a number of broad themes including: systems, strategic, participative, prototyping, structured, and data. Each of these broad themes gave rise to one or more specific methodologies.

General systems theory attempts to understand the nature of *systems*, which are large and complex. Organisations are open systems, and the relationship between the organisation and its environment is important. By simplifying a complex situation, we may be *reductionist*, and thereby distort our understanding of the overall system. The most well-known approach in the IS arena to address this issue is Checkland's soft systems methodology (SSM) [8]. It includes techniques, such as rich pictures, which help the users understand the organisational situation and therefore point to areas for organisational improvement through the use of IS.

Strategic approaches stress the pre-planning involved in developing IS and the need for an overall strategy. This involves top management in the analysis of the objectives of their organisation. These approaches counteract the possibility of developing IS in a piecemeal fashion. IBM's Business Systems Planning is an early example of this approach and business process re-engineering [9] is part of this overall movement.

In *participative* approaches, the role of all users is stressed, and the role of the technologist may be subsumed by other stakeholders of the information system. If the users are involved in the analysis, design and implementation of IS relevant to their own work, particularly if this takes the form of genuine decision-making, these users are likely to give the new IS their full commitment when it is implemented, and thereby increase the likelihood of its success. ETHICS [10] stresses the participative nature of ISD, following the socio-technical movement and the work of the Tavistock Institute and embodies a sustainable ethical position.

A *prototype* is an approximation of a type that exhibits the essential features of the final version of that type. By implementing a prototype first, the analyst can show the users inputs, intermediary stages, and outputs from the system. These are not diagrammatic approximations, which tend to be looked at as abstract things, or technically-oriented documentation, which may not be understood by the user, but the actual data on computer paper or on terminal or workstation screens. Toolsets of various kinds can all enable prototyping. These have become more and more powerful over the last few years. Rapid Application Development [11] is an example of an approach that embodies prototyping.

Structured methodologies are based on functional decomposition, that is, the breaking down of a complex problem into manageable units in a disciplined way. These approaches tend to stress techniques, such as decision trees, decision tables, data flow diagrams, data structure diagrams, and structured English, and tools such as systems repositories.

Whereas structured analysis and design emphasises processes, *data analysis* concentrates on understanding and documenting data. It involves the collection, validation and classification of the entities, attributes and relationships that exist in the area investigated. Even if applications change, the data already collected may still be relevant to the new or revised systems and therefore need not be collected and validated again. Information Engineering [12], for example, has a data approach as its centre.

In the 1990s there was what might be perceived as a second wave of methodologies. *Object-oriented* ISD became another 'silver bullet' [13] and has certainly made a large impact on practice. Yourdon [14] exposition argues that the approach is more natural than data or process-based alternatives, and the approach unifies the ISD process. It also facilitates the realistic re-use of software code. Coad and Yourdon [15] suggest a number of other motivations and benefits for object-oriented analysis, including: the ability to tackle more challenging problem situations because of the understanding that the approach brings to the problem situation; the improvement of analyst-user relationships, because it is not computer-oriented; the improvement in the consistency of results, because it models all aspects of the problem in the same way; and the ability to represent factors for change in the model so leading to a more resilient model. To some extent, therefore, it has replaced the singular process and data emphases on ISD.

Incremental or evolutionary development (often including prototyping) has also been a feature of 1990s development. Incremental development has the characteristic of building upon, and enhancing, the previous versions rather than developing a new system each time. Incremental development aims to reduce the length of time that it takes to develop a system and it addresses the problem of changing requirements as a result of learning during the process of development ('timebox' development, see [11]). The system to be developed is divided up into a number of components that can be developed separately. This incremental approach is a feature of DSDM [16]. Recently developing applications from components from different sources has gained popularity [17] as has obtaining open source software components (reflected in [18,19]).

Some methodologies have been devised for specific types of application. These specific-purpose methodologies include Welti [20] for developing ERP applications; CommonKADS [21] for knowledge management applications; Process Innovation

[22] for business process reengineering applications, Renaissance [23] supporting the reverse engineering of legacy systems and WISDM [24] for web development.

We characterise the above as the methodology era because of the apparent proliferation of different types of methodologies, and their increasing maturity. The work of IFIP WG 8.2 has tended to emphasize the human and organizational aspects of ISD (see for example [18,25]).

Many users of methodologies have found the waterfall model and the alternative methodologies outlined above unsatisfactory. Most methodologies are designed for situations, which follow a stated, or more usually, an unstated 'ideal type'. However, situations are all different and there is no such thing as an 'ideal type' even though situations differ depending on, for example, their complexity and structuredness, type and rate of change in the organisation, the numbers of users affected, their skills, and those of the analysts. Further, most methodology users expect to follow a step-by-step, top-down approach to ISD where they carry out a series of iterations through to project implementation. In reality, in any one project, this is rarely the case, as some phases might be omitted, others carried out in a different sequence, and yet others developed further than espoused by the methodology authors. Similarly, particular techniques and tools may be used differently or not used at all in different circumstances.

There have been a number of responses to this challenge. One response is to suggest a *contingency approach* to ISD (as against a prescriptive approach), where a structure is presented but stages, phases, tools, techniques, and so on, are expected to be used or not (or used and adapted), depending on the situation. Those characteristics which will affect the choice of a particular combination of techniques, tools and methods for a particular situation could include the type of project, whether it is an operations-level system or a management information system, the size of the project, the importance of the project, the projected life of the project, the characteristics of the problem domain, the available skills and so on. Multiview [26] is such a contingency framework.

Many attempts have been made to compare and contrast this diversity of methodologies. Olle [27] provides one example emanating from IFIP WG 8.1. Avison and Fitzgerald [1] compare methodologies on the basis of philosophy (paradigm, objectives, domain and target); model; techniques and tools; scope; outputs; and practice (background, user base, players, and product). In relation to the number of methodologies in existence, some estimates suggested that there were over 1,000 brand name methodologies world-wide, although we are rather skeptical of such a high figure, there is no doubt that methodologies had proliferated, although many of these were similar and differentiated only for marketing purposes. However, the characterization of this as the methodology era does not mean that every organization was using a methodology for systems development. Indeed, some were not using a methodology at all but most, it seems, were using some kind of in-house developed or tailored methodology, typically based upon or heavily influenced by a commercial methodology product.

5   Post-Methodology Era

We identify the current situation as the post-methodology era, in the sense that we now perceive methodologies as having moved beyond the pure methodology era. Now it seems that although some organisations still use a methodology of some kind there is enough of a re-appraisal of the beneficial assumptions of methodologies, even a backlash against methodologies, together with a range and diversity of non-methodological approaches, to justify the identification of an era of reflection.

Methodologies were often seen as a panacea to the problems of traditional development approaches, and they were often chosen and adopted for the wrong reasons. Some organisations simply wanted a better project control mechanism, others a better way of involving users, still others wanted to inject some rigour or discipline into the process. For many of these organisations, the adoption of a methodology has not always worked or been the total success its advocates expected. Indeed, it was very unlikely that methodologies would ever achieve the more overblown claims made by some vendors and consultants. Some organisations have found their chosen methodology not to be successful or appropriate for them and have adopted a different one. For some this second option has been more useful, but others have found the new one not to be successful either. This has led some people to the rejection of methodologies in general. In the authors' experience this is not an isolated reaction, and there is something that might be described as a backlash against formalised ISD methodologies.

This does not mean that methodologies have not been successful. It means that they have not solved all the problems that they were supposed to. Many organisations are using methodologies effectively and successfully and conclude that, although not perfect, they are an improvement on what they were doing previously, and that they could not handle their current systems development load without them.

Yet in the post-methodology era, there are many reasons why organizations are questioning the need to adopt any sort of methodology, as follows: *Productivity:* The first general criticism of methodologies is that they fail to deliver the suggested productivity benefits; *Complexity:* Methodologies have been criticized for being over complex; *'Gilding the lily':* Others argue that methodologies develop any requirements to the ultimate degree, often over and above what is legitimately needed.; *Skills:* Methodologies require significant skills in their use and processes; *Tools:* The tools that methodologies advocate are difficult to use, expensive and do not generate enough benefits; *Not contingent:* Methodologies are not contingent upon the particularities of the project; *One-dimensional approach:* Methodologies usually adopt only one approach to the development of projects, which does not always address the underlying issues or problems; *Inflexible:* Methodologies may be inflexible and may not allow changes to requirements during development; *Invalid or impractical assumptions:* Most methodologies make a number of simplifying yet potentially invalid assumptions, such as a stable external and competitive environment; *Goal displacement:* This refers to the unthinking use of a methodology and to a focus on following the procedures to the exclusion of the real needs of the project being developed. De Grace and Stahl [28] have termed this 'goal displacement' and Wastell [29] talks about the 'fetish of technique', which inhibits creative thinking; *Problems of building understanding into methods:* Introna and

Whitley [30] argue that some methodologies assume that understanding can be built into the method process. They call this 'method-ism' and believe it is misplaced; *Insufficient focus on social and contextual issues:* The growth of scientifically based highly functional methodologies has led some commentators to suggest that we are now suffering from an overemphasis on the narrow, technical development issues and that not enough emphasis is given to the social and organizational aspects of systems development [31]; *Difficulties in adopting a methodology:* Some organizations have found it hard to adopt methodologies in practice, partly due to the resistance of users to change; *No improvements:* Finally in this list, and perhaps the acid test, is the conclusion of some that the use of methodologies has not resulted in better systems, for whatever reasons. This is obviously difficult to prove, but nevertheless the perception of some is that 'we have tried it and it didn't help and it may have actively hindered'. The work of IFIP WG 8.6 on the diffusion of technology has much to teach us here.

We thus find that for some, the great hopes in the 1980s and 1990s, that methodologies would solve most of the problems of ISD have not come to pass. Strictly speaking, however, a distinction should be made in the above criticisms of methodologies between an inadequate methodology itself and the poor application and use of a methodology. Sometimes a methodology vendor will argue that the methodology is not being correctly or sympathetically implemented by an organization. Whilst this may be true to some extent, it is not an argument that seems to hold much sway with methodology users. They argue that the important point is that they have experienced disappointments in their use of methodologies.

One reaction to this is to reject the methodology approach altogether. A survey conducted in the UK [32] found that 57% of the sample were claiming to be using a methodology for systems development, but of these, only 11% were using a commercial development methodology unmodified, whereas 30% were using a commercial methodology adapted for in-house use, and 59% a methodology which they claimed to be unique to their organization, i.e. one that was internally developed and not based solely on a commercial methodology.

A variety of reactions to the perceived problems and limitations of methodologies exist and we now examine some of these. We begin by considering external development, but if the choice is made to develop internally, then users may demand that the methodology that they do use needs to be refined and improved (just as they were in the methodology phase). On the other hand, users may prefer to adapt the methodology according to the particular needs of each circumstance following a contingency approach, or even more informally and risky, an ad hoc approach. In some organizations speed as well as flexibility has become watchwords, and rapid and agile approaches have gained more adherents and the tendency towards more user and customer involvement strengthened. Finally we suggest that we are in a more stable environment than in any time since the early days of ISD methodologies and the foundation of IFIP TC8, and we see the immediate future being one of consolidation.

5.1   External Development

Some organisations have decided not to embark on any more major in-house system development activities but to buy-in all their requirements in the form of packages. This is regarded as a quick and relatively cheap way of implementing systems for organisations that have fairly standard requirements. A degree of package modification and integration may be required which may still be undertaken in-house. Clearly the purchasing of packages has been commonplace for some time, but the present era is characterised by some organisations preferring package solutions. Only systems that are strategic or for which a suitable package is not available would be considered for development in-house. The package market is becoming increasingly sophisticated and more and more highly tailorable packages are becoming available. Sometimes open source components can be 'packaged' to form the application.

Enterprise resource planning (ERP) systems have become particularly popular with large corporations since the mid '90s. The key for these organisations is ensuring that the correct trade-off is made between a 'vanilla' version of a standard package, which might mean changing some elements of the way the business currently operates, and a package that can be modified or tailored to reflect the way they wish to operate.

For others, the continuing problems of systems development and the backlash against methodologies has resulted in the outsourcing and/or offshoring of systems development. The client organisation no longer has any great concern about how the systems are developed. They are more interested in the end results and the effectiveness of the systems that are delivered. This is different to buying-in packages or solutions, because normally the management and responsibility for the provision and development of appropriate systems is given to a vendor. The client company has to develop skills in selecting the correct vendor, specifying requirements in detail and writing and negotiating contracts rather than thinking about system development methodologies.

5.2   Continuing Refinement and Improvement

One reaction to the criticisms that users of methodologies make is for authors and suppliers to 'get methodologies right'. For some there is the continuing search for the methodology holy grail. Methodologies will probably continue to be developed from time to time and, more likely, existing ones evolve. Most methodologies have some gaps in them or, if not complete gaps, they have areas that are treated much less thoroughly than others. For example, rich pictures, cognitive mapping, lateral thinking, scenario planning, case-based reasoning, and stakeholder analysis represent some of the techniques that are rarely included in methodologies, but we see good reasons for their inclusion [1]. Adams and Avison [33] suggest how analysts may choose between techniques as well as potential dangers in their use. Similarly, toolsets have developed greatly over the period from simple drawing tools to very comprehensive toolsets, some designed to support one particular methodology and others to support ISD as a whole.

In particular, methodologies are now appearing to deal with systems development for the web. This, it is argued, has some special characteristics, which make traditional methodologies inappropriate. Baskerville and Pries-Heje [34], for example, list these as time pressure, vague requirements, prototyping, release orientation, parallel development, fixed architecture, coding your way out, negotiable quality, dependence on good people, and the need for structure. The WISDM methodology [24] also addresses web development. Some of the methodologies devised for web development use the term 'agile' to characterise the need for flexibility and adaptability in web development which distinguishes them from traditional approaches (see section 5.4).

5.3   Ad-hoc Development and Contingency

This might be described as a return to the approach of the pre-methodology days in which no formalized methodology is followed. The approach that is adopted is whatever the developers understand and feel will work. It is driven by, and relies heavily on, the skills and experiences of the developers. Truex et al. [35] represents part of this backlash against conventional methodologies as they talk of amethodological and emergent ISD. This is perhaps an understandable reaction, but it runs the risk of repeating the problems encountered prior to the advent of methodologies.

We see a contingent approach as providing a positive response and see this as offering a good balance. A contingency approach to ISD presents a structure to help the developers, but tools and techniques are expected to be used or not (or used and adapted), depending on the situation. Situations might differ depending on, for example, the type of project and its objectives, the organization and its environment, the users and developers and their respective skills. The type of project might also differ in its purpose, complexity, structuredness, and degree of importance, the projected life of the project, or its potential impact. The contingency approach is a reaction to the 'one methodology for all developments' approach that some companies adopted, and is recognition that different characteristics require different approaches and we see it gaining increasing importance.

5.4   Agile Development

When following agile development, requirements are 'evolved' and, as the agile manifesto' [36] suggests, the approach emphasizes the involvement of users and customers in a joint approach to ISD more than processes and tools, working software over comprehensive documentation, customer collaboration over contract negotiation and responding to change over following a plan (see also [37]. Working software is delivered in smaller chunks than traditionally, but in a much shorter time span. Changing requirements are accepted as the norm and even welcomed. These principles conform more to today's ISD needs than many of the ISD methodologies of the 'methodology era', for example reacting to 'Internet speed development' [34]. These features are found in extreme programming (XP) and SCRUM as well as ISD approaches, such as DSDM [38].

5.5   Consolidation

In the previous three previous editions of Avison and Fitzgerald [1] published in 1988, 1995 and 2002, we discussed 9, 12 and 34 themes; 8, 11 and 37 techniques; 7, 6 and 12 tools; and 8, 15 and 32 methodologies respectively. Despite our best research endeavors, the numbers have not increased in the 2006 edition, indeed there has been a decline in numbers as some methodologies (and their associated techniques and tools) fall into disuse. However, this does not necessarily indicate a fall into disuse of frameworks and methodologies for ISD as a whole, but rather a consolidation process, indeed we see some methodology-era methodologies being used effectively and successfully as well as agile and contingent approaches to ISD. This may also suggest greater maturity in the field of IS generally and we see this consolidation process continuing.

6 Conclusion

This paper has attempted to review, albeit briefly, the history and drivers of ISD methodologies. We have used our analysis to reflect on and discuss the current situation, identified as the post-methodology era. This has involved the identification of various eras of methodologies. Our present era is perhaps best described as an era of methodology reappraisal, resulting in a variety of reactions. Although we believe that it is unlikely that any single approach will provide the solution to all the problems of ISD, we do now see a change. Diversity of methodologies and multiplication of similar methodologies has been replaced by some consolidation: ISD has entered a maturing phase of greater stability.

References

1. D.E.Avison and G.Fitzgerald. Information Systems Development: Methodologies, Techniques and Tools. 4th edition, McGraw-Hill, Maidenhead. (2006).
2. D.E. Avison and G. Fitzgerald. Where now for Development Methodologies?, Communications of the ACM, (January, 2003).
3. T.W. Olle, H.G. Sol, and A.A.Verrijn-Stuart (eds). Information Systems Design Methodologies: Improving the Practice, North Holland, Amsterdam (1986).
4. P.T. Quang and C. Chartier-Kastler. Merise in Practice. Macmillan, Basingstoke (1991).
5. M. Eva. SSADM Version 4: A User's Guide. McGraw-Hill, Maidenhead. (1994).
6. Yourdon Inc. Yourdon Systems Method: Model-Driven Systems Development. Yourdon Press, Englewood Cliffs (1993).
7. S. Brinkkemper, K. Lyytinen, and R.J. Welke (eds). Method Engineering: Principles of Method Construction and Tool Support, Kluwer, Boston (1996).
8. P. Checkland and J. Scholes. Soft Systems Methodology in Action. Wiley, Chichester (1990).
9. M. Hammer and J. Champy. Reengineering the Corporation: A Manifesto for Business Revolution. Harper Business, New York (1993).
10. E. Mumford. Effective Requirements Analysis and Systems Design: The ETHICS Method. Macmillan, Basingstoke (1995).
11. J. Martin. Rapid Application Development. Prentice Hall, Englewood Cliffs (1991).
12. J. Martin. Information Engineering. Prentice Hall, Englewood Cliffs (1989).
13. G. Booch. Object Oriented Design with Applications. Benjamin/Cummings, Redwood City (1991).
14. E. Yourdon. Object-oriented Systems Design, An Integrated Approach. Prentice Hall, Englewood Cliffs (1994).

15. P. Coad and E. Yourdon. Object Oriented Analysis. Prentice Hall, Englewood Cliffs (1991).

16. DSDM Manual Version 3 DSDM Consortium, Tesseract, Surrey (1998).

17. V. Sugumaran and V.C. Storey. A semantic-based approach to component retrieval, Database for Advances in Information Systems, 34, 3 (2003).

18. N.L. Russo, B. Fitzgerald, and J. DeGross (eds) Realigning Research and Practice in Information Systems development. Kluwer, Boston (2001).

19. J. Feller and B. Fitzgerald. Understanding Open Source Software Development, Addison Wesley, Harlow (2002).

20. N. Welti. Successful SAP R/3 Implementation, Addison-Wesley, Harlow (1999).

21. G. Schreiber, H. Akkermans, A. Anjewierden, R. de Hoog, N. Shadbolt, W. Van de Velde, and B.J. Wielinga. Knowledge Engineering and Management: The Common KADS Methodology, MIT Press, Cambridge (2000).

22. T.H. Davenport. Process Innovation, Harvard Business School, Boston (1993).

23. I. Warren. The Renaissance of Legacy Systems, Springer-Verlag (1999).

24. R. Vidgen, D.E. Avison, R. Wood, and A.T. Wood-Harper. Developing Web Information Systems, Butterworth-Heinemann, London (2002).

25. D.E. Avison, J. Kendall, and J. DeGross (eds). Human, Organizational and Social Dimensions of IS Development. North Holland, Amsterdam (1993).

26. D.E. Avison, A.T. Wood-Harper, R. Vidgen, and R. Wood. Multiview: A Further Exploration in IS Development, McGraw-Hill, Maidenhead (1996).

27. T.W. Olle. Information Systems Methodologies: A Framework for Understanding, Addison Wesley, Harlow (1988).

28. P. De Grace and L. Stahl. The Olduvai Imperative: CASE and the State of Software Engineering Practice. Prentice Hall, Englewood Cliffs (1993).

29. D. Wastell. The Fetish of Technique: methodology as a social defence. Information Systems Journal, 6, 1 (1996).

30. L. Introna and E. Whitley. Against method-ism: Exploring the limits of method, Information Technology and People, 10, 1, 31-45 (1997).

31. R. Hirschheim, H.K. Klein, and K. Lyytinen. Exploring the intellectual structures of information system development: A social action theoretic analysis, Accounting, Management and Information Technologies, 6, 1/2 (1996)

32. G. Fitzgerald, A. Philippides, and P. Probert. Information Systems Development, Maintenance and Enhancement: Findings from a UK Study, International Journal of Information Management, 40 (2), 319-329 (1999).

33. C. Adams and D.E. Avison. Dangers Inherent in the Use of Techniques: Identifying Framing Influences, Information Technology and People, 16, 2 (2003).

34. R. Baskerville and J. Pries-Heje. Racing the e-bomb: How the Internet is redefining IS development methodology, in N. L. Russo, et al. (2001)

35. D.Truex, R. Baskerville, and H. Klein. Growing Systems in Emergent Organizations, Communications of the ACM (42:8), (1999), pp. 117-123.

36. K. Beck et al. Agile Manifesto, available at http://agilemanifesto.org/ (2001).

37. J. Highsmith. Agile Software Development Ecosystems, Addison-Wesley, Harlow (2002).

38. J. Stapleton. DSDM: A Framework for Business Centred Development, Addison-Wesley, Harlow (2002).

Stakeholders Selection for Interorganizational Systems: A Systematic Approach

Luciana C. Ballejos[1] and Jorge M. Montagna[1,2]

1 CIDISI - FRSF Universidad Tecnológica Nacional
Lavaise 610 – (3000) Santa Fe - Argentina
lballejo@frsf.utn.edu.ar

2 INGAR – Instituto de Desarrollo y Diseño
Avellaneda 3657 – (3000) Santa Fe – Argentina
mmontagna@ceride.gov.ar

Abstract. Stakeholders identification is a critical task for successful software projects. In general, there are no methodologies that allow performing it in a systematic way. Besides, several facts must be analyzed when the project is carried out in a context formed by multiple organizations. The complexity of these environments makes the task extremely hard. To face these difficulties, stakeholders are defined and analyzed taking into account the characteristics of the interorganizational dimension. Also a methodology is proposed for carrying out their identification that allows systematically specifying all people, groups and organizations whose interests and needs are affected by the information system in all the involved dimensions.

1 Introduction

Stakeholders are the primary source of requirements for any software project [1]. They are defined as any group or individual that can affect or be affected by the achievement of an organization's objectives or that must be involved in a project because they are affected by its activities or results [2].

Big software projects involve a great number of stakeholders with different expectations that can be controversial [3, 4]. They can also be geographically dispersed. Thus, the action of appropriately involving the relevant ones is highly important for success [5, 6]. However, there are few authors that have studied the stakeholder concept applied to contexts formed by multiple organizations, generally called Interorganizational Networks (IONs), where usually opposed and competitive interests and cultures coexist. Some of the authors working in this area are Pouloudi [7], Sharp et al. [8] and Kotonya and Sommerville [9], who suggest integral definitions of the term. A holistic concept of all the others can be provided, which states that a stakeholder of an interorganizational information system (IOS) is any

Please use the following format when citing this chapter:

Ballejos, L.C., Montagna, J.M., 2006, in IFIP International Federation for Information Processing, Volume 214, The Past and Future of Information Systems: 1976–2006 and Beyond, eds. Avison, D., Elliot, S., Krogstie, J., Pries-Heje, J., (Boston: Springer), pp. 39–50.

individual, group, organization or institution that can affect or be affected (in a positive or negative way) by the system under study and that has direct or indirect influence on the requirements. This definition is similar to the traditional one, but extended to include also firms that interact in interorganizational (IO) contexts.

Even though there is a concept of stakeholder that may be applied to these environments, there are no practical models for their identification when the interorganizational dimension must be incorporated [10]. Pouloudi and Whitley [11], for example, present principles, without posing clear tasks to obtain concrete results with an adequate degree of consistency and reliability. To counteract this, a systematic approach for selecting stakeholders for these environments is presented.

2 Stakeholder Types

Different types of stakeholders exist in each project. In general, there is a lack of understanding regarding *types* and ideal candidates. This has incidence on the non-existence of systematic approaches for efficiently identifying them [12]. Bittner and Spence [1] propose to start involving stakeholders by first identifying different types. We define *stakeholder type* as the classification of sets of stakeholders sharing the same characteristics in relation to the context under analysis.

Traditional identification of types of stakeholders is focused on those inside the organization under study. This constitutes an inappropriate reference framework, since valuable information for a correct interpretation of the problem is missed [2, 13]. For IOSs there exists the need of incorporating the interorganizational dimension. It is also necessary to avoid focusing only on those stakeholders directly related to the development and use of systems, such as users and developers [5, 12, 14]. A more reality-adjusted one is necessary [11]. The traditionally used term "internal" must be extended. There are not only stakeholders inside the firm, but also stakeholders inside the ION, who will take care of the common objectives at network level. Stakeholders **inside each firm** represent some particular firm. Those **inside the ION** pursue interorganizational objectives, representing the network interests, which many times do not coincide with those of individual firms.

Another distinction can be made between **internal** and **external** stakeholders, depending on whether they are previously involved in organizations (manager, employee, etc.) or they are included because of having a necessary vision for this particular project (customers, suppliers, auditors, regulators, experts, etc.) [5, 13].

3 Stakeholder Roles

Besides the attributes held by stakeholders regarding the context in which they are included, it is necessary to take into account the roles they play during the project. A *stakeholder role* may be defined as a collection of defined attributes that characterize a stakeholder population, its relationship with the system and its impact or influence on the project.

Even though several authors focus role analysis on users and developers (or technicians) of an information system, there are others that should be studied as well [3, 12, 14, 15]. The most used in the literature are described in Table 1 [15, 16, 17, 18, 19]. They might be represented in any project.

Table 1. Stakeholder Roles.

Beneficiary: Those that benefit from the system implementation.
• Functional: Those that benefit directly from the functions performed by the system and its products or results. Other information systems that interact with the new one can be included in this role.
• Financial: Those that benefit indirectly from the system, obtaining financial rewards.
• Political: They benefit indirectly from the system, obtaining political gains in terms of power, influence and/or prestige.
• Sponsor: Those in charge of the project. They start the system development, collect funds and protect it against political pressures and budget reductions, etc. They are in charge of providing authority and guidance, and respecting priorities.
Negative: Those that undergo some kind of damage as a consequence of the system implementation or are adversely impacted by its development (for example, losing their jobs or power for decision making, physical or financial damage, etc.).
Responsible: They are in charge of the system development in all phases. This type includes people working with budgets and agreed times (e.g.: project manager, developers, responsible for selecting suppliers, etc.).
Decision-Maker: Those that control the process and make decisions to reach agreements. They define the way in which consensus is attained throughout the project.
Regulator: Also called "legislator" [8]. They are generally appointed by government or industry to act as regulators of quality, security, costs or other aspects of the system. They generate guidelines that will affect the system development and/or operation. For instance, health organisms that control standards, non-governmental organisms, organisms that defend rights, organisms related to legal, tax controls, etc.
Operator: They are also called "users" by many authors [14, 15]. They operate the system to be developed. They interact with the system and use its results (information, products, etc.). They are different from functional beneficiaries, even though their roles may overlap. An operator can benefit form the system or not.
Expert: They are familiar with functionalities and consequences of the system implementation. They widely know the implementation domain and can collaborate in the requirements elicitation to a great extent.
Consultant: Include any role dealing with providing support for any aspect of the system development. They are generally external to the organization and have specific knowledge on a particular area.

4 Methodology for Stakeholders Identification in IO Environments

Existing approaches for identifying stakeholders do not provide enough tools or concrete techniques, even in organizational environments [8]. Many consider stakeholders as a default product of a non-explained identification process [11]. But their selection is a key task, since all important decisions during the project are made by them. Thus, a methodology for guiding their identification in IO environments is proposed. It is composed by steps which are described in the following subsections.

4.1 Specify the Types of Stakeholders to be Involved in the Project

This step specifies the types of stakeholders the project will count on, analyzing the various existing contexts. Using the previously presented *stakeholder type* concept, a framework is introduced in Table 2. It allows performing an analysis by starting from different **criteria** applied to different **dimensions**, thus a profile characterization of the stakeholders to be involved is obtained.

After analyzing the specific needs in an IO context from different examples, a basic set of criteria was defined. It provides elements to characterize the stakeholders involved. Nevertheless, this set may be extended according to the specific needs of certain environments and IOSs. Each criterion identifies different points of view, needs or influences on the IOS development. They must be applied to each dimension in the work space (**organizational, interorganizational** and **external**).

Table 2. Multidimensional framework for stakeholders identification.

| | | SELECTION DIMENSION | | |
| | | INTERNAL | | EXTERNAL |
		ORG	ION	
SELECTION CRITERION	FUNCTION (functions or processes affected by the IOS)			
	GEOGRAPHICAL (geographical regions affected by the project)			
	KNOWLEDGE/ ABILITIES (abilities and knowledge about the IOS application domain)			
	HIERARCHICAL LEVEL (involved structural levels)			

4.1.1 Function Criterion

Implies the analysis of functions or tasks that will be affected by the IOS, either directly (because the system will support them) or indirectly (because IOS outputs and results will be used by them). Its application to the organizational dimension is intended to select stakeholders of each function affected by the IOS in each firm.

This criterion applied to the ION dimension identifies the main activities that take place in the network, basis for collaboration among organizations. Representatives of the integrated process must be involved, who will defend interorganizational interests, rather than individual or organizational ones. At external level, attention is focused on organizations that are external to the ION when the IOS somehow modifies their interaction with the network.

4.1.2 Geographical Criterion

This criterion identifies stakeholders located in different geographical places, with cultural and idiomatic differences, etc., since the organizations may be geographically dispersed. Organizational dimension considers geographical dispersion at firm level. It specifies the inclusion of stakeholders belonging to each branch or enclave of each firm. On the other hand, the network can have dispersed units, from which stakeholders must be selected. It will also be necessary to count on stakeholders that represent the geographical dispersion of external organizations whose relations with ION members will be modified by the IOS.

4.1.3 Knowledge / Abilities Criterion

This criterion is important to involve stakeholders having specific knowledge or abilities about the information universe underlying the IOS implementation domain. At organizational level, specific abilities for internal tasks in each organization must be analyzed. Attention must be placed on stakeholders having technical knowledge on modules or applications that will interact with the IOS. In the ION dimension, aspects to be taken into account are: interorganizational processes, supporting technologies, characteristics of interactions, etc. There may be also entities external to the ION with experience in the IOS implementation area or in the processes it will support, such as consultants or experts in technologies.

4.1.4 Hierarchical Level Criterion

The analysis is intended to involve stakeholders from every level affected by the IOS. Structures and decision flows must be studied. In the organizational dimension, stakeholders must be selected from every hierarchical level of each organization. At ION level, there is also a structure that can allow for different formalization degrees, according to each particular case. Each decision level must be involved. Also structures from external organizations must be included for the external dimension.

4.2 Specify the Roles to be Included in the Project

This step specifies the roles that will be included in the project. It is generic, since it has similar results in any example it is applied to. It can be performed simultaneously to the **Step 1**. Its results make the project manager become aware of the scope and time of participation of each particular role during the project.

The greatest possible quantity of the roles described in Table 1 will be represented. Charts like the presented in Table 3 must be generated. There Bittner and Spence [1] describe each role and present details of the associated responsibilities and participation frequency. "Participation" attribute significantly varies from one project to another, since it depends on the objectives of the project that is being executed and on personal estimations of the project manager.

Table 3. Information to be specified of each stakeholder role [1].

> - **Name:** Stakeholder Role Name.
> - **Brief Description:** Briefly describing the role and what it represents for the project. The stakeholder represents a group of stakeholders, some aspect of the participating organizations, or some other affected business area.
> - **Responsibilities:** Summarizing key responsibilities in relation to the project and to the system to be developed. Specifying the value the role will provide to the project team. For example, some responsibilities may be monitoring the project progress, specifying expenditure levels and approving funds spending, etc.
> - **Participation:** Briefly describe how they will be involved in the project and in which stages they will have influence.

4.3 Select Stakeholders

This task is based on Table 2 developed in **Step 1**. It has the objective of guiding the selection of entities having the characteristics identified previously. By analyzing the different criteria in the various dimensions, the project manager must identify concrete stakeholders that match that profile. The various profiles may be represented by individuals, groups, organizations, or a combination of them.

Characteristics of the selected stakeholders must be documented (Table 4). Rows show the different identified entities, through an ID and a name for each stakeholder, a brief description, the criteria used and the corresponding dimension. The last columns are completed in the following steps.

Table 4. Information to be gathered from each selected stakeholder.

| ID | STAKEHOLDER | Description | TYPE | | ROLE | INTEREST / IMPORTANCE | INFLUENCE |
			Criterion	Dimension			
S1							
S2							
Sn	...	...	...	...	...	...	...

4.4 Associate Stakeholders with Roles

The roles of the stakeholders selected in **Step 3** are specified, using the charts created in **Step 2** (Table 3). The first subtask is to restrict the set of roles each stakeholder can represent. Table 5 must be filled to associate the different **options** resulting from the analysis of the various **criteria** in all **dimensions** (rows) to the diverse **roles** a stakeholder with those attributes might play (columns).

The project manager must estimate the roles that can be played by certain criterion option and mark the corresponding intersection. Marked cells will represent the existence of a generic relationship between a particular stakeholder type and the roles it might be associated with, according to the attributes that define the type.

Table 5. Stakeholders Type-Roles Relationship.

| | | | ROLES | | | | | | | | | | |
| | | | BENEFICIARY | | | | | | | | | | |
DIMENSION		CRITERION	OPTIONS	FUNCTIONAL	FINANCIAL	POLITICAL	SPONSORING	NEGATIVE	RESPONSIBLE	DECISION-MAKER	REGULATOR	OPERATOR	EXPERRT	CONSULTANT
INTERNAL	ORG	Function												
		Geographical												
		Knowl./Ability												
		Hierarc. Level												
	ION	Function												
		Geographical												
		Knowl./Ability												
		Hierarc. Level												
EXTERNAL		Function												
		Geographical												
		Knowl./Ability												
		Hierarc. Level												

The second subtask is more concrete. During it, the manager must decide the role/s each stakeholder identified in Table 4 will play and record this in the **"Stakeholder Role"** column. To facilitate the analysis, Table 5 must be used. Paying attention to the different options of criteria and dimensions that gave rise to the selection of a particular stakeholder, the manager must decide which of the marked roles will be definitely represented by that entity.

Sometimes, the roles associated to a particular type of stakeholder may be contradictory. As a consequence, the manager will have to decide (possibly together with the stakeholders) on the role they will be definitely assigned.

4.5 Analyze the Importance and Influence of Stakeholders

Several authors propose the analysis of the importance (or interest) and the influence stakeholders have in a project before being included [20, 21, 22, 23]. The importance indicates the extent to which the project cannot be considered successful if his needs and expectations are not managed. The project success is important for some stakeholders (e.g. beneficiaries). Others have a relatively low importance. In the same way, some stakeholders have greater power and influence on the project decisions, which influences the project design, implementation and results. Anyway, it is important to have exact understanding of stakeholders' importance to determine interests' priorities at future stages of the project. The criteria and the distinction between roles associated to the stakeholders (**Step 4**) greatly facilitate this task.

With the aim of having a general view of the different degrees of importance and influence of all stakeholders, they are placed on the matrix shown in Table 6, where each stakeholder is located in some of the presented quadrants. Also, with this information, **Interest/Importance** and **Influence** columns of Table 4 must be filled.

Table 6. Stakeholders Matrix.

		INFLUENCE	
		HIGH	LOW
INTEREST / IMPORTANCE	HIGH	A Constitute the supporting base of the project.	B Need special initiatives.
	LOW	C Can influence results, but their priorities are not the same as those of the project. This may constitute a risk or an obstacle for the project.	D Least important stakeholders for the project.

Quadrant A: Some stakeholders may have much influence and even be very interested in the project. It is vital to understand these stakeholders' viewpoints, especially their potential objections. Such is the case, for example, of those that are sure that their interests and needs will be satisfied with the system and that have power for decision-making and/or influence on financing sources for the project.

Quadrant B: They are highly interested in the project, but their influence may be small. If they are in favor of it, they are valuable sources of information: they can accede to relevant documents and help in identifying challenges.

Quadrant C: They will not pay attention to the project details, since they consider that it does not affect them. However, they have influence on the project success: for example, they can vote for the project approval.

Quadrant D: The least possible amount of time must be devoted to these stakeholders. They are not interested in the project and are not in such a position that can help the project manager to perform his job.

Once these tasks are finished, concrete stakeholders having a particular interest in the IOS development have been identified. Also the roles they can play during the initial stages of the project were associated to each one, basing the analysis on their profiles. There is also an initial idea of the importance and influence they can have on the project. After this identification activity, the requirements elicitation remains.

5 Example

A project developed in the United Kingdom and encouraged by the National Health Service (NHS) has been selected to show the application of the presented methodology. It was previously used by other authors [2]. It has been enriched with information extracted from NHS webpage to have a more real vision of the problem [24]. It is a written case study where the proposed approach is applied in retrospect.

Authorities and Trusts are the different types of organizations that run the NHS at a local level. England is split into 28 Strategic Health Authorities (SHAs). They are responsible for managing local organizations on behalf of the English Department of Health. Within each SHA, the NHS is split into various types of Trusts that take responsibility for running different services in each local area. They group hospitals, organizations that work in health and social care, ambulance services, or first services (e.g.: doctors, dentists, pharmacists). All participating organizations will become part of a Trust and will be managed by an SHA. They are the main entities in the ION. Its external entities are patients, auditing committees, other government areas, medicines suppliers, educational institutions, etc.

The project is called Integrated Care Record Service (ICRS). It involves the design of an information system for managing a wide set of services that cover generation, movement and access to health files. It includes workflow capacities for managing and recording the movement of patients throughout all entities in the NHS. The main goal is the transformation of the current model of separated systems circumscribed to organizational structures into a globalizing model. ICRS will include e-prescribing, e-booking, delivering patient information such as test results and prescription information on-line and so on [25]. The previous utilization of information systems, applications and local data bases in member organizations should be taken into account. They must be integrated to the IOS.

The following lines present the results to be obtained if the methodology proposed is applied in this example. It does not constitute an exhaustive application. It is only intended to show its usefulness and some results that may be reached.

5.1 Step 1. Specify the Types of Stakeholders to be Involved in the project

Table 7 includes examples of the different criteria in the existing dimensions.

5.2 Step 2. Specify the Roles to be Included in the Project

A basic chart corresponding to the Operator role is shown as example (Table 8).

5.3 Step 3. Select Stakeholders

Various stakeholders can be identified with Table 7. Table 9 present some of them, with the information required for this step. It shows a unique occurrence of stakeholders with a certain profile. There may be cases in which different ones share the same profile but represent different organizations, regions, etc. Each of them will have a different input in the table.

Table 7. Types of Stakeholders for ICRS System.

		SELECTION DIMENSION		
		INTERNAL		EXTERNAL
		ORGANIZATION	ION	
SELECTION CRITERION	FUNCTION	Administrative Processes: Hospital Admission Process; Bed and Waiting list management; Master Patient Index maintenance; Booking. Clinical Processes: Special Services; Biochemical Analyses; Prescribing; Emergencies Management; Care Plans and Assessments.	- Planning Processes for stock management and medicines distribution. - Material Supplying. - Purchase of high complexity equipment. - National Integrated Process of urgencies and patients derivation. - SHAs: relations and partnerships with universities and education institutions.	- Patients. There exist diverse forums, commissions and committees for patients from which stakeholders can be selected: • Public Advisory Board (PAB). • Patients Forums. - Auditor Committees: to evaluate IOS results. - Government Areas that impose rules or conditions to the IOS functions and to the information that it will manage. - Laboratories and suppliers.
	GEOG.	Branches, dependencies, etc. of participating organizations.	- Medicines distribution centers. - Regional Health Departments. - Strategic Health Authorities.	- Geographical locations of the patients. - National branches of the laboratories that supply drugs and medicines to the ION organizations.
	KNOWLED.- ABILITIES	- Operators of the existing systems and that should interact with the ICRS. - Those in charge of the Informatics Area. - Organization's own standards.	- Health Improvement and Modernization Programmes. - Specialists in Health matters (e.g.: Quality Standards) - Promoters for the integrity of health information. - National analytical services (to provide expert intelligence to add value, through analysis and interpretation, and to promote Information sharing).	- Specialist in process redesign: to review issues of current practices, best practices guidelines and design new integrated processes. - National Clinical Advisory Board (NCAB). It is a committee to represent healthcare professionals (consultants, nurses, dentists, and pharmacists). - NHS Information Standards Board (ISB): to determine information standards for the system. - Universities and other education institutions. - Specialists in technology to be employed for IOS development.
	H.L.	Organizational authorities: hierarchical levels of each participating entity.	- English Department of Health. - Strategic Health Authorities. - Trusts.	- Hierarchical levels involved of the government areas, laboratories, suppliers, educational institutions.

Table 8. Example of Operator Role Description.

- **Name:** Operator.
- **Brief Description:** It represents people and groups that interact directly with the IOS.
- **Responsibilities:** It must express needs and requirements for the normal operation of the system to be developed. They must test proceedings adjustments and suggest modifications according to their experience. They must revise documentation of proceedings and functionalities.
- **Participation:** It will participate at different stages of the project:
  - Stage of functional and non-functional requirements elicitation (e.g. design/approval of use cases).
  - Stage of Proceedings Development after Design and Codification.
  - Stage of Transition and test of the system to be implemented.

5.4 Step 4. Associate Stakeholders with Roles

Table 10 associates possible roles to different criteria and dimensions previously specified. Then, the decided roles each stakeholder will play must be specified (Table 11). This must be included in the "**Role**" column of Table 9.

5.5 Step 5. Analyze the Importance and Influence of Stakeholders

Table 12 shows each stakeholder's interest and influence. This information must be reflected in the last two columns of Table 9 and is used to develop Table 13.

Table 9. Stakeholders Chart for ICRS (last 3 columns of Table 4 are omitted).

ID	STAKEHOLDER	Description	TYPE Criterion	TYPE Dimension
S1	Biochemists Group Organization X	They perform their activities in laboratories of Organization X. Their tasks will be modified.	Function	Organiz. (Hospital X)
S2	Patient A	Persons who will use health public services, whose information will be managed by the IOS. It will be associated to a particular region (Region A).	Function / Geograph.	External
S3	Director of the English Department of Health	Pursues political goals and interests of the government and National Health Department.	Hierarch.	ION
S4	Strategic Health Authority (SHA) Region 1	Pursues political goals and regional interests in health area (Region 1).	Hierarch.	ION
S5	Specialist in Process Redesign	To defend strategic issues for the performance improvement of the processes implemented with the IOS.	Knowl./Abil.	External
S6	In charge of Systems Compatibility Organization Y, Branch 1	Specify interaction requirements among information systems already existing in Branch 1 of organization Y and the IOS to be implemented.	Knowl./Abil. / Geograph.	Organiz. (Pharmacy Y)

Table 10. Stakeholders Types-Roles Relationship for ICRS.

DIMENSION	CRITERION	OPTIONS	FUNCTIONAL	FINANCIAL	POLITICAL	SPONSORING	NEGATIVE	RESPONSIBLE	DECISION-MAKER	REGULATOR	OPERATOR	EXPERRT	CONSULTANT
INTERNAL / ORG	Function	S1 - Information Management in Biochemical Laboratories. ...	√				√				√		
	Geographical	S6..Sn - Orgs-IOS Systems Compatibility. ...	√									√	√
	Knowl./Ability	S6..Sn - Orgs-IOS Systems Compatibility. ...	√									√	√
	Hierarc. Level	...											
INTERNAL / ION	Function	...											
	Geographical	...											
	Knowl./Ability	...											
	Hierarc. Level	S3- Director of English Health Department			√				√	√			
		S4..Sn – Strategic Health Authorities, SHAs.						√	√	√			
EXTERNAL	Function	S2..Sn - Order prescriptions, make bookings appointments on-line, access to test results and prescription information, etc. ...	√				√				√		
	Geographical	S2..Sn-Patients from particular regions. ...	√				√				√		
	Knowl./Ability	S5-Specialist in process redesign. ...										√	√
	Hierarc. Level	...											

Table 11. Stakeholder Roles for ICRS.

ID	STAKEHOLDER	ROLES
S1	Biochemists Group Organization X	Functional Beneficiaries, Operators
S2	Patient A	Functional Beneficiaries
S3	Director English Department of Health	Political Beneficiary, Decision-Maker
S4	Strategic Health Authority Region 1	Responsible, Decision-Maker
S5	Specialist in Process Redesign	Expert
S6	Responsible for Systems Compatibility Organization Y, Branch 1	Expert

Table 12. Stakeholders Interest and Influence for ICRS (Left).
Table 13. Stakeholders Matrix for ICRS (Right).

ID	STAKEHOLDER	INT. / IMP.	INFLUENCE
S1	Biochemists group **Organization X**	LOW	HIGH
S2	Patient **A**	HIGH	LOW
S3	Director English Department of Health	HIGH	HIGH
S4	Strategic Health Authority **Region 1**	HIGH	HIGH
S5	Specialist in Process Redesign	HIGH	LOW
S6	In charge of Systems Compatibility **Organization Y, Branch 1**	HIGH	LOW
S7	...	...	...

		INFLUENCE	
		HIGH	LOW
INTEREST IMPORTANCE	HIGH	S3 S4 ...	S2 S5 S6
	LOW	...	S1 ...

S2, S5 and S6 have high importance and low influence. Even though their viewpoint is essential, they have no control on the possibility of making crucial decisions for the project.

Regarding S3 and S4, their location in the quadrant denoting high importance and influence is due to the fact that they have power for decision making and influence on the project. In the NHS structure, they constitute different hierarchical levels. Politicians are the most interested parties and promoters of the project.

S1 was associated to high influence and low importance. According to the project manager's decision, requirements of this group do not constitute the main to be elicitated, and they have no influence on the decisions to be made in the project.

6 Conclusions

Stakeholders identification is a critical matter in software projects in general. IO environments introduce not only a new analysis dimension but also different interests and interactions that must be analyzed. This constitutes a challenge for the decisions that must be taken during the project at different levels. The existing related literature, however, does not provide practical guides to be systematically applied for selection in these environments. To overcome this, this work proposes a concrete methodology composed of steps for carrying out stakeholders' identification for interorganizational projects.

This proposal improves the already existing ones because is systematic, since it provides concrete tools to be applied considering all dimensions involved in these environments. It is also flexible, since new criteria for selection can be added to the methodology enhance the information and knowledge about the involved contexts. It is a concrete methodology that, in spite of being developed for contexts formed by multiple organizations, it may be also applied to traditional organizational contexts, avoiding the analysis of the proposed interorganizational dimension.

Acknowledgments: The authors want to thank the financial support from CONICET (Consejo Nacional de Investigaciones Científicas y Técnicas), Agencia Nacional de Promoción Científica y Tecnológica and UTN (Universidad Tecnológica Nacional) from Argentina.

References

1. K. Bittner, I. Spence, Establishing the Vision for Use Case Modeling, Use Case Modeling, Addison Wesley Professional, 2003.
2. A. Pouloudi, R. Gandecha, A. Papazafeiropoulou, C. Atkinson, How Stakeholder Analysis can Assist Actor-Network Theory to Understand Actors. A Case Study of the Integrated Care

Record Service (ICRS) in the UK National Health Service, Eltrun Working Paper Series, WP 2004-002, 2004.

3. J. Giesen, A. Völker, Requirements Interdependencies and Stakeholders Preferences, IEEE Joint International Conference on Requirements Engineering (RE'02), 2002.

4. B. Nuseibeh, S. Easterbrook, Requirements Engineering: A Roadmap, ICSE, Conference on The Future of Software Engineering, 2000, pp. 35-46.

5. G.S.C. Pan, Information Systems Project Abandonment: A Stakeholder Analysis, International Journal of Information Management, 25(2), 2005, pp. 173-184.

6. A. Papazafeiropoulou, A. Pouloudi, A. Poulymenakou, Electronic Commerce Competitiveness in the Public Sector: The Importance of Stakeholder Involvement, Int. J. of Services Technology and Management, 3(1), 2002, pp. 82-95.

7. A. Pouloudi, Aspects of the Stakeholder Concept and their Implications for Information Systems Development, 32 Annual Hawaii International Conference on System Sciences. 1999.

8. H. Sharp, A. Finkelstein, G. Galal, Stakeholder Identification in the Requirements Engineering Process, DEXA Workshop 1999, pp. 387-391.

9. G. Kotonya, I. Sommerville, Requirements Engineering: Processes and Techniques, J. Wiley & Sons Eds. 2003.

10. D. Chatterjee, T. Ravichandran, Inter-organizational Information Systems Research: A Critical Review and an Integrative Framework, 37th Hawaii International Conference on System Sciences, 2004.

11. A. Pouloudi, E.A Whitley, Stakeholder Identification in Inter-Organizational Systems: Gaining Insights for Drug Use Management Systems, European Journal of Information Systems, 6, 1997, pp. 1-14.

12. J. Coughlan, R.D. Macredie, Effective Communication in Requirements Elicitation: A Comparison of Methodologies, Requirements Engineering Journal, 7, 2002, pp. 47-60.

13. J. Jonker, D. Foster, Stakeholder Excellence? Framing the Evolution and Complexity of a Stakeholder Perspective of the Firm, Corporate Social Responsibility and Environmental Management, 9, 2002, pp. 187-195.

14. G. Khalifa, Z. Irani, L.P Baldwin, S. Jones, Evaluating Information Technology With You in Mind, Electronic Journal of Information Systems Evaluation, 4(1), 2001.

15. P. Gruenbacher, Integrating Groupware and CASE Capabilities for Improving Stakeholder Involvement in Requirements Engineering, Euromicro Workshop on Software Process and Product Improvement at 26th Euromicro Conference, 2000, pp. 2232-2239.

16. I.F. Alexander, A Better Fit – Characterising the Stakeholders, Requirements Engineering for Business Process Support (REBPS) 2004 Workshop, CAISE'04, 2004.

17. A. Kelvin, How stakeholders with various preferences converge on acceptable investment programs, Journal of Evaluation and Program Planning, 23, 2000, pp. 105-113.

18. J. Ropponen, K. Lyytinen, Components of Software Development Risk: How to Address Them? A project Manager Survey, IEEE Transactions on Software Engineering, 26(2), 2000.

19. V. Shankar, G.L. Urban, F. Sultan, Online trust: a stakeholder perspective, concepts, implications and future directions, J. of Strategic Information Systems, 11, 2002, pp. 325-344.

20. L. M. Applegate, Stakeholder Analysis Tool, Harvard Business Review, April, 2003.

21. J. Boutelle, Understanding Organizational Stakeholders for Design Success, Boxes and Arrows, May 2004. Available at: http://www.boxesandarrows.com/view/understanding_organi zational_stakeholders_for_design_success

22. A. Qualman, A Note on Stakeholder Analysis, Guidance Note on How to Do Stakeholder Analysis of Aid Projects and Programmes. Document prepared by the British Overseas Development Administration (ODA), Social Development Department. July 1995.

23. L.W. Smith, Project Clarity Through Stakeholder Analysis, CrossTalk, The Journal of Defense Software Engineering. December, 2000.

24. National Health Service, in: http://www.connectingforhealth.nhs.uk.

25. The Go Between Information for Information Users, 54, October, 2003. In: http://www. assist.org.uk/Branches/London/the_go_between/Go-Between%20-%20ISSUE54.pdf

Data Quality Management and Evolution of Information Systems

Carlo Batini[1], Barbara Pernici[2]

1 Università degli Studi di Milano Bicocca
Via degli Arcimboldi 8, Milano (Italy)
batini@disco.unimib.it
2 Politecnico di Milano
Piazza Leonardo da Vinci 32, Milano (Italy)
barbara.pernici@polimi.it
WWW home page: http://www.elet.polimi.it/people/pernici

Abstract. Information systems have been rapidly evolving from monolithic/ transactional to network/service based systems. The issue of data quality is becoming increasingly important, since information in new information systems is ubiquitous, diverse, uncontrolled. In the paper we examine data quality from the point of view of dimensions and methodologies proposed for data quality measurement and improvement. Dimensions and methodologies are examined in their relationship with the different types of data, from structured to unstructured, the evolution of information systems, and the diverse application areas.

1 Introduction

Managing data quality is a complex task, especially in modern organizations where information is ubiquitous and diverse. Information is processed inside organizations, but it can also be provided to other organizations and, hence, affect the quality of organizational services. Consequently, researchers have collected clear evidence that poor data quality can have a negative impact on customer satisfaction and, thus, competitiveness [1–3]. There is a general agreement in the literature on the business value of data quality (IQ) and on the cost implications of errors in information management for both internal and external users.

The evolution of information systems from systems which are accessed by a set of well identified users in a well defined context to services available online to different and unknown types of users has greatly increased the potential impact of poor data quality. Data quality requirements have changed accordingly to this different context of use, and information management has evolved and requires a more organized planning, monitoring, and control of data quality. The nature of data itself has

Please use the following format when citing this chapter:

Batini, C., Pernici, B., 2006, in IFIP International Federation for Information Processing, Volume 214, The Past and Future of Information Systems: 1976–2006 and Beyond, eds. Avison, D., Elliot, S., Krogstie, J., Pries-Heje, J., (Boston: Springer), pp. 51–62.

changed in information systems: different types of information, different types of information systems, wide increase of application domains are relevant issues.

The goal of this paper is to analyze data quality issues in information systems, in particular considering the evolution of information systems characteristics. Three coordinates of analysis are proposed: types of information, types of information systems, and application areas. Providing a complete map of the evolution of dimensions, techniques, methodologies, and tools is a complex issue. In the following sections we focus on a few representative dimensions, highlighting the evolution path of data quality dimensions and methodologies for data quality measurement and improvement among the three coordinates of analysis introduced above.

The paper is organized as follows: in Section 2, we discuss the main dimensions of data quality proposed in the literature. The three coordinates for analyzing data quality in information systems proposed in the paper are discussed in Sections 3-5. Finally, in Section 6 we discuss approaches being developed to improve data quality in information systems.

2 Dimensions of Data Quality

In the data-quality literature, various authors have proposed a rich set of possible data-quality dimensions, considering conformance to specifications, user requirements, context of use, and so on; however, a comprehensive list of commonly agreed quality dimensions is still not available. Dimensions are distinguished typically in two categories: schema quality dimensions, that refer to the quality of the intensional representation of data, the schema, and data quality dimensions, that refer to the quality of the extensional representation of data, i.e. their values. In the following we focus mainly on data quality dimensions, which are more relevant in influencing the quality of business processes and services, and we will interchange the terms data and information depending on the context.

Lists of data dimensions can be found in [4], [5], [1], [6] [7], and [2]. For a comparison of the different definitions and classifications see also [8]. Data quality dimensions reported by most authors in the field are:

- *Accuracy*: "inaccuracy implies that the information system represents a real world state different from the one that should have been represented". Inaccuracy refers to a garbled mapping into a wrong state of the information system, where it is possible to infer a valid state of the real world though not the correct one.
- *Timeliness*: refers to "the delay between a change of the real-world state and the resulting modification of the information system state". Lack of timeliness may lead to an information system state that reflects a past real world state. A particular form of timeliness is Synchronization among different time series concerns proper integration of data having different time stamps.

- *Completeness*: is "the ability of an information system to represent every meaningful state of the represented real world system". Completeness is of course tied to incomplete representations.
- *Consistency*: consistency of data values occurs if there is more than one state of the information system matching a state of the real world system, therefore "inconsistency would mean that the representation mapping is one-to-many".
- *Interpretability* concerns the documentation and metadata that are available to interpret correctly the meaning and properties of data sources.
- *Accessibility* measures the ability of the user to access the data as from his/her own culture, physical status/functions and technologies available.
- *Usability* measures the effectiveness, efficiency, satisfaction with which specified users perceive and make use of data.
- *Trustworthiness* (of an organization) measures how reliable is the organization in providing data sources.

3 Types of Data

Researchers in the area of data quality must deal with a wide spectrum of possible data representations. A basic classification proposed by several authors is to distinguish, implicitly or explicitly, three types of data:

1 *structured*, when the data are distinguished in elementary items, and each of them is represented with a format that can be described by a grammar.
2 *semi structured*, when data has a structure which has some degree of flexibility. Semi structured data are also "schemaless" or "self-describing" data (see [9-11]).
3 *unstructured*, when data are expressed in natural language and no specific structure or domain types are defined.

Dimensions and techniques for data quality have to be adapted for the three types of data described above, and are progressively more complex to conceive and use from structured data to unstructured ones. For structured and semi-structured data, the quality of data is usually measured by means of quality dimensions such as accuracy, completeness, and currency, since they are context independent and associated with consolidated assessment algorithms. For unstructured data, assessment techniques are less consolidated. For example, it is inherently difficult to evaluate the accuracy and completeness of a text. The evaluation of timeliness is instead easier and more common. The frequency of updates can be easily measured for a text and related to benchmarks [12].

A second point of view sees data as a particular manufacturing product. This point of view is adopted. In the Information Production Map (IP-MAP) model ([13], an extension of the Information Manufacturing Product model [14]; the IP-MAP model identifies a parallelism between the quality of data, and the quality of products as managed by manufacturing companies. In this model three different types of data are distinguished:

- *raw data items* are considered as the smaller data units. They are used to construct information and component data items that are semi-processed information;
- *component data items* are stored temporarily until the final product is manufactured. The component items are regenerated each time an information product is needed. The same set of raw data and component data items may be used (sometimes simultaneously) in the manufacturing of several different information products;
- *information products* are the result of a manufacturing activity performed on data.

Looking at data as a product, as we will see later in Section 6, allows exploiting well-established methodologies and procedures developed for quality assurance in manufacturing processes.

The third classification, proposed in [15], addresses a typical distinction made in information systems between elementary data and aggregated data. Elementary data are data managed in organizations by operational processes, and represent atomic phenomena of the real world (e.g., social security number, age, sex). Aggregated data are obtained from a collection of elementary data by applying some aggregation function to them (e.g. the average income of tax payers in a given city). This classification is useful to distinguish different levels of severity in measuring and achieving the quality of data. As an example, the accuracy of a field sex changes dramatically if we input M (male) instead of F (female); if the age of a single person is wrongly imputed as 25 instead of 35, the accuracy of the average age of a population of millions of inhabitants is minimally affected.

4 Types of Information Systems

Different criteria can be adopted in classifying the different types of information systems, and corresponding architectures; they are usually related to the overall organizational model and rules adopted in the organization or the set of the organizations that make use of the information system. In order to clarify the impact of data quality on the different types of information systems, we adapt the classification criteria proposed in [16] for distributed databases. Three different criteria are proposed: distribution, heterogeneity, autonomy.

Distribution deals with the possibility of distributing the data and the applications over a network of computers. *Heterogeneity* considers all types of semantic and technological diversities among systems used in modeling and physically representing data. *Autonomy* has to do with the degree of hierarchy and rules of coordination, establishing rights and duties, defined among the organization using the information system. The two extremes are: (i) a fully hierarchical system, where only one subject decides for all, and no autonomy at all exists; and (ii) a total anarchy, where no rule exists, and each component organization is totally free in its design and management decisions.

The three classifications are represented all together in the classification space of Figure 1. Among all possible combinations, five main types of information systems are highlighted in the figure: Monolithic, Distributed, Data Warehouses, Cooperative, Peer to Peer, Service-oriented.

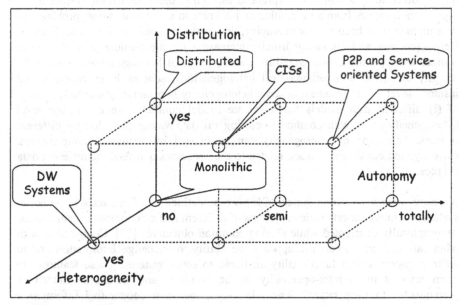

Fig. 1. Types of information systems

In a *Monolithic information system,* presentation, application logic, and data management are merged into a single computational node. Many monolithic information system are still in use. While being extremely rigid, they provide advantages to organizations, such as reduced costs due to homogeneity of solutions and centralization of management. In monolithic systems data flows have common format, decided at design time, and data quality control is facilitated by the homogeneity and centralization of procedures and management rules.

A *Data Warehouse* (DW) is a centralized collection of data collected from different sources designed to support management decision making. Data warehouses contain a wide variety of data that present an integrated and coherent picture of all data used in operational processes of an organization, eventually enriched with external sources, at a single point in time. Development of a data warehouse includes development of systems to extract data from operating systems plus installation of a warehouse database system that provides managers flexible access to the data. The most critical problem in DW design concerns the cleaning and integration of the disparate sources that are loaded in the DW, in that much of the implementation budget is spent on data cleaning activities.

A *Distributed information system* relaxes the rigid centralization of monolithic systems, in that it allows distribution of resources and applications among a network of systems, geographically distributed. Data design is usually performed centrally, but to a certain extent some degree of heterogeneity can occur, due to the impossibility to establish unified procedures. When the information system of an organization moves from a monolithic architecture to a distributed one, problems of data management become more complex, due to the reduced level of centralization. Heterogeneities and autonomy usually increase with the number of nodes. Data sources are typically characterized by various kinds of heterogeneities, that can be roughly classified into technological heterogeneities, schema heterogeneities and instance-level heterogeneities. Schema heterogeneity is principally due to the usage of (i) different data models that originate model conflicts, while Instance level heterogeneity deals with conflicts occurring on data values provided by different sources. This type of heterogeneity can be caused by accuracy, completeness, currency, and consistency errors, related to the processes that feed the different data sources.

A *Cooperative Information System* (CIS) can be defined as a large scale information system that interconnects various systems of different and autonomous organizations, geographically distributed while sharing common objectives [17]. Cooperation with other information systems presupposes the ability to exchange information and to make a system's own functionality available to other systems. These features are often referred to as inter-operability in the literature and should be treated as prerequisites to cooperation". The relationship between cooperative information systems and data quality is double face: from one side one can take profit of the cooperation among agents in order to choose best quality sources, and improve in such a way the quality of circulating data; from the other side, data flows are less controlled then in monolithic systems, and the quality of data, when not controlled, may rapidly decrease in time. In cooperative information systems it is difficult, although crucial for achieving data quality, to individuate a subject, usually called data owner, that is responsible for a certain data category. In fact, data are typically replicated among the different participating organizations, and one does not know how to state that an organization or subject has the primary responsibility for some specific data. These aspects make difficult for a new user of the information system to become confident and assess the reputation of other users. Trustworthiness issues are also related to identification of ownership of data. Another issue crucial for data quality becoming relevant in cooperative information systems is to keep track of the provenance of data. Data provenance is defined in [18] as the "description of the origins of a piece of data and the process by which it arrived in the database". The typical mechanism used to trace the provenance is using annotations. The annotation concept can be used to represent a wide spectrum of information about data, such as comments or other types of metadata, and, in particular, quality data.

In a *Peer to Peer information system* (usually abbreviated into P2P), the traditional distinction, typical of distributed systems, between clients and servers is disappearing. Every node of the system plays the role of a client and a server. The node pays its participation in the global exchange community by providing access to its computing resources, without no obligation on the quality of its services, and data. A P2P system can be characterized by a number of properties: no central coordination, no central database, no peer has a global view of the system, global behavior emerges from local interactions, peers are autonomous, and peers and connections are unreliable. It is clear that P2P systems are extremely critical from the point of view of data quality, since no obligation exists for agents participating in the system, and it is costly and risky for a single agent to evaluate the reputation of other partners.

In a *Service-oriented information system* the functionalities of information systems are provided as services to external and potentially unknown users. Services are published in registries and a service-oriented architecture provides the infrastructure to select and invoke services. Services may be annotated with information about their quality-of-service characteristics, including data quality dimensions (see e.g. [19]). In this way the service provider can declare which are the quality characteristics of the service it provides, and the service user can use these annotations, both to select the services to use and as an element to verify the trustworthiness of the service provider.

5 Application Areas

Data quality has a leading role in a wide number of application domains, under different perspectives. In the following, we discuss the role of data quality in some of the most relevant application areas, selected among a wide spectrum of domains, and, specifically, e-Government, web applications, and Life Sciences.

5.1 e-Government

The main goal of all e-Government projects is the improvement of the relationship between government agencies and citizens, as well as between agencies and businesses, through the use of information and communication technologies. E-Government projects must face the problem that similar information about one citizen or business is likely to appear in multiple databases, each autonomously managed by different agencies that, historically, have never been able to share their data about the citizens and businesses. The problem of data quality in e-Government is worsened by the many errors usually contained in the legacy databases of agencies, due to many causes. First, due to the nature of the administrative flows, several citizens' (and businesses') data (e.g., addresses) tend to become stale and are not updated for long periods of time. Also, errors may occur when personal data are stored. Furthermore, data provided by distinct sources differ in format, following local conventions, that can even change in time and result in multiple versions. One major consequence of having multiple disconnected views for the same information, is that citizens and businesses experience consistent service degradation during their interaction with the agencies.

5.2 Web Applications

Web applications are characterized by the presentation to a wide audience of a large amount of data, the quality of which can be very heterogeneous. There are several reasons for this variety, but a significant reason is the conflict between two needs. On the one hand information systems on the web need to publish information in the shortest possible time after it is available from information sources. On the other hand, the most relevant dimensions are, form one side, accuracy, currency, and completeness, relevant also in the monolithic setting, form the other side a new dimensions arises, namely trustworthiness of the sources. With the advent of internet-based systems, web information systems, and peer to peer information systems, sources of data increase dramatically, and provenance on available data is difficult to evaluate in the majority of cases. This is a radical change with respect to old centralized systems (still widespread in some organizations, such as banks), where data sources and data flows are accurately controlled and monitored. So, evaluating trustworthiness becomes crucial in web information systems. Several papers deal with this issue, see e.g. [20] and [21]. These two requirements are in many aspects contradictory: accurate design of data structures, and in the case of web sites, of good navigational paths between pages, and certification of data to verify its correctness are costly and lengthy activities, while publication of data on web sites requires stringent times. Web information systems present three peculiar aspects with respect to traditional information sources: first, a web site is a continuously evolving source of information, and it is not linked to a fixed release time of information; second, the process of producing information changes, additional information can be produced in different phases, and corrections to previously published information are possible. Such features lead to a different type of information with respect to traditional media.

Interpretability is a dimension whose importance has increased dramatically while moving from monolithic systems to cooperative and internet based systems. More and more data and information is exchanged within flows in which the meaning of data is not explicitly represented.

Accessibility is also a major quality issue in web systems to guarantee understandability and feasibility when navigating and querying the web.

5.3 Life Sciences

Life sciences data and, specifically, biological data are characterized by a diversity of data types, very large volumes, and highly variable quality: data are available through vastly disparate sources and disconnected repositories, and their quality is difficult to assess and often unacceptable for the required usage. Biologists typically search several sources looking for good quality data, for instance in order to perform reliable experiments. However, the effort to actually assess the quality level of such data is entirely in the biologists' hands; they have to manually analyze disparate sources, trying to integrate and reconcile heterogeneous and contradictory data in order to identify the best ones.

As an example, a typical activity of a biologist is to analyze a set of genes, with the objective of understanding their functions. The biologist may perform a web search on a site that is known to contain gene data for the particular organism under consideration. Once the data is obtained, the biologist must assess its reliability; in order to do so, he may perform a new web search in order to check if other sites provide the same gene information. It may happen that different sites provide conflicting results. The biologist has also to check that the provided results are up to date, i.e., if a gene is "unknown" in the queried sites, or no recent publication on that gene is available, e.g. through Pubmed (see [22]). In order to overcome such problems, Life Sciences and Biology need for a robust use of data quality techniques.

6 Methodologies for Data Quality

Two types of recovery actions are proposed in case of insufficient data quality: reactive recovery actions and proactive recovery actions. Reactive recovery actions are performed contextually with the execution services of the information system and allow the recovery of running services. Proactive recovery actions are mostly based on data mining techniques and can only be executed in an off-line mode; proactive recovery actions are complex and require the support of an environment that is able to execute services, detect runtime faults, and perform recovery actions without compromising the running instances of the monitored Web services. A long term approach to improvement is adopted, where recovery actions have the goal to improve services and applications in order to avoid future failures. Process-oriented methods allow the identification of the causes of data errors and their permanent elimination through an observation of the whole process in which data are involved.

In the following, we discuss first a proactive approach, while in the subsequent section reactive approaches are illustrated.

6.1 Quality as Manufacturing of Information Products: IP-UML

As mentioned in Section 2, an information product approach to data quality can be the basis for proactive process-based methods for data quality improvement. The IP-UML approach [26] proposes to define a UML profile for data quality within a methodology that is based on the IP-MAP framework, with some original additional proposals: (i) the artifacts to produce during the improvement process are defined using UML elements defined in the profile for data quality; (ii) it uses IP-MAPs not only in order to assess quality and to detect the need for improvement actions, but also as a diagrammatic way to design improvement actions. The starting concepts are the ones defined in the IP-MAP framework. The Information Quality profile consists of three different models, namely: (i) the Data Analysis Model, identifying which data are of interest, (ii) the Quality Analysis Model, identifying the quality requirements for each data type, and

(iii) the Quality Design Model, modeling data and processes together in order to model process-based improvement actions. As for techniques to produce artifacts, design patterns for quality improvement are proposed. Quality improvement is a complex activity that typically requires investments in terms of money and of people skills. The reuse of solutions and experiences can be very useful in supporting quality improvement, and can reduce time and costs considerably. For instance, a variety of techniques for data improvement are proposed in the literature and can be adopted as the basis for design patterns. The most straightforward solution suggests the adoption of data-oriented inspection and rework techniques, such as data bashing or data cleaning [10]. These techniques focus on data values and can solve problems related to data accuracy and data consistency quality dimensions [10]. A fundamental limitation of these techniques is that they do not prevent future errors. They are considered appropriate only when data are not modified frequently [10]. On the other hand, a more frequent use of data bashing and data cleaning algorithms involves high costs that can be difficult to justify.

A Process to Improve data quality is proposed, consisting of three distinct phases: Data Analysis, Quality Analysis and Quality Improvement Design. The Data and Quality Analysis phases are inspired by the IP-MAP framework, and are simply explained by the specific UML artifacts that should be produced in each phase in conformance with the Information Quality profile. The Quality Improvement Design phase consists of two distinct sub-phases, namely: the Quality Verification phase and the Quality Improvement phase. The former is inspired by the IP-MAP framework; while, the latter has been introduced with the specific aim of using IP-MAPs to explicitly model improvement processes. The task of data quality improvement needs to be adequately supported by software tools. Such tools can be classified as follows: Modeling tools, supporting non-automatic activities, such as modeling and design. Measurement tools, implementing quality measurement techniques. Ad-hoc tools.

6.2 Self Healing Systems

Self healing systems are proposed in [27] to provide repair actions when faults in the information system are identified. Among the possible faults we consider in the present paper data level faults as a type of application-level faults. Internal data level faults include data quality faults that are related to the data manipulated during the execution of a specific service. It is important to evaluate the quality of information flow along a specific service since failures can be caused by incorrect or missing information.

The healing approaches proposed are based on repair actions defined for the different types of faults, leveraging on adaptivity mechanisms at the web-service and application levels. In particular, we focus on healing mechanisms based both on service selection and substitution and on the addition of new services in composed processes to support self-healing functionalities. For each diagnosed fault, one or more recovery actions are executed and, with respect to the way in which these actions are performed.

Run time recovery actions in data quality require the identification of the causes of data errors and their permanent elimination through an observation of the whole process in which data are involved. Data tracking methods are required in order to determine the exact stage or steps in information process where the causes of data quality decreasing occur[6].

Tools are being proposed for data quality monitoring, analysis, and improvement. For instance, the Poliqual Quality Factory [28] allows performing both (i) *on line evaluation*: the property quality values and aggregate quality values are computed using the corresponding algorithms, as illustrated above, and (ii) *off-line evaluation*: aggregate quality values are precomputed and stored in a quality repository. Moreover, decision rules for applying the above mentioned evaluation techniques can be designed, focusing in particular on evaluation of quality metadata and improvement actions.

7 Concluding Remarks

Evolving characteristics of information systems pose new requirements with respect to data quality. Poor data quality has implications in terms of additional costs, both for data quality improvement actions and for indirect effects of poor data quality such as, for instance, reduced trustworthiness of providers of information system services. Additional research is needed to evaluate which are the most relevant quality dimensions according to the different characteristics of a specific information system. Moreover, cost implications need further investigation and techniques for planning, monitoring, and controlling data quality, both with reactive and proactive approaches are still being investigated.

References

1. T. Redman. Data Quality for the Information Age. Artech House (1996)
2. T. Redman. Data Quality The field guide. The Digital Press (2001)
3. L.P. English. Improving data warehouse and business information quality: methods for reducing costs and increasing profits. John Wiley & Sons, Inc., New York, NY, USA (1999)
4. Y. Wand and R. Wang, R. Anchoring data quality dimensions in ontological foundations. Communications of the ACM 39(11) (1996)
5. R. Wang and D. Strong. Beyond Accuracy: What Data Quality Means to Data Consumers. Journal of Management Information Systems 12(4) (1996)
6. M. Bovee, R. Srivastava, and Mak, B. A Conceptual Framework and Belief-Function Approach to Assessing Overall Information Quality. In: Proceedings of the 6th International Conference on Information Quality. (Boston, MA, 2001)
7. M. Jarke, M. Lenzerini, Y. Vassiliou, and P. Vassiliadis, P., eds. Fundamentals of Data Warehouses. Springer Verlag (1995)
8. M. Scannapieco, P. Missier, and C. Batini, C. Data Quality at a Glance. Datenbank Spectrum 14 (2005) 6–14

9. S. Abiteboul, P. Buneman, and D. Suciu. Data on the Web: From Relations to Semistructured Data and XML. Morgan Kaufmann Publishers (2000)

10. P. Buneman. Semistructured data. In: Proceedings of PODS '97, Tucson, Arizona (1997)

11. D. Calvanese, D.D. Giacomo, and M. Lenzerini. Modeling and querying semistructured data. Networking and Information Systems Journal 2(2) (1999) 253– 273

12. B. Pernici and M. Scannapieco. Data quality in web information systems. J. Data Semantics 1 (2003) 48–68

13. G. Shankaranarayan, R. Wang, and M. Ziad. Modeling the Manufacture of an Information Product with IP-MAP. In: Proceedings of the 6th International Conference on Information Quality (ICIQ 2000), (Boston, MA, 2000)

14. R. Wang, Y. Lee, L. Pipino, and D. Strong. Manage your information as a product. Sloan Management Review 39(4) (1998) 95–105

15. P. Missier, G. Lack, V. Verykios, F. Grillo, T. Lorusso, P. Angeletti. Improving data quality in practice: a case study in the italian public administration. Parallel and distributed Databases 13(2) (2003) 135–160

16. M.T. Ozsu, P. Valduriez. Principles of Distributed Database Systems, Second edition. Prentice Hall (2000)

17. G. De Michelis, E. Dubois, M. Jarke, F. Matthes, J. Mylopoulos, M. Papazoglou, K. Pohl, J. Schmidt, C. Woo, E. Yu. Cooperative Information Systems: A Manifesto. In Papazoglou, M., Schlageter, G., eds.: Cooperative Information Systems: Trends & Directions. Accademic-Press (1997)

18.   P. Buneman, S. Khanna, W. Tan. Why and where: A characterization of data provenance. In: Proceedings of the International Conference on Database Theory (ICDT). (London, United Kingdom, 2001) 316–330

19.   B. Pernici. ed. Mobile Information Systems. Springer (2006)

20.   L. De Santis, M. Scannapieco, T. Catarci. Trusting Data Quality in Cooperative Information Systems. In: Proceedings of 11th International Conference on Cooperative Information Systems (CoopIS 2003). (Catania, Italy, 2003)

21.   A.F. Cardenas, R. Pon. Data quality inference. In: IQIS '05: Proceedings of the 2nd International Workshop on Information Quality in Information Systems, New York, NY, USA, ACM Press (2005)

22.   U.S. National Institutes of Health (NIH). (http://www.pubmedcentral.nih.gov/)

23.   H. Krawczyk, B. Wiszniewski. Digital document life cycle development. In: ISICT 2003: Proceedings of the 1st International Symposium on Information and Communication Technologies, Trinity College Dublin (2003) 255–260

24.   H. Krawczyk and B. Wiszniewski. Visual GQM approach to quality-driven development of electronic documents. In: Proceedings of the Second International Workshop on Web Document Analysis (WDA2003) (2003)

25.   International monetary fund. (http://dsbb.imf.org/)

26.   M. Scannapieco, B. Pernici, E.M. Pierce. IP-UML: Towards a methodology for quality improvement based on the IP-MAP framework. In: IQ. (2002) 279–291

27.   D. Ardagna, C. Cappiello, M. Fugini, P. Plebani, B. Pernici. Faults and recovery actions for self-healing web services (2006)

28.   C. Cappiello, C. Francalanci, and B. Pernici. A self-monitoring system to satisfy data quality requirements. In: OTM Conferences (2). (2005) 1535–1552

Panel: OASIS in the Mirror: Reflections on the Impacts and Research of IFIP WG 8.2

Kenneth E. Kendall[1] (panel chair), David Avison[2],
Gordon Davis[3], Julie E. Kendall[4], Frank Land[5], and
Michael D. Myers[6]

[1] Rutgers University, US, ken@thekendalls.org
[2] ESSEC Business School, France, avison@essec.fr
[3] University of Minnesota, US, gdavis@csom.umn.edu
[4] Rutgers University, US, julie@thekendalls.org
[5] London School of Economics and Political Science, UK,
FLandLSE@aol.com
[6] University of Auckland, NZ, m.myers@ auckland.ac.nz

Abstract. What has IFIP contributed to the field of information systems and organizations through the activities of Working Group 8.2, its central working group in information systems? What has WG 8.2 delivered to its constituents? What have the results and impacts of the WG 8.2 been on the larger community? This panel will not shy away from controversy as it discusses the history, contributions, and unrealized potential of research spawned by this working group over the past 30 years.

1 Introduction

The central IFIP working group in information systems is IFIP Working Group 8.2. OASIS is the acronym adopted by Working Group 8.2 to stand for Organizations and Society in Information Systems. One definition of *oasis* refers to it as a fertile spot in a desert or wasteland. Another definition implies that an oasis is a retreat or place of refuge from unpleasant or chaotic surroundings. Working Group 8.2 titles its semi-annual newsletter as "OASIS" as well as calling its informal workshops preceding ICIS meetings "OASIS."

What has IFIP contributed to the field of information systems and organizations through the activities of Working Group 8.2, its central working group in

Please use the following format when citing this chapter:

Kendall, K.E., Avison, D., Davis, G., Kendall, J.E., Land, F., Myers, M.D., 2006, in IFIP International Federation for Information Processing, Volume 214, The Past and Future of Information Systems: 1976–2006 and Beyond, eds. Avison, D., Elliot, S., Krogstie, J., Pries-Heje, J., (Boston: Springer), pp. 63–66.

Kenneth E. Kendall[1], David Avison[2], Gordon Davis[3], Julie E. Kendall[4], Frank Land[5], and Michael D. Myers[6]

information systems? What has WG 8.2 delivered to its constituents? What have the results and impacts of the WG 8.2 been on the larger community?

Within the foregoing framework of this broad topic, this panel of past and present chairs of WG 8.2, and past and present IFIP officers and national representatives, will discuss the nature, methodologies, and direction of research related to the interaction of organizations and society with information systems and IT from inception of the working group until the present.

The panel will engage in debate on some of the hallmark debates resonating through IS and WG 8.2 including the relative merits of qualitative versus quantitative research; the question of rigor versus relevance; and whether technical or nontechnical approaches are superior.

Questions to be examined by the panel also include: Has the research originating from WG 8.2 members been fertile? Has WG 8.2 visibly altered the academic landscape? Or are the premier journals, deans of business schools, and junior faculty in IS still taking conservative (or safe) approaches identical to those held prior to the inception of Working Group 8.2? Additionally, have we been inclusive or exclusive in the way we accept innovative ideas, paradigms, methodologies, tools or even IS researchers?

Among the participants in this panel are four Past Chairs WG 8.2, a Past Chair of TC8, and the Current Chair of WG 8.2.

About the Panelists

Kenneth E. Kendall, Ph. D., (panel chair) is a professor of ecommerce and information technology in the School of Business-Camden, Rutgers University. He is one of the founders of the International Conference on Information Systems (ICIS) and a Fellow of the Decision Sciences Institute (DSI). He is currently the President-Elect of DSI and a Past Chair of WG 8.2. Dr. Kendall has been named as one of the top 60 most productive MIS researchers in the world and recently co-authored a text, *Systems Analysis and Design*, sixth edition and *Project Planning and Requirements Analysis for IT Systems Development*. Dr. Kendall has had his research published in *MIS Quarterly, Management Science, Operations Research, Decision Sciences, Information & Management, CAIS* and many other journals. For his mentoring of minority doctoral students in information systems, he was named to the *Circle of Compadres* of the Ph.D. Project, which was begun by the KPMG Foundation a decade ago to increase the diversity of business school faculty. Professor Kendall's research focuses on studying push and pull technologies, ecommerce strategies, and developing new tools for systems analysis and design. His email is ken@thekendalls.org.

Dr. David Avison is Professor of Information Systems at ESSEC Business School, Paris, France after being Professor at the School of Management at Southampton University for nine years. He is joint editor of Blackwell Science's *Information Systems Journal*. He has over twenty books to his credit (plus one translation from the French). Recently he published four books, including the third edition of the text *Information Systems Development* (jointly with Guy Fitzgerald). He has published a large number of research papers in learned journals, edited texts, and conference papers. He served as vice chair of IFIP technical committee 8 and was past Chair of IFIP WG 8.2. He was past President of the UK Academy for Information Systems and also chair of the UK Heads and Professors of IS. Recently he was a Program Chair of ICIS 2005 in Las Vegas. He researches in information systems development and on information systems in their natural setting, in particular using action research, though he has also used a number of other qualitative research approaches. His email is avison@essec.fr.

Gordon B. Davis is the Honeywell Professor of Management Information Systems at the Carlson School of Management, University of Minnesota. He received his MBA and Ph.D. from Stanford University. He also holds honorary doctorates from the University of Lyon, the University of Zurich, and the Stockholm School of Economics. He is a Fellow of the Association for Computing Machinery. He is the U.S.A. representative of IFIP Technical Committee 8 (Information Systems) and has served as chairman of TC8. He serves on the editorial boards of major journals in the field. He has published extensively and written 20 books in the MIS area. His areas of research include MIS planning, information requirements determination, conceptual foundations for IS, control and audit of information systems, quality control for user-developed systems, in-context assessment of information systems, and management of knowledge work. Gordon can be reached by e-mail at gdavis@csom.umn.edu.

Julie E. Kendall, Ph. D., is an associate professor of ecommerce and information technology in the School of Business-Camden, Rutgers University. Dr. Kendall is the immediate Past Chair of IFIP Working Group 8.2 and was awarded the Silver Core from IFIP. Professor Kendall has published in *MIS Quarterly, Decision Sciences, Information & Management, CAIS, Organization Studies* and many other journals. Additionally, Dr. Kendall has recently co-authored textbook, *Systems Analysis and Design*, sixth edition. She is also a co-author of *Project Planning and Requirements Analysis for IT Systems Development*. She co-edited the volume *Human, Organizational, and Social Dimensions of Information Systems Development* published by North-Holland. Dr. Kendall is a Senior Editor for *JITTA* and is on the editorial boards of the *Journal of Database Management* and *IRMJ* and was Co-Coordinator of the DSI Doctoral Student Consortium in 2003. She also serves on the review board of the *Decision Sciences Journal of Innovative Education* and was a functional editor of MIS for *Interfaces* and an associate editor for *MIS Quarterly*. Dr. Kendall is researching policy formulation for ICTs in developing countries, and agile methodologies for systems development. Her email is julie@thekendalls.org.

Frank Land received his Bsc (Econ) from the London School of Economics in 1950. In 1952, he joined J. Lyons, the UK food and catering company that pioneered the use of computers for business data processing, building its own computer, the LEO (Lyons Electronic Office). He stayed with LEO until 1967 when he was invited to establish teaching and research in information systems at the London School of

66   Kenneth E. Kendall[1], David Avison[2], Gordon Davis[3], Julie E. Kendall[4],
        Frank Land[5], and Michael D. Myers[6]

Economics. In 1982, he was appointed Professor of Systems Analysis. In 1996, he became Professor of Information Management at the London Business School. On his retirement in 1992, he was appointed Visiting Professor of information Management at the LSE. Frank is a past Chairman of IFIP WG 8.2. He can be reached by e-mail at FLandLSE@aol.com.

Michael D. Myers is a Professor of Information Systems in the Department of Management Science and Information Systems at the University of Auckland, New Zealand. He is currently the Chair of IFIP Working Group 8.2 and President-Elect of AIS. Michael has published widely in the areas of qualitative research methods, interpretive research, ethnography, and information systems implementation. He is editor of the *ISWorld Section on Qualitative Research,* senior editor of *MIS Quarterly,* an associate editor of *Information Systems Journal,* and Editor in Chief of the *University of Auckland Business Review.* Michael can be reached by e-mail at m.myers@ auckland.ac.nz.

Design of the Organization of Information Services in Large Public Organizations

J.P. van Wamelen
Ordina Consulting, prof Evertslaan 130b,
Delft, 2628XZ, Holland
E-mail: johan.van.wamelen@ordina.nl

Abstract. The design of the organization of information services in large public organizations must be improved to give a better answer on the changing political, administrative and social demands being made on large public bodies. At the moment it is not clear how the organization of the information services should function in this respect. Up until now the organization of the organization of the information services is part of the operations organization. The distance to the strategic function in a public organization is therefore large. To make better use of IT it is necessary to bridge these gap. In the last year investigation is done if and how these gap can be bridged and a first new design was made.

1   Background

These days, the significance of developments in information and communications technology (IT) has a great influence on public organizations. Those developments have now reached the stage where they can be regarded as one of the major factors to influence the changing political, administrative and social demands made on public organizations. These changes are creating a need for public organizations to innovate. Something that affects not only their operational management, but also their mission.

In the past period IT within the public sector has mainly been used to increase the effectiveness and efficiency of operational management. But developments in IT mean that it must be applied to the same ends in business processes to serve the changing political, administrative and social demands made on public organizations. As far as the public sector is concerned, this is the case in two such processes: policy development and services.

Until now, the organization of information services within the public sector has reflected the original function of IT within organizations: support for operational management. This becomes clear by the fact that the IT function often forms part of the operations organization, or even technical services. That distances it from the strategic function. As a result, only limited use can be made of IT's innovations and it is difficult to predict accurately what the repercussions

Please use the following format when citing this chapter:

van Wamelen, J. P., 2006, in IFIP International Federation for Information Processing, Volume 214, The Past and Future of Information Systems: 1976–2006 and Beyond, eds. Avison, D., Elliot, S., Krogstie, J., Pries-Heje, J., (Boston: Springer), pp. 67–75.

would be for the business. To enable better use of IT, investigation is needed into how the IT function within the public sector should be organized.

In these respect the main question is: How should the information service in large public organizations be organized in a way that it is possible to bridge the gap to the strategic function.

2   Research Objectives

To answer this question, we first looked at the extent to which IT can bring about innovation within the public sector. In order to pose a picture of this notice should be taken of the changing political, administrative and social demands being made on large public bodies; for example, new requirements in respect of demand-based leadership, integration and policy co-production against the backdrop of such developments as social emancipation, internationalization and technological developments – including IT itself [1-3]. The innovations being referred to here concern the way in which policy comes about and is implemented, as well as the content of that policy and the resulting services.

The influence of IT in this area is difficult to determine because, on the one hand, its development underlies the changing demands being made and, on the other, it is one of the tools used to remove the problems, which they create. Moreover, the deployment of that tool creates more problems, which can then be solved through the further application of IT [4].

Furthermore, in order to understand these relationships, it is necessary to know more about the innovative power of IT. This is not easy, since it is a relatively recent technology, the full scope of which has yet to be appreciated. As part of this study, then, we first tried to paint a broad picture of the situation from two different angles: IT as social change and IT as a virtual world. This made it clear that there is indeed a complicated relationship. To investigate this, we opt to take a small section of reality and look at how the information services related to it are organized. In the first instance, four projects were examined at the ministry of education, which is striving to achieve policy innovation.

3   Development of Analytical Framework

The next step consists of the development of an analytical framework to start the research. The analytical framework is made up of the following components:

*   Two theoretical frameworks, by which the influence of IT's innovative strength can be revealed and the organization of information services described;
*   An analytical method, to determine the actual relationship between the influence of IT's innovative strength and the organization of information services.

As the basis for the first framework, the influence of IT was defined in more detail and subdivided in terms of value and significance. These aspects are defined using five characteristics of technology in the network society [5] and five intrinsic properties [6,7] associated with them.

*   Value of IT, defined in terms of:
    o   Importance/meaning;
    o   Broad applicability/pervasiveness;

o   Use of network logic/networking logic;
o   Independence of process sequences/flexibility;
o   Ability to integrate/convergence.
- Significance of IT, defined in terms of:
o   Horizontalization;
o   Virtualization;
o   Deterritorialization;
o   Multimediatization;
o   Interactivity.

We then investigated the individual influence of these characteristics and properties. On the one hand, these involve opportunities in order to work more efficiently, more effectively and differently; on the other hand, they relate to organizations' ability to change such aspects as time, space and relationships. Based upon this investigation, a first theoretical framework was constructed [8,9].

A second such framework was then developed, which can be used to describe the organization of information services. Here, a distinction was drawn between the structure of the IT organization and its place within the institution as a whole [10-12]. In this framework a distinction is made in:

- Functions of IT
o   Decision making
o   Policy development
o   Administration
o   Service supply
o   Innovation
o   Control
- Governance of IT
o   Business monarchy
o   ICT monarchy
o   Feudal
o   Federal
o   Duopoly
o   Anarchy
- Products of IT
o   IT policy and strategy
o   Investment and priorities
o   Architectures
o   Infrastructures
o   Applications

Based upon these two theoretical frameworks, an analytical method was developed. This was used to investigate the extent to whether, in practice, there is an identifiable link between the degree of cohesion created in IT innovation and policy renewal on the one hand, and the organization of information services on the other. In doing this, a cyclical innovation model was used [13]. To analyze our findings in this research this methodology can be used because

- The cyclical innovation model was developed to study processes of innovation which matches the focus of our analysis;
- As a result of technological developments IT can be considered to be a strongly growing knowledge area;
- The potential value or 'promise' of IT can (in the model) be regarded as some form of applied knowledge.

From this model, four situations that characterize the relationship between policy renewal and IT innovation could be distinguished.

1. One-dimensional and driven: there is no relationship between IT innovation and policy renewal, and the value and significance of IT are only considered to a limited degree;
2. One-dimensional and co-coordinated: there is a relationship between IT innovation and policy renewal, but the value and significance of IT are only considered to a limited degree;
3. Multidimensional and driven: there is no relationship between IT innovation and policy renewal, but the value and significance of IT are considered to a high degree;
4. Multidimensional and co-coordinated: there is a relationship between IT innovation and policy renewal, and the value and significance of IT are considered to a high degree.

4   Application of the Analytical Framework to three Case Studies

We then turned our attention to several different programs and projects at Dutch departments of state, clustered to form three case studies, to see how they draw upon IT's power to innovate in their own organization. The case studies concerned: the ministries of Health, Welfare and Sport, Justice and Transport Public Works and Water Management. Some of these were in the area of policy development and implementation, others covered operational management issues. For each case study, we first revealed our findings and then presented a number of observations and conclusions. All of these were derived from the analytical method we have developed. We used the method from the perspective of the concerned IT-expert and the business manager involved. It pointed pout that in each of the ten studied aspects different answers were given. The following results were booked:

1. The importance of information: IT's value in the network society is first of all defined by the extent that the usage of information is considered of more importance than the underlying technology, used for retrieval, processing and distribution of that information. In general it seems that project managers and involved experts, concerned with the actual content (of an issue, problem or work process), value the information itself more than IT experts do. A shared and supported vision as a basis for decision-making in favor of the role of information instead of technology is hardly seen. In addition it can be noticed that IT experts as well as other experts value a properly working, technical infrastructure. It is not always evident to what extent the lack of this technology actually forms an obstacle. Not having an underlying vision makes it difficult to emphasize the importance of information in a more structural matter.

2. Broad applicability: Secondly IT's value is determined by its usage in different areas. A distinction can be made between its use in operations, policy making and policy implementation. In each of these three areas IT can be used in an all-embracing, comprehensive way or only for specific tasks. The ideas concerning the applicability of IT are

ambiguous.   The dominant idea however, supports a limited applicability. In several cases one deliberately chose for limited use of IT. In other cases this was done more implicitly, by emphasizing IT use in operations and the underlying technical infrastructure. Only in a few cases a universal applicability was recognized and in one case this was based on an underlying vision.

3.   Use of network logic: Thirdly, IT's value is determined by the degree of involvement of elements of the network society in the application of IT. In a network society (work) processes take place in layered and branched networks more and more. This makes the positioning of used information difficult and also leads to an increase in unstructured information. In nearly none of the studied project and programs, architectures are considered or propositioned as a tool to make use of network logic. The application of architectures is mostly based on technical basic assumptions, for instance to form different (technical) modules or provide a solid base for building a technical infrastructure. As a result mostly IT experts are concerned with architectures, while other involved experts or project managers are not. Another consequence is that the results of projects and programs in the long term will not be flexible enough to react to, or adapt to changing needs and conditions.

4.   Independency of sequence in processes: Before processes were run in a certain sequence in order to get the desired products. Using IT, the sequence in these processes becomes irrelevant and can be shuffled or reversed. By doing this in many cases the efficiency and effectiveness of a process can be improved. The degree to what this advantage of IT is accounted for also determines the value of IT. In the majority of the studied projects and programs this possibility of changing the sequences of a process is recognized. In one of the cases it will actually be done. In approximately half of the cases this possibility is seriously taken in consideration. No clear distinction can be made between the role and opinion of IT experts or other involved experts and project managers regarding this value of IT. It is also unclear how this actual application of IT can be realized.

5.   Integrating ability: The use of IT can have different faces. A distinction can be made between different forms of communication such as using a regular ('wired') connection versus wireless, different standards, different sorts of work stations, emphasizing speech, data or text and applying web technology or not. IT's value in a network society is also determined by the degree of different forms of communication that can be used uncomplicated and at the same time. In only one case this value was recognized and used. The reason for this was obvious. The involved project managers indicate that mostly well-tested technology is used instead of (relatively new) concepts that intend to integrate different techniques. Another reason can be found in the fact that most of the studied projects started some time ago, when not all of today's possibilities were available yet. A third reason may be based on the project managers' need to match with the technology already used in their sector. By making only limited use of the integrating ability of IT

the results of the studied projects and programs may be considered outdated on a relatively short term.

6. Horizontalization: The meaning of IT in a network society is firstly visible in the way this society operates. This implies that government's traditional role will change and become more coordinate. The studied projects should fit into a society that is functioning on the basis of new administrative steering directives in the near future. This makes it important to investigate to which degree the set of instruments that is developed, fits in such a society. The majority of projects show that they take account of this changing role of the government. This can be read from the reasons for starting these projects, the way the projects are carried out and the use of the results after finishing the projects. In the actual content of the projects this is less visible however. The majority of the projects and program's focus on improvement of existing processes. As a result the traditional way of working is redesigned with the opportunities of a government in a network society.

7. Virtualization: The growing use of IT can increasingly create any thinkable reality in a virtual world. Because of this dematerialization identities and meanings can be (re)created and manipulated. For the public administration this meaning is of great importance because of its consequences for authenticity, reliability and unequivocality. These three values cannot be taken for granted anymore. One reaction to this could be intensifying the demands on these three values and making such arrangements that the traditional standards can still be met. A different reaction could be the recognition of this meaning of IT and anticipation on this fundamental change in society. An overall agreement exists regarding the consequences and possibilities of virtualization. All studied projects and programs decided to react in a repressive way, which meant that questions regarding authenticity, reliability and unequivocality are prominent items on the agenda. A discussion regarding an alternative attitude in order to be able to anticipate on this meaning of IT in a network society was not seen in any of the studied projects. IT experts as well as project managers and other involved experts did not seem to be interested in such a discussion.

8. Deterritorialization: As a result of dematerialization, the physical place of action will lose its value. Activities and transactions are not reducible to a certain physical place anymore, which leads to an increase as well as a decrease in scale. IT connects dispersed actors, physical places and activities. Organizations can become lose from or independent of a (physical) territory, which influences their external operating as well as their internal design. The studied projects and programs only partly take account of the meaning of deterritorialization. To what degree they do so and what aspects are seen as important vary. The majority strives for concentration of activities, places and actors regarding control tasks and technical support. Ideas regarding possibilities for scaling down in the sense of custom-made solutions and opportunities were only seen in a few cases. In addition these organizations were rather forced to these ideas by the circumstances instead of having them supported by an underlying vision.

9. Multimedia: The fourth meaning of IT concerns multimedia, or the possibility to communicate in an endless series of different combinations, which offers much more opportunities than was the case in the recent past. The studied projects and programs do not or hardly show any use of multimedia. Only one project mentions the possibility. This is rather awkward, since especially in public domains, accessibility should be aspired. None of the studied projects and programs indicated any form of anticipation on this meaning in the near future. This counts for the IT experts as well as the project managers and other involved experts.

10. Interactivity: Interactivity may be well the most intriguing meaning of IT. The possibility to rapidly start all thinkable relationships, actions and reactions in an endless range of different variants, is the actual reason or cause for the existence of the network society. This creates a society in which the standard is abundance. Projects directed at improvement of the performance of the government must take account of this meaning. This is seen in two of the studied projects and programs, which have included this meaning as one of the characteristics of the project. In the other projects neither IT experts nor project managers or other involved experts pay any attention to this meaning of IT.

Next, based on these case studies, several generic conclusions were drawn. In general, it can be concluded that policy renewal and IT innovation do not yet go hand in hand in the vast majority of the programs and projects studied.

Based upon our findings, observations and conclusions in respect of the programs and projects studied at each case study, we also produced an overall assessment of the IT function's position within them. These painted three different pictures.

- At the first case study, the picture is a checkered one. IT is meaningful in some respects, but subservient in others;
- At the second case study, the picture is more coherent. IT's position here is somewhere between that of a cost centre and subservience;
- At the third case study, the conclusion can be drawn that IT's primary position is as a cost centre where the costs are not regarded as that important.

In other words, in virtually none of the cases studied the IT function occupies a meaningful position. To change this, improvements must be made in the organization of information services in such a way that it becomes possible to conduct programs and projects in a more co-coordinated, multidimensional way and so to allow the IT function to assume a position of greater significance. To make this possible a design framework was constructed.

5   Practical Test of the Design Framework and Conclusions

To take proper account of the characteristics and properties of IT in a network society, the necessary demands to the organization of information services identified in analyzing the case studies must come in the following areas.

- More emphasis on a market-based strategy rather than a functional one;

- The use of process control in combination with information architectures, with less emphasis on operational IT issues;
- Introducing cohesion by enhancing the tactical authority of the managers concerned, with less emphasis on supply-led control.

We then positioned these demands in terms of the so-called "nine-cell model" [14]. From that, a design approach covering the following points was described.
- Improving the mutual cohesion of business strategy and IT implementation;
- Improving the relationship between strategy and implementation, in respect of both the business and the IT;
- Improving the relationship between business and IT at both the strategic and the operational level.

The expectation was that, if this rules were used to make the improvements, the information services could be organized in such a way that better use be made of the innovative powers of IT.
To test this approach, we now applied it at three pilots. The pilots concerned: The Immigration and Naturalization Service, The Food and Consumer Product Safety Authority and the National Police Services Agency
It can be stated that none of these had reached a stable final situation at the end of the work. All have made a start on the change, but none have completed it. Our experiences in applying the design framework resulted in several conclusions.

1. Solving everyday problems usually had priority. This can be explained by the fact that the organizations were behind in their development and implementation of information management and that they, at the same time, strongly depended on a properly working information household. Because in most cases it was often unknown what caused the occurring problems, the starting point (of changes) could not be clearly defined and information management was merely led by ad hoc solutions for presently occurring problems.
2. Besides the unclearness of the present situation, the future of the organizations is diffuse as well. This is related to or even caused by changing social, administrative and political conditions and the incompetence to predict (the consequences of) the development of e-government and e-governance or the influence of the implementation of process management.
3. The gap between the present and (near) future, as far as both can be fully understood, is rather large. This gap can prevent those concerned to look into the future or to take account of the present.
4. New instruments or other means must be developed to overcome this gap. This can be a difficult job however, because such means (for instance an information architecture) usually do not directly contribute to present problems and cannot realize the desired situation in a short period of time.
5. Bridging the gap by taken small steps in the right direction can be hard to realize, because the need for such an approach is difficult to concretize. Moreover the managers are not eager to be involved in making a strategy or vision operational, while IT experts are not that willing to give priority to functionality over technology (due to a lack of knowledge and experience outside their own field).

The approach developed thus seems to be inadequate as a solution to the research question. This may be caused by the fact that the organization of the information services should be changed by the innovative power of IT; improved products and processes alone are not enough. Nor is it sufficient to develop and produce a new blueprint. Rather, the right institutional conditions have to be created to enable the necessary improvements. Therefore, the research question for this study needs to be redefined as follows: What conditions should be created to organize the information services at large public bodies in a network society?

6   Recommendations for Further Research

The study reveals that many questions remain unanswered. In particular, whether information services will be better organized once the structure has been changed and, even more importantly, whether public bodies will then be able to meet the other political, administrative and social demands being made of them. Consequently, this study can perhaps best be regarded as a starting point for further research. In this respect, three questions are important.

- How can an information services architecture be designed to improve the process of automation?
- Is it possible to use business rules as a solution for steering the information services?
- Can a competence centre be a useful tool for bridging the gap?

References

1. J. Donovan. The second industrial revolution, reinventing your business on the web, Prentice Hall (1997).
2. M.A. Gross. A call for revolution, New York (1993).
3. P. Keen. Competing in chapter 2 of internet business, Delft (1999).
4. D. Tapscott. Governance in the digital economy, Toronto (1999).
5. M. Castells. The information age: economy, society and culture, Volume I, II, III. Londen (1996).
6. P. Frissen. De lege staat, Amsterdam (1999).
7. J. De Mul. Kunst en nieuwe technologie, prolegomena voor een digitale esthetica, Rotterdam (1999).
8. B. Hooff and W. van der, Moone. Beter, sneller, anders, Informatie en informatiebeleid N4 (1999).
9. J.P. van Wamelen. Creating conditions for the realization of e-government, New Orleans (2004).
10. M. Broadbent and P. Weill. Effective IT governance by design (2003).
11. L. Groth. Future organisation Design, Wiley (1999)
12. H. Mintzberg. Structures in five: Designing effective organizations, Newe York (1983).
13. G. Berkhout. The dynamic role of knowledge in innovation, Delft. (2000)
14. M. Abcouwer. Contouren van een generiek model voor informatiemanagement, Amsterdam (1997).

Business Process Reengineering Role in Electronic Government

Rodrigo L. Martín and Jorge M. Montagna

CIDISI – Centro de Investigación y Desarrollo en Ingeniería en Sistemas de Información, FRSF, UTN - Lavaisse 610 – (3000) Santa Fe – Argentina

rmartin@epe.santafe.gov.ar, mmontagna@ceride.gov.ar

Abstract. Business Process Reengineering (BPR) came up as a key concept in the 1990s, with a high impact on management and transactions of private companies. However, it has not been so well accepted in public administration. Nowadays, many projects for changes in government are related to electronic government. According to this, this article discusses the role of BPR in this context, its contribution to this kind of initiative, and if it is a required element to go forward. Also, the difficulties in carrying out the BPR in the particular case of e-government are analyzed, taking into account the characteristics of this kind of project, the stages that are generally involved and the environment in which it is performed. Finally, a basic structure for the development of e-government is provided, specifying the insertion of BPR for reaching a more efficient, effective and foreseeable management of new projects.

1   Introduction

Internet has influenced our way of living and working. One of its effects on government is what we call electronic government or e-government. There are many definitions, but in a simplified way it consists of introducing the Internet and computer networks into the actions of government.

However, e-government experiences have shown poor results when compared with those achieved in the private sector. A series of errors are produced, with a high rate of failures [1]. Many difficulties come up from the need of transforming the way in which the activities of the public sector were traditionally executed to take advantage of these new technologies. This forces the use of transformation tools, like Business Process Reengineering (BPR), to carry out the changes.

Please use the following format when citing this chapter:

Martín, R.L., Montagna, J.M., 2006, in IFIP International Federation for Information Processing, Volume 214, The Past and Future of Information Systems: 1976–2006 and Beyond, eds. Avison, D., Elliot, S., Krogstie, J., Pries-Heje, J., (Boston: Springer), pp. 77–88.

Public services require changes starting from the introduction of Information Technology (IT); but its advantages have been poorly taken bearing in mind certain characteristics of the public sector:

- Processes are highly structured: information requirements, methods for processing information and desired formats are known precisely. Also, criteria for decision making are completely understood, with clearly defined and repetitive steps. It is hard to have these old and complex procedures transformed.
- Government is the only one that provides public services. Interaction with government is not a matter of choice. These requisites inhibit the introduction of customer satisfaction criteria, services improvement, quality management, etc.
- In general, the characteristics of the public sector differs from those of other fields. There is less flexibility to carry out modifications, limited culture of change, etc.
- There is a big fragmentation of workflows.
- There are many levels of decision-making and centralized control. All agencies work in an isolated manner, managing their own resources [2].
- In general, political leaders ignore matters related to IT and its capabilities, and delegate them to technical experts [3].

Government faces serious restrictions in carrying out the required transformation related to BPR projects to take advantage of the IT capabilities.

The present work studies the role of BPR in the development of e-government. Different stages are posed and the influence of BPR at each stage is analyzed, particularly for the case of one-stop e-government. Also, a basic framework for the e-government application is considered and the role of BPR is specifically studied in relation to each step so as to assure an effective BPR use.

2 Electronic Government

E-government can be defined as any governmental activity based on the use of computer networks. Different types of interactions of the government can be identified: G2C (to Citizens), G2B (to Business), G2G (to Government), etc. Some definitions provide very broad meanings: Lenk and Traunmuller [4] consider as e-government any proposal of modernization of the public sector. In a more limited definition used in this work, the term refers just to the administrative processes.

One-Stop Government (OSG), a concept related to e-government, consists of the integration of services from the viewpoint of users (citizens, business and public servers) [5]. Public services are structured according to specific citizens' life-events and business situations. So, new products are generated to satisfy users' demand for flexible access, without the usual distance and time restrictions. OSG requires the complete integration of the usually fragmented public agencies because services are provided from only one access portal.

In the traditional access, it was compulsory for the user to go through agencies following the logics of operative procedures. In the case of OSG, all services are integrated in a unique entrance portal (Figure 1). Not only front-office is affected, but also the processes need to be restructured. OSG requires more coordination between agencies to integrate processes. BPR is a natural tool to achieve this. However, BPR has not proved to be efficient in government so far.

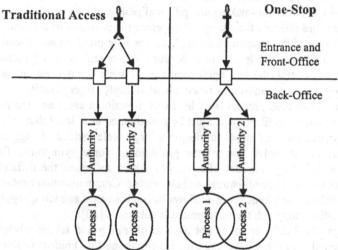

Fig. 1. Traditional access to state-owned services vs. one-stop government

3   BPR Difficulties in Government

Due to special characteristics of public processes, the experiences of the private sector with BPR cannot be directly transferred to government. Indeed, some authors argue that a successful BPR is not possible in the public sector [6]. According to Heeks [1], 35% of BPR projects fail completely (they are given up or never implemented), 50% fail partially (main objectives are not achieved) and only 15% are successful. Scholl [7] analyzes BPR practices in government. Table 1 presents the most common difficulties that usually appear in BPR projects in government.

Table 1. BPR difficulties in the state-owned sector

Attitude	Willingness to apply the radical changes derived from BPR.
Scope	Changes depth. The more drastic the change, the wider its scope.
Extension	Amount of functional areas and entities included in business processes.
Knowledge	Abilities of leaders and team members in charge of BPR.
Leadership	Project leader influence and authority.
Objectives	Definition degree of objectives to be attained with the project.
Institutional Restrictions	Legislation and standards that restrict the development of new proposals.
Resources	Availability of human and financial resources.
Techno centrism	Focusing on technological uses and ignoring other organizational aspects.

Attitude: Not everyone accepts the changes posed by the BPR. Unnecessary work is eliminated. There is an on-going conflict between the need of modifying labor guidelines upheld for a long time and the lack of contribution from affected people. Project BacenSenado [8] is an example of human factor value. The main reason of its failure was the senators refusal to use the system on the grounds that their obligations were decision-making and political relationships.

Scope: the more relevant the change, the greater the potential of reaching significant benefits. Many of the innovative IT applications take place on superficial aspects of processes. They are easily accepted because the organizational structure remains intact [9]. In general, the first applications of IT were focused on task automation. Deep changes generate more resistance, but also imply larger benefits.

Extension: A business process includes many functional areas and the participation of its stakeholders. BPR projects must be coordinated at a level that is high enough to identify problems and opportunities on a large scale instead of suggesting partial improvements that solve part of the problem or some symptoms. This implies working with a large number of agencies, which increases the difficulties. Each agency has its own special features and objectives. Communication problems arise to break boundaries and generate workflows through several agencies, regulations, and legal limitations to which the government is subjected [10].

Knowledge: the Public sector is not used to changing and taking advantage of IT. Then, internal areas that have experience to manage this kind of problems are not usual. Anyway, in the last years, new methodologies and approaches (for example New Public Management) have encouraged the development of specific offices to study these subjects without resorting to external consultants.

Leadership: A top-down leadership, which manages motivated people doing non-standard tasks, is required for the BPR. This is difficult when carrying out changes in high administrative positions as a result of elections. BPR efforts can be rejected or abandoned by the new authorities. Even when being continued, BPR is likely to have a different leader, and consequently going forward becomes quite difficult because there may be changes in interests, available resources, etc. BPR implies changes extended in time and risks that must be led by the same person.

Objectives Definition: Many BPR projects fail because corporative goals are not taken into account [11]. BPR involves many agencies with different interests and it is hard to arrive to consistent objectives that match all their needs. In this sense, highly fragmented processes and the change of authorities are very significant constraints. In contrast to the private sector, it is very difficult to assess benefits such as customer satisfaction, growth, result improvements, etc. This situation makes it hard to show the BPR benefits and to justify the associated risks.

Institutional restrictions: The institutional dimension has a very important role as an inhibitor of innovations. Redesigned processes are affected by restrictions that current legislation imposes. Government bases its behavior on standards that inhibit redesign. Administrative processes are subject to financial, legal, etc. restrictions, that strengthen the adopted bureaucratic structure [9]. Institutional constraints are usually more strict than those in the private sector, thus drastically limiting the possibility of redesign.

Resources: Experience shows that BPR generally takes more time than what has been estimated, involves more people and resources than the available ones and always comes up with unexpected problems. There is a series of problems: annual budgets handling in projects with a larger duration, resources correct estimation, the need of sharing resources among several areas, shared management, etc.

Techno centrism: Likely, IT incorporation increases bureaucracy and generates dependence on a specific technology [5]. Many organizations have spent a lot of money on IT to automate existing processes without determining if they were necessary or not. BPR includes IT with the aim of implementing innovative solutions but demanding, as well, changes in organizational level. The risk of not exploring solutions which implies organizational changes is high.

4 The Need of BPR in E-government Framework

Transformation projects in the public sector revolve around e-government and BPR is a methodology to redesign taking advantages of IT capabilities. So, it is interesting to relate both concepts to find out the extent to which using BPR in e-government initiatives is necessary.

Several studies have analyzed e-government implementation based on models with development stages (Table 2). Lisbon European Council [12] identified four levels of e-government evolution. The first level just consists of the information presentation about public services; the second level provides downloadable forms from the website; the third level allows online processing of forms; and finally the fourth level provides integrated e-services and the possibility of making online transactions. Layne and Lee [13] include levels of catalogue, transaction, vertical integration and horizontal integration. Reddick [14] considers only two levels. The first level involves the initial efforts of government to establish online presence, presenting information about its activities on the Internet. The second level is the transactional stage, in which government shows online databases, allowing citizens to interact for the payment of taxes, etc.

Table 2 Models of e-government levels

MODELS	LEVELS			
Lisbon European Council [12]	Information	Interaction	Interactive	Transaction
Layne y Lee [13]	Catalogue	Transaction	Vert. Integration	Horiz. Integration
Reddick [14]	Information		Transaction	

It is possible to find equivalences between models. The aim is to specify stages that show the degree of e-government progress and the increasing difficulty of its implementation. Nowadays, the number of e-government initiatives of level 1 in any of the models is greater than those of other levels. An important element to be taken into account is the quality of the offered services, which is notorious when transactions are involved. This is related to the increased implementation complexity. The effort required to provide information online is not the same as the effort needed to offer transactional services.

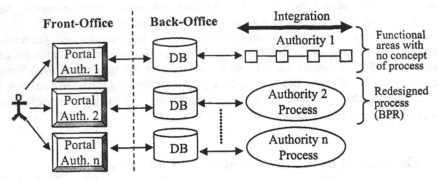

Figure. 2. Stage 1 of e-government

Projects start at the first level as a result of individual and isolated initiatives of each agency, basically focused on technical matters (performance, security, tools for the portal development, equipment, etc.) and front-office questions (website content, how it looks, formats, etc.) (Figure 2). Back-office remains without changes. Starting from the need of offering new services and improve the current ones, there is an evolution towards higher levels. Technical matters and business processes must be considered, though difficulties are always greater during the process integration.

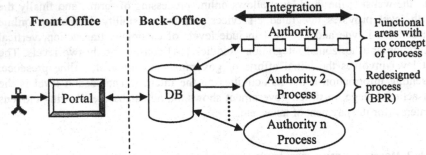

Figure. 3. Stage 2 of e-government *(OSG with BPR per Authority)*

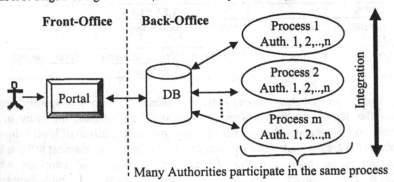

Fig. 4. Stage 3 of e-government (OSG with BPR between Authorities)

Figure 2 shows an unequal evolution of e-government initiatives in its first steps, depending on each agency authorities. There is no connection between different projects. In the first portal, an initiative that is still at the initial stage, back-office shows a group of tasks that has not been integrated with a significant fragmentation. The second portal, an initiative at a higher level, shows that the authority has redesigned the process. The tasks composing the process have been integrated. The difference between projects shown in Figure 2 is marked by the vertical integration of activities of each business process in the back-office. It will remain at an initial stage of e-government, while these tasks are not integrated. Moving to a higher level requires working with a complete process. The application of a radical redesign is closely related to difficulties detailed for BPR in Section 3. Figure 3 shows an initial stage in an OSG solution. Usually, authorities detect many individual initiatives. This creates a series of problems: duplication of efforts, low quality portals, loss of institutional image due to poor design or low performance, incompatibilities of initiatives, etc, leading to an OSG proposal that integrates different initiatives.

The OSG integration is different to the previous cases. Its development is independent from individual agencies and a coordinated approach is required. To abstract the citizen from government fragmentation, on the one hand, a strong technologic infrastructure must be provided. On the other hand, views, contents, formats, etc. must be standardized when portals of different agencies are integrated. Data must be combined in a unique consistent database or, at least, must have a common access to the data sources. Information systems from different agencies must be compatible. Figure 3 shows an intermediate stage of this evolution, integrating front-offices from different initiatives. Basic guidelines are generated about contents, formats, etc.; and the requirements each agency initiatives must meet are standardized and included in this global portal. Then, OSG advances on back-office. Basically, it works first on front-office since it is directly related to e-government initial levels.

The evolution to higher levels of OSG requires interaction among agencies, through a horizontal integration among current processes. In many cases, agency existence can be discussed. Many of them have been created in a fragmented government to perform tasks that have now disappeared because information is now available online (Figure 4). This new stage requires a different process redesign. Starting from the analysis of the interactions of the n existing processes, many of them are not now required, because they are combined, others disappear, etc., with a tendency towards wider processes integrating more agencies. This will be enabled by digital media for performing tasks instead of the traditional papers. Figure 4 shows the shift from previous n processes to new m processes, with $m < n$. Besides, the process owners must be considered because the interaction between agencies forces them to define the scope of the tasks and who are in charge of performing them.

4.1 One-stop E-government Difficulties

The need for integrating business processes and systems increases in the OSG. The changes are very complex due to a series of difficulties that may arise:

- *Technical*: the lack of standards and coordination in the equipment incorporation, the existence of independent systems, etc. are the main problems. Government is a large geographically dispersed and barely coordinated organization.
- *Political*: authorities are not involved. They lack knowledge on this issue and consider it is a technical problem. In the OSG, difficulties are bigger because of the need of coordinating different areas and solving conflicts arising from this interaction.
- *Integration processes*: Business processes from different agencies need to be integrated horizontally as much as vertically to implement OSG, and then BPR is required. However, the previously analyzed problems must be considered. Until now, the structure of public agencies has been stable, almost without changes.

The existence of many participants and the previous processes lacking a good coordination increase the complexity. These projects are new and there is not much experience related to their development. The lack of knowledge on methodologies for adequate change management is a severe restriction for the pursued integration.

Coordinating several independent agencies becomes a problem. It may arise when dealing with complementary activities as well as similar activities performed by agencies with different locations or different jurisdictions. For this reason, it is quite difficult to clearly specify BPR objectives. Coordination problems among several agencies are moved to resource management. Getting resources for an adequate change management is very difficult; even more if the organizational frontiers of the project do not adjust to the usual assignment. Agencies integration requires solving many legal barriers and even changes in laws because services integration implies information exchanging that are not consistent with the current legislation. Many of the quoted problems limit the application scope of the OSG approach. Due to the difficulties in solving these issues, the extent of changes is erroneously reduced and e-government remains at initial levels.

4.2 A Framework for Successful BPR Incorporation

Different alternatives are proposed to simplify e-government application [9] [12]. Wimmer [5] presents an interesting approach that shows the insertion of BPR into a global politics of e-government (Figure 5).

At the first stage, e-government is considered as a *vision*, whose scope must be determined (objectives, social development, etc) so as to reach political support. At the *strategies* stage, the decisions for making the suggested vision come true must be made, including an adequate e-government architecture:

- Guidelines and norms for the incorporation of IT, protocols and standards, etc.
- Security requirements, performance, access speed, etc.
- Criteria specification to generate an appropriate legal framework.
- Definition of the service characteristics to be provided.
- Specifying the mechanisms for agencies to solve conflicts in a coordinated way. As regards BPR, some points to be taken into account are:
- Methodology selection for BPR application.
- Specifying a mechanism for project management involving several agencies, specifying resources assignment, change management, etc.

• Identifying tools and standards to be used in the different projects.

Once the adequate infrastructure is reached, specific initiatives must be generated and selected [15]. The correct evaluation of advantages, benefits, and involved risks is a critical point. The use of BPR is one of the reasons why e-government levels are limited. Therefore, when assessing alternatives, its feasibility must be taken into account, regardless of the adjustment to the vision and suggested strategies. Therefore, initiatives must include the need of carrying out BPR, mechanisms to overcome difficulties and the necessary resources so as to assure feasible initiatives of high levels with an adequate evaluation of the involved risks.

At the *projects* stage, approved initiatives are implemented. The challenge is the effective execution of the project as regards goals attainment budget fulfillment, schedule, etc. This is closely related to the effective application of BPR. Many of the BPR problems arise during the implementation. A successful completion is more likely if an appropriate framework has been generated for the development of the projects at the strategy stage, taking into account technical, political and process integration difficulties.

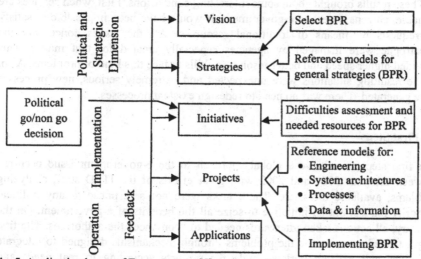

Fig. 5. Application layers of E-government [5]

Finally, in the level of *applications*, services are provided through the Web. continuous monitoring of their progress is needed to correct errors, improve the services and adjust them to the new needs of citizens and public authorities.

5 Example

The steps taken in e-government are analyzed in an Argentine provincial state.

5.1 Background

Between 1995 and 1999, out of individual initiatives, the first websites in agencies were developed. They were made according to the needs of the agency authority. From a technical point of view, each agency had its own IT expert group that depended on an IT Provincial Direction (ITPD). Therefore, all areas had a sense of autonomy to carry out their projects. The aim of these websites was to present the area on the Internet. This spontaneous development led a series of problems: there was no institutional image of the province, there were no quality standards, etc. Each agency had a website of different quality and performance.

As no services were offered, websites were barely visited. However, visits significantly grew when more than 150,000 inhabitants were affected by a flood in one important city of the province. There were missing people, huge damages in houses and firms. This forced government to provide immediate answers to new requests. The possibility of obtaining updated information through the Internet made the access to websites jump from 800 to 20,000.

These results brought about some interesting conclusions. First, when services are valuable, citizens access to e-government. It would have been impossible to satisfy all requests by means of traditional resources. All the issues concerning the catastrophe were managed by agencies especially created for that matter. This provided higher speed and better resolution skills to face this kind of problems. Also, as the resulting situations were unexpected and extremely serious, new processes were generated. There was no need to redesign existent processes.

5.2 First Steps

The first steps to achieve a global approach to the e-government issue occurred between the year 2000 and 2002 with great efforts of the ITPD staff, analyzing problems, available tools, etc. These tasks were not a response to any political authority request but an initiative to seize all the benefits of e-government. On the contrary, all actions taken afterwards needed to "convince" the authorities. The first stages tended to overcome the problems through mechanisms designed to integrate initiatives and existing portals, guide the projects according to real needs and develop an institutional image. From a technical point of view, the emphasis was placed on standards and platforms definition, selection of tools to deal with contents, training, etc. From a political point of view, the aim was to make the responsible ones be aware of the need of an integral e-government approach. In general, political authorities showed no interest in the issue.

Based on this evaluation, a series of initiatives started. From the technical point of view, the intention was to eliminate the gap between ITPD and the IT groups of each agency who were responsible for the current proposals, to create a general strategy on the subject. This showed the difficulties of shifting from the scenario of Figure 2 to that of the Figure 3.

In the year 2000, the first set of rules is issued, establishing basic definitions to standardize the information and develop websites. The results were not the ones expected; agencies were reluctant because they continued operating with their websites according to their own needs. In this situation, the objective was to cut down anarchy. A positive element was the participation of the authorities: the Coordinating Ministry considered this subject for discussion.

5.3 Towards a Consolidated E-government Approach

In 2003, new authorities were in charge and this allowed dealing with the subject with new enthusiasm. Even though there is no real advance on a formal proposal like that of Figure 5, works go in a similar direction. A specific agency was created, whose first task was to generate norms. A basic plan was developed, including subjects such as resource availability, contents and services development, technical infrastructure, etc. The aim was to move forward in the development of solid proposals that allow evaluating all benefits so that all areas are convinced of adding their services to a new general portal on the OSG approach.

As the lack of conviction was considered a weakness, a provincial e-government Committee was created so as to develop an e-government strategic plan. It is interesting to consider that the aforementioned agency did not succeed in solving the political inconveniences, which compels for the finding of another solution.

5.4 E-government Levels and BPR

An analysis of the different initiatives shows that most proposals are in Level 1 [12]. Proposals of higher levels started to present problems with the current processes. When working on back-office, there were difficulties in the proceedings: differences in forms, dissimilar interpretations, lack of standardization, etc. Taking into account these problems, tasks remained at the front-office, at Level 2 (Interaction): development of unified forms. Also, there are Level 3 examples (Interactive); however, proceedings standardization among different jurisdictions is emphasized. This has delayed the advancement on back-office, mainly on proposals implying proceedings redesign, taking advantage of IT capabilities. The current situation may be associated to the scenario of Figure 3.

Nowadays, proposals on back-office are still originated individually. It may have happened with other subjects; when repeated problems are addressed, tools and rules will be generated so as to standardize all developments.

In order to uniform developments on front-office, standardized rules were originated through glossaries, a style guide book, norms and rules to be followed (for example Contact Us option), etc. Better results were obtained when coordinating efforts. For example, areas did not provided services of the same quality to satisfy all requests from citizens and companies. A database was generated so as to keep record of the contacts of all jurisdictional websites, making it possible to verify the level of attention provided, for example, response time. Additional services were developed and the present websites were improved after detecting the FAQ.

So far, BPR has not been considered for the two types of integration analyzed in this work. The difficulties of previous levels avoid suggestions about it. On the other hand, advanced level projects have not been presented. Commissions and those responsible for e-government policy do not worry about these issues, since there are more urgent issues to solve in this matter. A deep analysis will be carried out in the future when moving to interaction and transaction stages; and then proceedings, good practices, tools, etc. will be required.

6. Conclusions

E-government success will mainly depend on the improvement obtained as a result of BPR implementation. Reaching higher e-government levels is related to business processes redesign to take advantage of IT capabilities. One portal working on front-office to receive requests is not enough; government must now be prepared to provide quick and high quality services.

The development of OSG brings about much more benefits. However, this means a new level of integration that agencies must face, requiring the use of BPR. However, many current e-government applications appear on the basic levels, regardless of the future benefits that may appear at superior levels. This delay is the result of the difficulties in implementing BPR in the public sector. Consequently, in order to accomplish real e-government benefits, authorities should generate appropriate tools and mechanisms for the use of BPR in the process integration.

References
1. R. Heeks, Most eGovernment-for-Development Projects Fail: How Can Risk be Reduced?, Working Paper Series Nº. 14, (2003)
2. J. Burn, G. Robin, A Virtual Organization Model for E-Government, Australian Journal of Information Systems 9 (2), 104-112 (2002).
3. The Harvard Policy Group on Network-Enabled Services and Government, J. F. Kennedy School of Government, Eight Imperatives for Leaders in a Networked World (2000).
4. K. Lenk and R. Traunmüller. Perspectives on Electronic Government, IFIP WG8.5 Working Conference on Advances in Electronic Government, Zaragoza, España (2000).
5. M. Wimmer, A European perspective towards online one-stop government: *the eGOV project* Electronic Commerce Research and Applications 1, 92-103 (2002).
6. N. Kock, R. McQueen, Is Re-engineering Possible in the Public Sector? A Brazilian Case Study, Business Change and Re-engineering 3 (3), 3-12 (1996).
7. H. Scholl, E-Government-Induced Business Process Change (BPC): An Empirical Study of Current Practices, International Journal of E-Government Research 1 (2), 27-49 (2005)
8. A. Joia, Developing Government-to-Government enterprises in Brazil: a heuristic model from multiple case studies, Internat. Journal of Inform Management 24, 147-166 (2004).
9. J. Fountain, Building the Virtual State, Brooking Institution Press (2001).
10. R. Allen, Assessing the impediments to organizational change A view of community policing, Journal of Criminal Justice 30, 511-517 (2002).
11. I. L. Wu, A model for implementing BPR based on strategic perspectives: an empirical study, Information & Management 39 (4), 313-324 (2002).
12. eEurope, An information society for all. Action Plan. http://europa.eu.int/information_society/eeurope/2002/news_library/documents/eeurope2005/eeurope2005_en.pdf (2002).
13. K. Layne, J. Lee J., Developing fully functional E-government: A four stage model Government Information Quarterly 18 (2), 122 (2001).
14. C. Reddick, Citizen interaction with e-government: From the streets to servers?, Government Information Quarterly 22, 38-57 (2005).
15. J. Montagna, A Framework for the Assessment and Analysis of Electronic Government Proposals Electronic Commerce Research and Applications 4 (3), 204-219 (2005).

The Evolution of IS:
Treasury Decision Support & Management
Past, Present & Future[*]

Alankar Karol[1,] Mary-Anne Williams[1] and Steve Elliot[2]

1 Innovation and Technology Research Laboratory, University of
Technology, Sydney, NSW 2007, Australia
{alankar.karol,mary-anne.williams}@uts.edu.au
2 School of Business, University of Sydney, NSW, 2006, Australia
s.elliot@econ.usyd.edu.au

Abstract. This paper contributes to the discipline of Information Systems (IS) by illustrating the continuing evolution of IS applications to a single, core business function. Historical developments in IS and the major global treasury activity, foreign exchange trading, have been examined to establish the context. Findings from a seven year research project into the impact of ICT on financial services and the development of a next generation agent-based treasury management system prototype have been applied. Possible future developments in IS applications are explored in terms of the capabilities of emerging technologies to address current treasury challenges. The implications for practitioners in an increasingly complex, global market are discussed and sustainable research issues, particularly for IS research, identified.

1 Introduction

Achieving organisational efficiencies and strategic positioning are key challenges for all firms [1] but those engaging in global markets are confronted by additional challenges, including the necessity for foreign currency exchange. Organizations selling or purchasing internationally outside common currency blocks (e.g., the European Union), require foreign currency exchange as a core business function. These activities are typically undertaken by a corporate treasury department (see section 5 for a description of this function). Developments in Information Systems (IS) over time have presented opportunities for innovation in decision support and management of foreign exchange transactions. Information Systems is a term with

[*] This research was conducted under the auspices of a Research Project on Business Innovation funded by the *Danmarks Nationalbank*, the central bank of Denmark and the Australian Research Council.

Please use the following format when citing this chapter:

Karol, A., Williams, M.-A., Elliot, S., 2006, in IFIP International Federation for Information Processing, Volume 214, The Past and Future of Information Systems: 1976–2006 and Beyond, eds. Avison, D., Elliot, S., Krogstie, J., Pries-Heje, J., (Boston: Springer), pp. 89–100.

many definitions, but the essence of an Information System is that they are applications of Information Technology to meet a challenge or to address a problem.

The research questions are: how has, and can, IS evolve in a core business function? This paper has three aims: to illustrate the continuing evolution of IS through examination of the nature and impact of IS in a single, core business function; to identify sustainable research issues and themes in IS by investigating related IS applications over time; and to assist treasury management (TM) succeed in an increasingly complex, global market by highlighting how next generation IS applications might address its challenges in the future. A multiple method research approach has been adopted with a review of literature, interviews from a seven year research project into the impact of ICT on financial services [2-5] and the 'proof of concept' development of a prototype future generation agent-based treasury management system [6].

Related publications from this project have examined, in increasing detail, the technical solutions available or possible to meet current challenges confronting treasury risk management. This paper was prepared specifically to commemorate the 30th anniversary of IFIP TC8: The past, present and future of Information Systems. It takes a reflective, evolutionary analysis of past and present risk management system solutions and then considers the empirical and theoretical implications of likely future developments. The structure is: context is established through an overview of IS roles in management and brief histories of foreign exchange markets and IS; the evolution of treasury management over time is examined; the current status of treasury systems identified; requirements for future treasury management systems determined; the implications for IS research and practice considered and discussed.

2   The Role of IS in Management

Five classical functions of management have been identified, (i) Decision Making, (ii) Planning, (iii) Organising, (iv) Coordinating, and (v) Controlling [7].

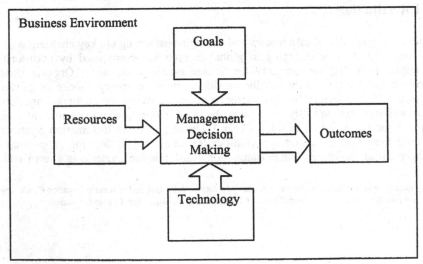

Figure 1: IS supporting decision making in Management.

The role of IS over time is and has been to provide management with sufficient information to make informed decisions that assist in achieving the five management functions. IS play a crucial role within and across organisations and industries, e.g. they enable, transform, and shape organisational and industry innovations and structures, see Figure 1.

Management can be conceptualised in terms of a goal-directed system of decision processes that take resources such as information, funds, commodities as inputs and produce decision outcomes. Decision making in organisations is typically goal directed, e.g. in pursuit of sustained strategic competitiveness and above-average. Management decision making can be more effective if technology is used appropriately to support management decisions.

Decision making is an essential management activity, and it can be divided into three types: strategic, tactical and operational [4,7]. Operational decision making concerns low level decisions with a short term time horizon, i.e. day to day decision making about operational issues. Tactical decision making is concerned with decisions with a medium term horizon, and strategic decision making focuses on long term high level issues. Strategic management involves deciding on the objectives, resources and policies of the organisation. A major challenge for strategic decision making is anticipating the future opportunities for the organization within a likely environment, to achieve strategic positioning and operational effectiveness.

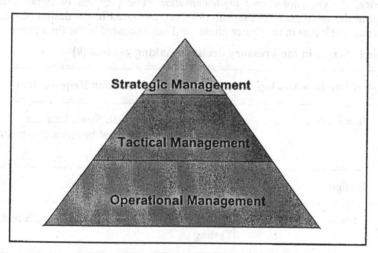

Figure 2: Management hierarchy based on decision making required

Strategic decisions typically have implications for the resource base of the enterprise, i.e. its capital equipment, its work force, its technological base etc, over a medium period of time. Tactical decisions are concerned with efficiency and effectiveness, ensuring resources are properly utilized and the performance of operational units is competitive. Tactical decisions involves close interaction with people performing the tasks of the organisation; ideally it takes place within the context of broad policies and objectives set out by strategic decision making and planning processes. Operational decision making is concerned with specific tasks set forth by strategic and tactical management, including determining which units or individuals in the organisation will carry out specified tasks, establishing criteria of completion and resource utilization, and evaluating outcomes. Operational decisions focus on how the enterprise should undertake day-to-day operations in the business environment.

Decisions can also be classified, into three classes: structured, semi-structured and unstructured. Unstructured decisions are typically the highly complex they occur in a context where the problem being addressed is not well understood, e.g. major influence factors may be unknown, uncertain or incomplete. They are often novel, significant, and non-routine, and there is no well-understood procedure for finding the best solution. At the other end of the spectrum structured decisions take place when the decision problem is well understood and all the relevant information is available. They are repetitive, routine, and involve a straightforward procedure [7].

Structured and unstructured decision making and problem solving occurs at all levels of management. In the past, most of the success in most IS came in dealing with structured, operational, and management control decisions. However, gains have been made over time and at present IS has been able to provide significant assistance in the area of semi-structured decision making particularly as technological capabilities have be developed. In the future IS is expected to make some inroads into providing support in assisting decision making in dynamic and complex environments.

According to Simon [8] decision making involves a number of phases: *intelligence, design, choice and implementation*. The problem or opportunity is identified in the intelligence phase, solutions are proposed in the design phase, and one solution is selected in the choice phase, and implemented in the final phase.

Table 1: Stages in the Treasury decision making process [9]

	Phase of Decision Making	Treasury Information Requirement
1	Intelligence	Business need (e.g. cash flow), business opportunity, International business contract and associated risk
2	Design	Modeling, financial information
3	Choice	Hypothetical Reasoning, Simulations, Stress Testing
4	Implementation	Hedge, Option, Swap, FX derivative

Table 1 indicates the types of information required for each of the decision-making phases. IS need to take into account the needs of managers at each stage of the decision making process since each stage has different requirements.

3   A Brief History of Foreign Exchange Markets

A concise review of foreign exchange markets will help to place TM developments into context. Different currencies and the need to exchange them have existed since ancient times. The Second World War saw a decline in the trade of foreign exchange, the fall of the British Pound as the major trading currency and the rise of the US Dollar as the new international standard for foreign exchange. In 1944 the Bretton Woods system for exchange rate management made the US dollar as the world's benchmark currency and pegged it to the price of gold at USD 35.00 per ounce. As a consequence all other currencies were pegged to the US dollar and were not allowed to fluctuate more than 1% on either side of the pegged rate. If any currency did move by more than 1% then the central bank of that country intervened in the market until the exchange rate returned to the 1% band. In 1971 The Bretton Wood system was replaced by the Smithsonian system and almost simultaneously the European Community formed the European Joint float in 1972 to break free of the dollar. Both systems collapsed in 1973 resulting in the free floating system. In 1979 the European Monetary System was formed which allowed most of the countries of the European Union to link their currencies to avoid large fluctuations. That system failed in 1993 when the UK withdrew and this led to the formation of the European Central Bank which formally floated the Euro in 1999 as the common currency for most of the nations of the European Union. Today the foreign exchange rates of the different countries are a mix of free floating currencies for the developed nations and currencies of the developing countries pegged to major currencies.

These changes in the foreign exchange markets have most of the major currencies floating freely which has given rise to increased volatility in exchange rates. Some of the most important factors that effect exchange rates are the GDP, the level of business activity, the level of employment, interest rates, inflation rate, trade deficits and even the political climate in either of the two countries involved.

Besides being one of the most volatile markets in the world the foreign exchange market is the largest market in the world with an average daily trading volume of USD 1.9 trillion in April 2004 as compared to USD 650 billion in April 1998 [10]. The foreign exchange market is exceptional due to high liquidity, geographical dispersion, large number and variety of traders and long trading hours.

4   A Brief History of Information Processing and Systems

The evolving technological infrastructure helps to place IS developments into a technological context. The history of IS can be divided into four major periods which are characterized by a principal technology used to solve the input, processing, output and communication problems of the time: (i) manual, (ii) mechanical, (iii) electromechanical, and (iv) electronic. The premechanical manual age (3000 B.C. - 1450 A.D) was driven by hand writing enabled by paper and pens. The first abacus, developed some time before 300BC (http://en.wikipedia.org/wiki/Abacus).

From an IS perspective the printing press heralded the beginning of the Mechanical Age (1450 – 1840), later slide rules and other algorithmic devices were introduced, and this period culminated in the Babbage machine. The discovery of electricity lead to the Electromechanical Age (1840 – 1940) where information could be converted into electrical impulses for transmission via telegraph, telephone and radio. The first computer was built in 1942, and so the so-called Electronic Age extends from then until the present time.

The first generation computing systems (1951 -1958) were based on vacuum tubes as their main logic elements, punch cards to input and *externally* store data, rotating magnetic drums for *internal* storage of data and programs which were written in machine language and assembly language. The Second Generation (1959 1963) computers were typically based on transistors. Magnetic tape and disks began to supplement punched cards as external storage devices. High-level programming languages like, FORTRAN and COBOL were introduced. The Third Generation (1964-1979) computers used integrated circuits. Operating systems were developed and more advanced languages were developed. The Fourth Generation (1979- 1990) is based on large-scale and very large-scale integrated circuits with microprocessors, and CPUs on a single chip. PCs appeared in the 1970s. Fourth generation language software products include Visicalc, Lotus 1-2-3, dBase, Microsoft Word, etc. Computing was transformed by database management systems and personal computers. Fifth generation systems, characterised by higher levels of abstraction in the programming languages, began to emerge in the mid-1980s. Declarative languages like SQL, object-oriented languages like C++ and Java, agent-oriented systems such as BDI, and mark up languages such as html, XML, RDF, OWL emerged. Future technologies will be characterized by agility, biological integration, mobile, pervasiveness and ubiquity [8,11].

5 Evolution of Treasury Management

Corporate treasurers are responsible for establishing policies for financial risk management, executing the related practices and then subsequently tracking and reporting the results of the programme. As a result most treasury departments see maintaining adequate access to liquidity, improving working capital utilizations, enhancing cash flow forecasting and monitoring, refining hedge strategies and processes, minimizing transaction costs and rigorous error and compliance checking as their major responsibilities [9,12].

However with the breakdown of the pegged currency systems, globalization of the financial markets, complex derivative instruments on the exchanges and the enhanced volatility of the environment due to threats of global terrorism, the treasury department of most companies find themselves facing new challenges. Expansion into international trade has left more and more companies exposed to foreign exchange exposures and transformed the nature of the key traditional activities of the treasury departments.

The IS capabilities to assist TM have changed with the rapid development in the mathematical models available for the pricing of certain exchange traded instruments like futures and some over the counter instruments like exotic options. The rapid development in mathematical models for the complex derivatives developed in the last two to three decades have shown the limitations of the conventional spread sheet and increased the risk exposure of many companies. The need for non-linear analysis for measuring the risk exposure and hedging strategies has created a need for integrated treasury IS. Important aspects of past, present and future treasury management systems are summarized in Tables 2, 3 and 4.

Over the last 30 years treasury management systems have moved from entirely manual systems to systems that rely on stand alone PC's with spreadsheet software. Banks have introduced large corporate wide software but still have difficultly managing their systems, e.g. rogue trading.

A survey [10] of 200 leading financial services companies into how they were perceiving and responding to the eBusiness revolution showed concerning mismatches between the reality of eBusiness today and the reaction of the industry to its potential. Many established financial services companies were not responding to

Table 2: Summary of Treasury Management systems, over time [2,3,9,12]

The Past 1976 – 2005	
Information System Type	Manual, Electromechanical
Requirements	Manual advice form
Information Gathering	Printed Newspaper for rates and directives from management
Level of Management	Mainly operational
Transaction Technologies	Telephone, Telefax, Letter Confirmation
Transaction Execution	Manual bank transfer
Type of Trades	Simple trades, no derivatives
Outcome	Gain and losses at the markets will
Nature of Risk	No ability to offset risk and exposures
Risk Management	Hand held electronic calculators
The Present 2006	
Information System Type	Electronic and 4th Generation Software
Requirements	Manual and electronic advice forms
Information Gathering	World Wide Web (e.g. Bloombergs), telephone discussions with broker, and directives from management
Level of Management	Operational and tactical
Transaction Method	Telephone, Telefax, Letter Confirmation
Transaction Execution	Electronic prior funds transfer, , SWIFT Global Network
Type of Trades	Simple trades, options, futures, and other derivatives
Outcome	Limited capacity to manage gains or losses
Nature of Risk	Increasingly sophisticated modeling needed to offset risk and exposures
Risk Management	Electronic Spreadsheets
The Future 2006 and beyond	
Information System Type	Electronic and next generation software e.g Agents, Semantic Web
Requirements	Policy driven risk management strategies with scope to develop highly customized solutions
Information Gathering	World Wide Web (e.g. Bloombergs), telephone discussions with broker, directives from management, proactive software looking for potential opportunites and matching trades, agent assisted price discovery and analysis. Simulations and interactive models
Level of Management	Operational, Tactical and Strategic
Transaction Method	Agent-to-agent and agent mediated
Transaction Execution	Electronic prior funds transfer, SWIFT Global Network
Type of Trades	Simple trades, options, futures, and other derivatives trend towards customized derivatives
Outcome	Reduced risk, increased opportunity
Nature of Risk	Increasingly sophisticated modeling needed to offset risk and exposures
Risk Management	Electronic Spreadsheets

the implications of eBusiness for their business. General perceptions included; that eBusiness doesn't involve much change and that existing platforms, marketing approaches and organizational structures were adequate to meet eBusiness challenges.

Table 3: Developments in Treasury IS systems (source: original research)

	Past 1976 -	Present 2006	Future 2006 -
Treasury IS underlying Technology	Manual	Electronic isolated reactive systems, e.g. spreadsheets	Electronic integrated agent-oriented, proactive
Treasury IS Type	Transaction	Management IS	Intelligent Decision Support Tools and Executive IS
Nature of Management Decision Making appropriately supported	Operational	Tactical	Strategic
Nature of Risk that can be effectively managed	Operational	Tactical	Strategic

Table 4: Developments in IS compared with Treasury Management Systems [3].

	Past 1976 -	Present 2006	Future 2006 -
IS	Electronic and largely limited by Hardware Capabilities	Electronic and 4th and 5th Generation Computing Systems	Electronic, Mobile, Pervasive, Ubiquitous, Agile,
Treasury Management Systems	Manual focus on transaction processing	Electronic focus on transaction processing	Electronic focus on strategic and legal issues

6 Treasury Management Systems Today

Treasury Management Systems have come a long way from the traditional spread sheet systems of yesteryears where the data was collected and entered manually into the software. Besides being prone to human error the system was limited by its capabilities. Although spreadsheets have come a long way since their development in the 1970s they are still limited in the context of treasury management since they are unable to provide support for non linear analysis of the mathematical models that are now prevalent in the industry. The evolution of Database Management Systems gave rise to one point of entry for the data and made the vast amounts of data more manageable. However the treasurers still relied heavily on the use of spread sheets for the analysis to gauge hedge positions and risk exposures.

The changing philosophy of risk management and the role of treasury in the organization has placed a greater emphasis on consolidated risk management. Consolidated risk management – sometimes also called integrated or enterprise-wide risk management – generally refers to a coordinated process for the measurement and management of risk on a firm-wide basis. The conventional wisdom dictates that consolidated risk management will help companies assess risks and returns of different business lines and thus allow them to make more informed decisions about where to invest scarce resources to maximize profit [9].

Consolidated risk management can be clearly understood if we make a distinction between risk measurement and risk management. Risk measurement entails the quantification of risk exposures such as Value-at-risk, earnings-at-risk, stress scenario analyses, duration gaps, etc. depending upon the type of risk being measured and the degree of sophistication of the estimates. In contrast, risk management refers to the overall process that a company follows to define a business strategy, to identify the risks to which it is exposed, to quantify the risks and to understand and control the nature of the risks it faces. Risk management is a series of business decisions, accompanied by a set of checks and balances, risk limits, risk reporting, review and oversight by senior management and the board. Thus consolidated risk management involves not only an attempt to quantify risk across a diversified business but also a much broader process of business decision making and support to management in order to make informed decisions about the extent of risk taken both by individuals and the business as a whole [9].

As a result the present day treasury management systems offer some key features:
- Multi-currency capability for viewing, printing and exporting data.
- Improved search interface to narrow selected criteria quickly and efficiently.
- Standardised format for data collection across the business network.
- Local account information including subsidiary account-profiles, local policy summaries, etc.
- Reporting capabilities.

These systems in general provide ease of data management and manipulation, reduced costs through minimization of coverage overlap, increased efficiency from the automation of historically paper-based processes, reduced exposures, increased productivity, access to real-time account information so decisions can be based on most up-to-date information and gives a consolidated "big-picture" view of the global coverage.

7 Next Generation Treasury Management Systems

Innovative companies have realised that they can not wait for the future to happen and they have to actively position themselves accurately in the future to manage the risk which arises from such a volatile environment. For example, if a company has to predict with a high accuracy what it expects its sales to be in the future, what would be the cost of the fuel in the future and also what the exchange rates would be, a next generation system would require:

1. **Learning:** The ability to learn directly from decisions or tasks they have to perform. The IS should be able to derive a model of business practice purely by

analyzing the data. Typically such knowledge is held by operational personnel with many years of experience. Genetic Algorithms and Neural Networks have the capability to perform such a task. This is in strict contrast to the earlier systems where the knowledge required to perform these tasks had to be explicitly specified by human intervention. This learning technique also overcomes the limitation set due to different opinions of different experts and as such is more consistent.

2. Adaptation: Businesses and business processes are constantly changing due to changes in the macro-economy, competitive pressures, government regulations and as such Intelligent Systems providing decision support should be able to adapt. Such systems should be able to monitor their own performance and revise their knowledge consistently with the changing environment. For example interest rates can fluctuate over a very short period of time. The Intelligent system should be able to learn from the market and be able to adapt to such changes before making any recommendations.

3. Flexibility: Experienced personnel can make decisions even when the available information is unclear, imprecise or incomplete -- a characteristic often seen in financial markets. Most traditional computer programs are inefficient under such constraints. Any Intelligent system should then have the flexibility to make recommendations and support business decisions in such an environment.

4. Transparency: Intelligent systems that automate many different decision making tasks should be transparent in their decision making process so that they could easily be understood by humans. This has become even more important recently with the legal requirements imposed by legislation such as IAS 39 which holds the board accountable for the decisions of the company specifically for the use of options and other derivatives for hedging. Moreover this transparency is required to enable the Intelligent system to adapt to future changes. This also allows easy interaction with the experts if models have to be changed.

5. Proactive: The Intelligent systems should offer the possibility of discovering new business processes or relationships that were previously unknown. This could potentially give rise to new trading and hedging strategies. Traditional systems which are conventionally operated by humans provide no such opportunity [6,12].

8   Issues for IS Research

The necessity for a multidisciplinary research focus is apparent in a specialist business function like treasury. Finance and treasury have a rich research tradition but not usually in adoption, diffusion, implementation and evaluation of enabling technologies for TM functions. These represent an IS focus. The intersection of the disciplines does reveal some research interest. Treasury risk management is concerned with the need to assess the impact of emerging technologies, models and model risk.

The major lesson for IS research is a reminder that technology cannot be analyzed in a vacuum, and that business and environment factors as well as inhibitors and drivers of technology adoption play a crucial role [6] This caution is particularly pertinent where ICT is developing so rapidly. There is a temptation to focus on the changing technology and to treat it as something new whereas the IS focus is on applications of the technology and how these may be more successfully accomplished.

Researchers reviewing Tables 2, 3 and 4 and the requirements for TM systems in sections 6 and 7 will note a myriad of research implications. A better understanding of technology adoption is important especially in light of the fact that resistance may be anticipated [10] particularly with the introduction of disruptive technologies [3].

9 Issues for Treasury Management Practice

Confronted by volatile global markets creating severe business challenges and dynamically developing technological capabilities that may be able to address their challenges, business management as a whole and treasury management in particular needs to establish mechanisms to monitor, evaluate and successfully innovate to realize the potential benefits from technology. A key prerequisite in acquiring this innovative capability is a willingness to change and to learn from these experiences.

Surveys [10] have revealed a puzzling resistance in firms to embrace necessary change, to explore better, cheaper and faster ways of doing business. Perhaps this is a corporate manifestation of Darwin's survival of the fittest! Such developments need not be technology-based. Consolidation and integration of treasury management at organisational and inter-organizational levels are an option. Smart companies are relinquishing ownership of non-core specialist value chain activities [13, p7] where business benefits are available. Ultimately, the technology-based opportunities presented in Tables 2, 3 and 4 will need to be compared with the possible requirements listed in sections 6 and 7. Innovative management will be thinking about further opportunities to improve current practice: "Technology offers possibilities for business we hadn't considered in the past." [14]

10 Discussion

This paper seeks to contribute to the discipline of Information Systems by illustrating the continuing evolution of IS in a single, core business function. Historical developments in IS and the major global treasury activity, foreign exchange trading, have been examined to establish the context. Possible future developments in IS applications have been explored not as wildly speculative guesses but based on the capabilities of emerging technologies to address current treasury problems as described by reviews of the literature, results arising from a seven year research project into the impact of ICT on financial services and the development of a next generation agent-based treasury management system prototype..

Sustainable research issues and themes in IS are identified and activities to assist Treasury Management succeed in an increasingly complex, global market are presented. Next generation IS applications are considered for how they might address Treasury Management challenges in the future.

As with many business functions, treasury has experienced small, incremental changes over the last 30 years. Until quite recently. Substantial changes in current practice are sweeping across corporations and treasury departments will not be excluded. So what might the next 10 years hold in store? More upheaval! 'The disruption to a lot of traditional businesses has only just begun [6].

References

1. M.E. Porter. Strategy and the Internet, Harvard Business Review; March, Vol. 79 Issue 3, 62-78 (2001)

2. S. Elliot, and M-A. Williams. Intelligent Agent and Semantic Web enabled Innovation in the Wholesale Financial Services Industry, *Proceedings of Collector Conference* (Toulouse, April 2002).

3. S. Elliot, M-A. Williams, and N. Bjørn-Andersen. Strategic Manage*ment of Technology-enabled Disruptive Innovation: Next Generation Web*, in the Proceedings of the International Conference on Intelligent Agents, Web Technology and Internet Commerce, IEEE Computer Society Press, (2005).

4. A. Karol and M-A. Williams. Understanding Human Strategies for Belief Revision: An Empirical Study, in the Proceedings of the Tenth conference on Theoretical Aspects of Rationality and Knowledge (TARK X) Halpern, J. and Van der Meyden (eds), (2005).

5. V. Zwass. Electronic Commerce and Organizational Innovation: Aspects and Opportunities, International Journal of Electronic Commerce, Volume 7, Number 3, Spring, pp. 7-37 (2003).

6. M-A. Williams and S. Elliot.   An Evaluation of Intelligent Agent-based Innovation in the Wholesale Financial Services Industry,   Proceedings of Second IFIP WG 8.4 Working Conference, Kluwer, 91 – 106, (2003).

7. S. Haag, M. Cummings, and D.J. McCubbrey. Management Information Systems for the Information Age, 5th edition, McGraw Hill Publishers, (2005).

8. H.A. Simon. Rational Decision Making in Business Organizations, American Economic Review, American Economic Association, vol. 69(4), pages 493-513 (1979).

9. C. Cumming and B.J. Hirtle. The Challenges of Risk Management in Diversified Financial Companies *Federal Reserve Bank of New York* Economic Policy Review / (March 2001).

10. Arthur Andersen. Thriving in the New Economy: Perception vs. reality, Financial Services Report, Issue no. 2 | January, Executive Summary (2000)

11. C.S. Amaravadi The world and business computing in 2051, Journal of Strategic Information Systems 12 (2003) 373–386

12. M-A. Williams and S. Elliot. Corporate Control of Rogue Traders: An Evaluation of Intelligent Agents for Improved eBusiness Treasury Risk Management in Elliot S., Andersen K.V. and Trauth E. (eds) *Multi-Disciplinary solutions to Industry & Governments' E-Business Challenges* (Trauner, Austria, 2004).

13. A. Barua and A. Whinston. Measuring the Internet Economy, CISCO Systems and the University of Texas. June 6, www.internetindicators.com (2000).

14. G. Cox. Business computing 2001—the state of the art, Journal of Strategic IS 12 (2003) 285–294

Panel: The Identity and Dynamics of MIS

Tor J. Larsen and Linda Levine
Norwegian School of Management, Norway
Software Engineering Insitute, Carnegie Mellon University, U.S.A.
e-mail: Tor.J.Larsen@BI.NO

Abstract. In this panel, we address the identity and dynamics of MIS, including myths and taboos in the history of the field, interdisciplinary identities, intradisciplinary perspectives, and empirics on coherence and change in the discipline.   Panelists are   Frank Land, London School of Economics, UK Michael D. Myers, University of Auckland Business School, NZ Robert Zmud, Michael F. Price College of Business, University of Oklahoma, OK and Linda Levine, Software Engineering Institute, Carnegie Mellon University, PA. Panel Moderator and Point of Contact:Tor J. Larsen

Introduction

No end appears to be in sight for the now familiar and longstanding discussions on the status of the field of Management Information Systems (MIS)[1] —its identity and its value, with respect to its role as a field, within the university, and in relation to industry practice.This ongoing debate and relentless self-examination reveals two persistent themes. The first focuses on coherence in MIS and in framing questions such as: Does MIS have a core and overarching theory? A cumulative tradition? Are other disciplines referencing MIS. The second theme revolves around the matter of rigor versus relevance, which is also occasionally expressed as a debate between academic and practical concerns—where a further refinement focuses on degrees of purity in the use of research methods. If we are to come to grips with these issues we

---

[1] Different labels are used to refer to the field, for example: Information Technology (IT), Information Communication Technology (ICT), Information Systems (IS), Management Information Systems (MIS), and Information Management (IM). Each term has its proponents; however, the terms are often used interchangeably. For the sake of clarity and consistency, we use the term Management Information Systems.

Please use the following format when citing this chapter:

Larsen, T.J., Levine, L., 2006, in IFIP International Federation for Information Processing, Volume 214, The Past and Future of Information Systems: 1976–2006 and Beyond, eds. Avison, D., Elliot, S., Krogstie, J., Pries-Heje, J., (Boston: Springer), pp. 101–105.

need to consider some of the myths, taboos and misconceptions which have grown up within our discourse.

Further refinement on the nature of MIS has examined its core and sub areas. One approach distinguishes between the internalist view and the externalist view. The internalist view builds on Kuhn's notion of a dominant paradigm in the tradition of normal science, which is interspersed with periods of revolution. This dominant paradigm takes the form of an overarching theory, which is subscribed to by a research community. The externalist view treats a discipline as a "complex network of interacting researchers whose ideas may stem from a number of disciplines who therefore form an intellectual community". Many characterize this network as a "fragmented adhocracy." Another example of the externalist view is expressed through Porra's notion of "colonial systems." Vessey et al. demonstrate that there is considerable diversity in MIS research in the topics addressed, research approaches employed, reference disciplines used, and levels of analysis. Their findings dispute the internalist view.

Benbasat and Zmud argue that a definition of the IS artifact can serve as the platform for defining appropriate MIS research. Ives, Parks, Porra, and Silva present a strong counter argument. They advocate the field of MIS research is best seen as a "colonial system" where colonies have strong inner ties but loose outer connections. They assert that the glue in MIS is a common interest in information technology and information systems. Similarly, King describes the discipline of MIS as driven by "…a shared interest in a phenomenal event—the rise and consequences of radical improvement in information technology." … and any, "attempt to build a long-standing academic field on a phenomenon, especially a revolutionary phenomenon, will fail". As Fitzgerald aptly observes: "In IS, we stand with our backs to the technology, the computer, the machine or whatever, and look outward towards the world at large.".

We agree with our colleagues in MIS who argue that "letting a thousand flowers bloom" is a necessary prerequisite for developing theories and expanding our knowledge. The continuous surge of new technologies and fads also contributes to this abundance. However, the current state of a thousand flowers does not absolve us of the need to examine patterns in the composition of MIS and its areas of work.

In this panel, we address the identity and dynamics of MIS, including myths and taboos in the history of the field, interdisciplinary identities, intradisciplinary perspectives, and empirics on coherence and change in the discipline.

Myths, Taboos and Misconceptions in the IS Domain Frank Land.

It is just over 50 years since computers began to be used as practical tools for business and administration, and about 40 years since MIS began to establish it self as a distinct academic discipline. In that time the discipline has grown to become a major component of the academic calendar. As a new discipline, often driven by a rapidly developing technology, it has sought to define its subject matter and its boundaries. That debate has been ongoing and even today fills the pages of some of its best journals. But in some senses MIS is a flawed discipline. In the 50 or so years of its existence the discipline has accumulated an array of myths, taboos and misconceptions. Some are deeply embedded in the mindsets of our peers. Some are transient, but have important impacts on what research gets carried out in a particular time. Many stem from not fully understood borrowings from our reference disciplines. Some take the form of tacit assumptions widely held, but because they are not articulated, they are also not tested. Of course all disciplines have these problems.

In this panel discussion I want to point to a selection of the myth, taboos, and misconceptions which disfigure our disciplines and hope that by highlighting some we can, as a community, begin to be aware of what we need to do.

Interdisciplinary Identities: MIS and Reference Disciplines Michael D. Myers,

In his presentation Michael will present a review of the history of the IS field and show how the IS field has developed its own unique identity, a unique research perspective and its own research tradition. He will argue that the time has come for IS researchers to stop seeing other fields as "reference disciplines" (i.e. fields which we look up to for theories, methods and exemplars of good research). Rather, IS researchers should see the IS field as one amongst others. However, this new found identity does not mean that IS researchers should cut themselves off from other related disciplines. On the contrary, IS researchers should be encouraged to conduct interdisciplinary work with scholars from other fields – but as equal partners in the important work of knowledge creation .

Intradisciplinary Perspective Robert Zmud,

Benbasat and Zmud articulated an intensively debated position on the desirability of establishing boundaries for the MIS discipline – boundaries that are intimately defined in terms of the IT artifact and its immediate context. Here, this position will be both clarified and extended. While this refined position maintains the earlier-stated position, it more explicitly recognizes that such a boundary invariably shifts to reflect concomitant changes in the nature of the phenomena subsumed within the boundary and the emergence of new phenomena. The issues raised by the emergence of new phenomena are particularly challenging, especially as it relates to disciplinary boundaries for an interdisciplinary field such as MIS. Of central importance is the necessity to distinguish whether 'new phenomena' are in fact 'new' or instead variants of phenomena already subsumed within existing scholarly disciplines. The implications of such challenges to the MIS discipline are examined and interpreted within the refined position.

Empirics: Coherence and Change in the Discipline Linda Levine

The research questions we pose here ask: what themes or ideas represent the center of MIS or its zones of coherence – or is diversity and fragmentation the rule? And will the center or zones change over time? Within MIS research, is there evidence of theory building that contributes to a cumulative research tradition? Using a co-word analysis approach—to analyze the patterns in discourse by measuring the association strengths of terms representative of relevant publications—the researchers found 62 specific centers of coherence. The data documented a high degree of change in centers of coherence over time. Evidence of theory building was extremely weak. A cumulative research tradition remains elusive. MIS centers of coherence change over time—we think, partly in response to practical pressures. We suggest that MIS opens a richer and more difficult debate on its theory, practice, and identity as a discipline in the 21st century university.

Biographies

Frank Land has spent almost his entire career working with IS/IT. After graduating from the LSE in 1950 he worked for 16 years with the pioneering business computer offshoot of the large British food and catering company J. Lyons and company. He was appointed Professor of Systems Analysis in 1982 and later joined the London Business School as Professor of Information Management. On retirement, he returned to the LSE as an Emeritus Professor. Frank received the AIS LEO Award, an AIS Fellowship and an IFIP Outstanding Service Award. He is currently working in the field of Knowledge Management and researching the relevance of Complexity Theory to understanding aspects of the IS phenomenon.

Tor J. Larsen received his Ph.D. in Management Information Systems (MIS) from the University of Minnesota, U.S.A., 1989. Since then he has worked as associate professor at the Norwegian School of Management, Department of Leadership and Organizational Management. He has acted as its Head of Department since 2003. Dr. Larsen's publications are found in, for example, Information & Management, Journal of MIS, and Information Systems Journal. His professional memberships include AIS, IFIP WG 8.2, and WG 8.6. His present research interests are innovation, diffusion, innovation outcome specification, MIS, and technology mediated learning.

Linda Levine is a senior member of the technical staff at the Software Engineering Institute. Her research focuses on acquisition of software intensive systems, agile software development, and diffusion of innovations. She holds a PhD from Carnegie Mellon University. Levine has over 60 publications in a wide range of journals. including: *IEEE Software, Information Systems Journal, Michigan Telecommunications and Technology Law Review, and Scandinavian Journal of Information Systems*. She is a member of the IEEE Computer Society, AIS, National Communication Association, and cofounder and vice chair of IFIP WG 8.6 on Diffusion, Transfer and Implementation of Information Technology.

Michael D. Myers is Professor of Information Systems and Associate Dean at the University of Auckland Business School. His research interests are in information systems development, qualitative research methods in information systems, and the social and organizational aspects of information technology. He has won Best Paper awards in *MISQ and Information Technology & People*. Dr. Myers served as a Senior Editor of *MISQ* (2000-2005), as an Associate Editor of *Information Systems*

Research (2000-2005). He currently serves as President of AIS and as Chair of the IFIP WG 8.2.

Robert Zmud is Professor and Michael F. Price Chair in MIS, Division of MIS, Michael F. Price College of Business, University of Oklahoma.   His research interests focus on the organizational impacts of information technology and on the management, implementation and diffusion of information technology. He currently is a Senior Editor with *Information Systems Research* and *MISQ Executive* and he sits on the editorial boards of *Management Science, Academy of Management Review* and *Information and Organization.* He is a fellow of both AIS and DSI. He holds a Ph.D. from the University of Arizona and a M.S. from M.I.T.

Enterprise Applications:
Taking the Open Source Option Seriously

Nicolás Riesco B. and Jaime Navón C.
Computer Science Dept., P. Universidad Católica de Chile
{nriesco,jnavon}@ing.puc.cl

Abstract. Free and Open Source Software (FOSS) is becoming more popular. Nevertheless most CIOs wouldn't even consider this option for their enterprise information technology needs. We found that the three main concerns about FOSS have to do with legal issues, costs and support. We propose an initial framework to look at FOSS in a balanced, unbiased and systematic manner that can be used for evaluation of specific scenarios from very small companies to large ones.

1 Introduction

The interest for Free and Open Source Software (FOSS) has been growing in the last 5 years. Nevertheless, at the enterprise level, only a few companies use FOSS as their main software platform. They either buy proprietary enterprise application suites (ERP, World Class) or choose instead between Microsoft's .Net and J2EE platforms. Among the reasons often given by CIOs for this situation are:
- Fear of legal consequences
- It could end up being even more expensive
- Lack of technical support (no one to call)
- Doubts about critical issues such as performance, reliability, scalability, etc.
- Insufficient information to perform an in-depth analysis

We believe that this early ruling out of the FOSS option is a bad idea. There are many scenarios where this option represents in fact the best or even the only reasonable option. This is especially true in developing countries where there are few big enterprises but many small to medium size companies (in Chile these companies are known as PYMES).

We propose a framework that helps in the decision making process. First, we analyze the needs and requisites of enterprise software and the main concerns about FOSS related to these needs. Then, we examine the distinctive characteristics of FOSS in depth. Finally, we focus on the most important issues to develop metrics that allow us to say, more or less, how adequate would be FOSS for a given scenario.

Please use the following format when citing this chapter:

Riesco B., N., Navón C., J., 2006, in IFIP International Federation for Information Processing, Volume 214, The Past and Future of Information Systems: 1976–2006 and Beyond, eds. Avison, D., Elliot, S., Krogstie, J., Pries-Heje, J., (Boston: Springer), pp. 107–118.

2   The Enterprise Applications Habitat

An enterprise is an organization of people or entities that work together towards common goals; usually, large corporations. Enterprises often have important information technology related needs: information storage and retrieval, resource planning, customer management, accounting, etc. The software that supports these needs is called enterprise software or Enterprise Application (EA)[1].

Historically, EA used to run on mainframes, using proprietary systems such as HighExPlus, BancsConnect, and EX[1]. Nowadays, the mainframe approach has evolved first into the client-server computing model and then to an "n-tier" architecture where the presentation is separated from the business logic, and the business logic from the data.

EA does not run over bare machines. Many other software products could be operating between the EA and the hardware itself: the operating system, web servers (including special modules and plugins to support different programming languages), database servers, application servers, etc. Moreover, software development tools, libraries, IDEs, etc. represent also software products that should be considered. This paper is especially useful in choosing FOSS for this kind of software.

Since the above mentioned software will be supporting the EA, it is important to know whether there are special requirements that we need to take care of. Emmerich et al.[2] point out special requirements associated to enterprise software: high availability, scalability, reliability, performance, changeability and security.

According to the Gartner Group unplanned application downtime is caused: 20% by hardware, 40% by application failures (bugs, performance issues or changes to applications that cause problems) and 40% by operator errors[3]. If we leave aside human mistakes we would still have to consider both hardware and software faults. Since hardware problems are independent on whether we are using FOSS or not, we focus here in software faults only.

Replication, redundancy and clustering (including farms) are just a few of the techniques that can be used to respond to the above mentioned requirements. Generally speaking, all those terms refer to duplicating resources in order to achieve a certain degree of availability and/or to provide a faster response. All these techniques are available through proprietary products, but they are not exclusive to the proprietary software world; FOSS can provide them too.

3   Facts about Free and Open Source Software

Open Source Software (OSS) is any software that has its source code available[2]. It is based on the principles of Free Software, which defines four levels of freedom:[3]
- Freedom 0: To run a program, for any purpose.
- Freedom 1: To study how a program works, and adapt it to your needs.

---

[1] We will refer to EA and enterprise software as synonyms
[2] A formal definition at http://www.opensource.org/docs/definition.php
[3] http://fsf.org/licensing/essays/free-sw.html

- Freedom 2: To redistribute copies of a program to help your neighbor.
- Freedom 3: To improve the program, and release your improvements to the public, so that the whole community benefits.

In other words, Free Software is "The freedom to run, study, copy, redistribute and improve software". We will consider Free Software equivalent to OSS, and refer to them as FOSS.

3.1 Type of License

Licensing is very important when using a piece of software. Using FOSS does not make you the owner of the code; you can use it but with certain restrictions. Some important facts about licenses to take into account are:
- Author takes no responsibility for the software.
- There is no Warranty for the program.
- You are not required to accept the license, since you have not signed it. However nothing else grants you permission to modify or distribute the program[4].
- You may not sublicense the program except as expressly provided under the License[4].

A complete description of the different Open Source licenses can be found on the Open Source web site[4]. The more popular flavors are GPL, BSD and LGPL. Other flavors are, in general terms, variations of those three.

GPL stands for "GNU Public License" which gives you the right to use, distribute and modify any GPL software, as long as if you distribute it (whether you have modified[5] it or not) you must include the source code with it. That means the software stays free forever, and any improvements will be eventually available to anyone. This is called "Copyleft". As defined by the GNU, "is a general method for making a program or other work free, and requiring all modified and extended versions of the program to be free as well"[5]. Proprietary software cannot be based in part upon GPL software. If so, it cannot be distributed without the source code. GPL software should not be used on proprietary software (that would be senseless).

Thanks to these features, GPL license can be considered "viral", because any software released by the GPL license is "infected" with it. A "marketing-oriented" meaning for this is that the GPL software spreads at the speed a virus does, because it is free, good and users recommend it to other users.

LGPL (Lesser General Public License) works like the GPL license but applied to libraries. A program that is linked to a LGPL library, may be distributed without including its source code, but the library itself, must be distributed with it. Drivers usually fall in this category. MySQL connector, a driver/API provided by MySQL AB, had LGPL license once, but is now distributed under the GPL license. The consequence of this license change, is that, if you use the driver on your project, then your project must be released under the GPL license. This change is also known as GPLed (that code has been GPLed).

---

[4] http://www.opensource.org/licenses/index.php
[5] Lawyers call this "derivative work"

A BSD (Berkeley Software Distribution) license gives you the right to use, distribute and modify the software. No need to distribute the source code along with the binaries, but you must keep the original information about the author and some other stuff.

In a Dual Licensing scheme, an author willing to authorize other users to benefit from his work can freely determine the type of license to use. He is not obliged to give equal rights to all users and can therefore use several licenses[6]. FOSS vendors usually offer a GPL version of their software for public use and a proprietary version for those that might have problems with copyleft. Dual licensing can be considered as a licensing scheme that allows software vendors to provide a high quality enterprise-compatible FOSS product, with which they can profit. It also allows legal concerns about the origin of the software to be dismissed.

3.2   Legal Risks

Before we get into the legal risk analysis we need to remember a few things. First, the fact that the software is free does not imply property. No matter if the software was obtained for free or paying money for it. Second, there is no warranty. Third, modification is allowed, but it has to be explained within the concept of distribution. Finally, distribution is allowed as long as it fulfills the license's requirements. By using GPL, any derivate work must be distributed as GPL. By using LGPL you are allowed to link libraries into non-free programs, without "infecting" it, and by using BSD you are not forced to distribute the source code. Table 1 shows a comparison between restriction levels among licenses.

Table 1. Restriction level by License

License	Distribution
BSD	Non Restricted
LGPL	↑↑
GPL	↓↓
Proprietary	Restricted

Let's get now into the legal issues. Starting with the intellectual property (IP), companies need to be very careful about infringing IP rights when using FOSS. In the US, copyrights have been filed for not only lines of code, but also for topics such as look and feel, technical, or operational processes[7]. Copyrights can be infringed easily, what makes it difficult to manage. On the other hand, GPL itself has never been challenged in court[8, 9, 10], lawyers can offer only theories, not facts[9].

Including FOSS as proprietary: CherryOS, a MacOSX emulator for Windows, was discovered to use GPL code on its proprietary software. As a result they had to release its software under GPL. Recently, MySQL sued NuSphere for GPL violation. The case was settled out of court[10].

The recent SCO case and the following controversy contributed to increase the public awareness about the legal issues involved with FOSS. A lot has been said, nothing is really clear and SCO has been unable to prove actual IP infringement. Is the opinion of R. Stallman that if SCO was "right", then it would be enough to remove some small part of the Linux code and the problem would be over. If SCO's intention was to generate FUD (Fear Uncertainty and Doubt), they might have succeeded[10]. Companies like IBM, HP, RedHat and JBoss offer insurance for this kind of legal problems on their products. Other companies like OSRM[6] provide insurance services to mitigate Open Source License risks and related IP issues.

Some people, like OSDL's CEO Stuart Cohen, think that the SCO controversy "was the best thing that ever happened to Linux"[11], giving Linux a boost. A detailed timeline of the SCO Controversy can be found at Linux.org's site[7].

4 Towards a Decision Framework

As we said before, there are many factors involved in the decision to use or to rule out the use of FOSS in the enterprise: costs, support, control and flexibility, open standards, product maturity, security, scalability, legal issues (unexpected license costs and possible lawsuits like SCO), etc. Of all these factors there are three that to many are considered as "fundamental factors":

- Legal: according to Gartner[12] legal concerns are at the top of the list of "fear factors of Open-Source Adoption". Forrester[13] considers "unexpected license costs" as an important concern too.
- Costs: according to Forrester[13] and Dravis[14] cost is a significant factor.
- Support: lack of it is considered by 57% as the biggest concern[13].

Other good reason to focus only on these three fundamental factors is that the rest depends more on the specific product we are considering. The "Business Readiness Rating for Open Source", which is being proposed as a new standard model for rating FOSS or the "Open Source Maturity Model (OSMM)"[15] and "CapGemini Open Source Maturity Model" may all be used to this end.

Let's focus then on those fundamental factors. First, each of these three factors is more or less relevant depending on what stages of software development we are considering: Planning, Deployment or Operation. As table 2 shows, "Legal Concern" is mainly associated to the Planning stage, meanwhile "Cost Factors" and "Support" are more relevant during Deployment and Operation.

Table 2. Fundamental Factors v/s Stages

	Planning	Deployment	Operation
Legal	*		
Cost		*	*
Support		*	*

4.1 Legal Aspects

If we want to avoid "Unexpected license costs and possible lawsuits" it is critical to pick the right license type. There are some other issues to be considered that have

---

[6] http://www.osriskmanagement.com
[7] http://www.linux.org/news/sco/timeline.html

been analyzed and explained in [9, 16, 17], but the fundamental decision involves finding out what type of license is adequate or "compatible" with our company.

One way to go is to perform a rigorous legal analysis of every license of every piece of software that is offered to us. This process could be expensive and time consuming. A better way to go is to conclude the type of license we need from a strategic analysis of our business and then get only products that offer these licenses.

Here we propose a framework that can be used to determine the compatibility that the different kinds of licenses have with a given company. This framework, that we call OSCoM (Open Source Compatibility Metrics)[8] is based on a series of questions that must be answered by managers or people who really know the company. The questions are grouped into categories according to:

–   The use that the software is going to have[9]
–   Whether we plan to perform modifications to the software
–   The type of distribution the software is going to have

Each question has several alternatives, which might have a sub-question, allowing to divide a complex question into a series of simple ones. The sub-questions inherit the category of the "father". Figure 1 shows the idea.

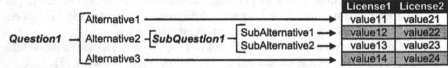

Fig. 1. Example Question

Another way to see it is trough a "n-ary" tree (Figure 2a) in which each level contains questions and answers and each leaf contains an option without sub-question (Figure 2b).

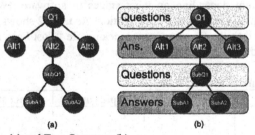

Fig. 2. Questions Tree (a) and Tree Structure (b)

Every leaf has some associated info. Each license is categorized into "best", "ok", "no" and "warning". These words represent different numeric values as shown in (1), (2), (3) and (4). For each license we can also keep some additional comments.

---

[8] http://oscom.sourceforge.net
[9] It is not the software itself what is important, but what we are going to do with it

It is possible then to go down through the tree to get the number and comments associated with a license when we arrive to a given leaf. This process is repeated three times for use, modification and distribution to obtain a total number and a final compatibility value that goes from 0 to 100. A negative value means incompatible **Scores:**

$$best \; = \; 100 \,/\, totalQuestions \qquad\qquad (1)$$
$$ok \; = \; best \,/\, 2 \qquad\qquad (2)$$
$$no \; = \; -100 \qquad\qquad (3)$$
$$warning \; = \; [\, no \mid ok \mid best \,] \qquad\qquad (4)$$

About the numbers: (1) The total number is distributed among all the questions. (2) A percentage of the best, we take 50%. (3) More than the number itself the important thing here is that any incompatibility must show up clearly, even if it is only one. We take the value -100 so the total score will always be negative. (4) By default it corresponds to the "no" value, but it gets a new value if it is fixed.

Notice that although the analysis is not dependent on a particular piece of software, it is dependent on the use, modification and distribution that we have in mind. It is completely different, for instance, software for development (e.g. Eclipse), for in-house use (e.g. OpenOffice) for service providing (e.g. Compiere) or for selling. In this last case FOSS is not an option but we might opt for a dual licensing scheme.

4.2 Cost Issues

When considering costs, no matter if it is FOSS or proprietary software, we have to be very careful. It is wrong, for instance, to think that because there is no need to pay for the licenses the associated costs of the FOSS based solution is zero or near zero. The total cost in that case could even be higher than the costs of the licenses for a proprietary alternative.

Most people think that the best way to consider the cost variable is to take the "Total Cost of Ownership" (TCO). Another option would be the "Return Of Investment" (ROI) but here we are more interested in comparing alternatives than in knowing if the money we are spending in technology is well spend.

If we are taking TCO as our comparison criteria, it is necessary to consider each stage of the process (Planning, Deployment, Operation). Each of those has its own costs that need to be identified (some are of a fixed amount and some are variable), for example:

- Fixed Costs: Planning (*Research, Consulting*) and Deployment (*Acquisition, Installation, Training*)
- Variable Costs: Maintenance (*Basic Configuration, Reconfiguration, Specialized Support, Internal Support Personnel*)

Figures 3 and 4 show a possible cost structure. Among the acquisition costs we can find for example the licenses. Installation costs will include initial configuration of the systems and the integration with other existing systems.

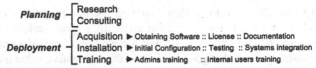

Fig. 3. Fixed Costs Structure

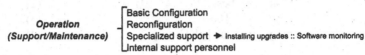

Fig. 4. Variable Costs Structure

There are other issues that might be necessary to consider in the TCO analysis. For a more detailed analysis see for instance "Managing Your IT Total Cost Of Ownership"[18]. The authors include downtime, futz, virus resistance and power consumption in the list. They also explain that "only a 20% of TCO lies in initial acquisition costs and the rest lies in administration costs" which is coincident with what we said about the danger of putting to much emphasis in license costs.

An example of the use of TCO to compare Linux v/s Windows solutions can be seen in Cybersource's study[19]. It shows that, in this case, the FOSS alternative produces up to 36% in savings. Another study by IDABC[20] found savings of 66% and Robert Frances Group found even larger savings[21]. Finally, Forrester, taking into account a sample of 14 companies, concluded "software costs for Linux proved to be less expensive, on a per-server basis, than Windows by at least 60%"[7].

Not all studies found such big cost advantages for FOSS; Bearing Point concludes that costs within medium and enterprise scenarios over a five year period do not significantly differentiate Windows Server 2003, Red Hat Enterprise Linux 3 or Novell/SUSE LINUX 8[22]. They also say that "Areas of differentiation to consider include such factors as value-added functionality, vendor support, productivity advantages, and the costs to deploy, manage and maintain an infrastructure".

So the cost aspect ends up being a tricky business. The important thing to remember is that we must perform TCO calculations considering as many variables as possible. The results will depend on many factors like business size, period of time and service level considered.

4.3   Support

Support has always been an important component in enterprise software. We could argue that support is already taking into account when considering costs. Comments like "the number of people I have assigned to Linux is almost double my Windows staff for the same number of servers"[7] or "maintenance and support was 3-14% higher on companies using mixed operating systems environment than those using only Windows"[7] show that cost and support are indeed related one to the other.

We believe however that this is an issue that needs to be considered by itself. Consider for instance a solution that involves a piece of FOSS for which it is very difficult (almost impossible) to get support no matter how much money we are ready to pay. Managers would probably rule out immediately the use of any unsupported piece of software.

IT companies are taking advantage of a business opportunity. In fact, support has become an important source of income for IT companies that are finding more and more difficult to make money just by selling the hardware or the associated software. In some cases the product is FOSS and cannot be sold without a license violation, so they give away the software and charge for support. Companies like JBoss, RedHat, and Suse represent just a few examples of this.

Other companies like MySQL, Sleepycat (Berekely DB) and Trolltech (QT) offer a dual licensing scheme for companies where "copyleft" is not an option. Other interesting initiatives include Spike Source, which offers pre-tested FOSS stacks and Source Labs offering maintenance and support for FOSS. Dell has announced support for MySQL and JBoss software that run in their "Power Edge" servers. There is even a support search engine[10].

Although in many cases the hardware/software vendor also provides support (because it is good business) we are not forced to this. Any person or company with the relevant knowledge could do it. In that case FOSS poses a small additional challenge: documentation is often poor or even inexistent (FOSS projects struggle to get people who are willing to do documentation) making it very hard to fix uncommon problems. At this time Linux skills are harder to find compared to Windows but this may change in the future[7].

Contrary to what many CIOs may think, defect density in FOSS releases will generally be lower than commercial code that has only been feature-tested, that is, received a comparable level of testing. From other side, FOSS developments exhibit very rapid responses to customer problems. In successful FOSS projects, a group larger by an order of magnitude than the core will repair defects, and a yet larger group (by another order of magnitude) will report problems[23]. There is no methodology for evaluating support that we are aware of. We suggest the use of a sequence of steps as shown in Figure 5.

The first step is to decide whether we are going to use internal or external support. In the case of contracting external services we must assure not only availability but also the credentials of the provider, experience, service level options, etc. The internal support option requires answers to questions such as:

-   Do we already have a support department? Do we want to create one?
-   Do we have the knowledge or experience in-house?
-   Do we have the necessary people? Gurus?

[10] http://www.findopensourcesupport.com/

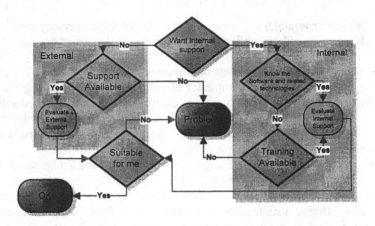

Fig. 5. Support Evaluation Diagram

4   Results

So, is FOSS appropriate for us? This is the question we started with. We have proposed a more structured way to answer the question that requires a view from three different sides: legal, cost and support. For each of them we need to look at the special characteristics of our company and the specific scenario where the decision is being taken.

Let's say we are considering a very small company (micro company) with one or two people using just one computer connected to the internet, used for reading emails, word processing and spreadsheets. The OSCoM analysis would show that all the licenses get similar scores and therefore license compatibility is not significant.

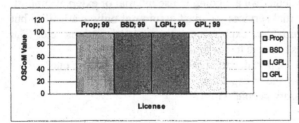

Category	Answer
Use	Normal
Modifications	Simple
Distribution	No
Future-Dist.	No

Fig. 6. OSCoM Analysis for Micro Size Company

The Cost analysis shows that the use of applications with no associated license fees produces important savings (OpenOffice instead of Office). Finally with respect to support, there is only one computer running well known application software. Probably all that is needed is to make a call in case of any problem. Although it might be a little harder to find a Linux expert compared to someone who can solve a Windows problem it is not indeed a big issue.

Now, if we consider a small company, the scenario may involve a LAN with one computer acting as a mail-web-db server. If the company chose FOSS it would be a combination of Linux, Apache, MySQL and PHP. Otherwise it could be Windows+IIS+SQLServer. It is not uncommon to start thinking in intranets and Web based applications which could involve the use of a more complete platform like .Net or J2EE (J2EE usually considered too complex for this type of scenario).

The OSCoM analysis is now a little more elaborated:

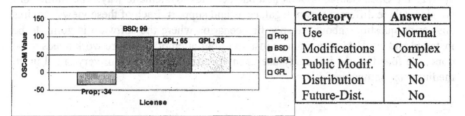

Category	Answer
Use	Normal
Modifications	Complex
Public Modif.	No
Distribution	No
Future-Dist.	No

Fig. 7. OSCoM Analysis for Small Size Company

Proprietary licenses that do not allow access to the source code make special purpose solutions hard to do. If we compare BSD with GPL and LGPL, the first one is the best if we do not plan to make all our changes and modifications public.

Cost analysis is also more complex. The use of a solution like Apache+MySQL might appear ridiculously low compared to a IIS+SQL Server equivalent but we showed that this is not the only cost that has to be taken into account. Support issues also start to be important. We may have no people inside that can assume a support role at all. In that case we should consider to put together a support group or find an external service. It should not be hard to find the needed support in case it is needed.

For a medium size company, we can find not only web servers but application servers and all the components of a full size software platform like J2EE or .Net. A decision to go open source is even harder if the critical applications are already running in one of these proprietary platforms (Java being easier than .Net). Here is an OSCoM scheme for this new scenario:

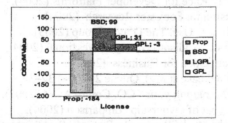

Category	Answer
Use	Extension
Program Use	Proprietary
Modifications	Special
Public Modif.	No
Distribution	No
Future-Dist.	Yes

Fig. 8. OSCoM Analysis for Medium Size Company

Here, future distribution potential increases the differences compared to the previous scenario. LGPL is now better than GPL because of the extensions to proprietary software.

5 Conclusion

Free and Open Source Software represents a big opportunity not only to individuals or small companies. Very good quality software with functionality and performance similar or even better than expensive proprietary software is available with no license payment associated to it. Nevertheless CIOs and IT managers often fail to even consider this option. We have proposed a framework that can be used to analyze the Open Source options in a balanced and systematic way. The framework considers three different views: legal, costs and support. Each of these views requires answering questions about the specific scenarios where the software is going to be installed and used. Although this is just an initial attempt and more work needs to be done, we found that it is already useful in specific scenarios from very small up to medium size companies.

References

1. A. Gokhale, D.C: Schmidt, B. Natarajan, and N.Wang. Applying model-integrated computing to component middleware and enterprise apps. Comm. ACM 45 (2002).
2. W.Emmerich,E.Ellmer, and H.Fieglein. Tigra - an architectural style for enterprise application integration. In: ICSE '01, IEEE Computer Society (2001) 567–576.
3. D. Scott. Making smart investments to reduce unplanned downtime. Gartner 1999.
4. GNU. Gnu general public license (2005) http://www.gnu.org/copyleft/gpl.html.
5. GNU. What is copyleft? (2005) http://www.gnu.org/copyleft/.
6. P.E. Schmitz and Castiaux, S. Pooling Open Source Software. IDABC (2002).
7. J. Giera. The Costs And Risks Of Open Source. Forrester Research (2004).
8. B. Fitzgerald and G. Bassett. Legal Issues Relating to FOSS (2003).
9. J. Michaelson. There's no such thing as a free (software) lunch. Queue 2 (2004).
10. A.G. González. The calm before the storm? legal challenges to open source licences. In: Proceedings of the Int. Conference on Open Source Systems (2005).
11. ZDNet-UK: Sco was the 'best thing that ever happened' to linux. http://news.zdnet.co.uk/0,39020330,39190780,00.htm (2005).
12. M. Driver. .NET, Java and OS: A 3-Way Race for Developer Platforms (2004).
13. T. Schadler. OS Moves Into The Mainstream. Forrester Research (2004).
14. P. Dravis. OSS: Case Studies Examining its Use. The Dravis Group (2003).
15. B. Golden. Succeeding with Open Source. Addison-Wesley Professional (2004).
16. P. Gustafson and W. Koff. Open Source: Open for Business (2004).
17. D. Ascher. Is os right for you? (a fictional case study). Queue 2 (2004) 32–38.
18. J:S. David, D.Schuff, and R.S. Louis. Managing your TCO. Comm.ACM (2002).
19. Cybersource: Linux vs. windows total cost of ownership comparison (2004).
20. S. Hnizdur, K. Matthews, E. Bleasdale, A. Williams, A. Findlay, S. Atkinson, and C. Briscoe-Smith. The IDA Open Source Migration Guidelines. IDABC (2003).
21. Robert Frances Group. TCO for Linux in the Enterprise (2002).
22. BearingPoint. Server op. system licensing and support cost comparison (2004).
23. A. Mockus, R. Fielding. Two case studies of open source software development: Apache and Mozilla (2002).

Understanding the Future of Global Software Production

Investigating the Network in India

Pratyush Bharati
Management Science and Information Systems
College of Management
University of Massachusetts, Boston
Boston, MA 02125-3393 USA
Pratyush.Bharati@umb.edu
WWW home page:
http://www.management.umb.edu/faculty/bharati_pratyush.php

Abstract. The software industry in India that mostly exports information technology (IT) services has emerged in the last decade as an important constituent of the world software industry. The industry is organized into MNC networks, whose structural, relational, and territorial dimensions has been investigated. The quasi-disintegration and internationalization of MNC production activities, the commodification of services, the availability of highly skilled low cost personnel, and Indian IT services firms link with MNCs have aided in the emergence of IT services industry in India. The research elucidates that MNCs are key drivers in this complex and inter-dependent network that involve important Indian firms. This is the first study to investigate the Indian IT services industry in the context of global software production network.

1 Introduction

The software industry in India that mostly exports information technology (IT) services has emerged in the last decade as an important constituent of the world software industry. The world IT services market spending was estimated to be $ 415.1 billion in 2004 [1]. The Indian share of this market increased from 1.5 % in 2000-2001 to 1.9 % in 2002-2003 as the growth rate of Indian IT services exports was 22 % while the world IT spending grew only at a rate of 1-2 %. In 2004, IT services industry in India was $ 9.2 billion constituting about 2.2 % of world IT services industry [2,3]. The focus of the IT services industry in India is exports. In 2002, 79.2% of revenues were from exports with exports revenue growing at 30% and domestic revenue at 13% [4]. Although IT services work comprises from application outsourcing to IT consulting but Indian industry only has a noticeable

Please use the following format when citing this chapter:

Bharatti, P., 2006, in IFIP International Federation for Information Processing, Volume 214, The Past and Future of Information Systems: 1976–2006 and Beyond, eds. Avison, D., Elliot, S., Krogstie, J., Pries-Heje, J., (Boston: Springer), pp. 119–129.

presence in custom application development and application outsourcing segments of the market.

The organization in the Indian software industry has not been investigated in detail. This research studies the organization of the Indian firms and Multi-National Corporations (MNCs) in the software industry. It investigates the firms in the IT services industry, specifically studies the structural, relational and territorial dimension of the IT services network. The research questions that are being investigated are: What are the different economic agents and their links in the network? What is the governance structure in the network? What is the spatial dispersion or concentration of production units, location of suppliers and clients?

2 Brief Literature Review

The MNCs are the major clients and owners of the Indian IT services industry. The growth of IT services is largely driven by the Multi National Corporations' (MNCs) desire to outsource their IT services. The organization of IT services industry into MNC networks and the network's structural, relational, and territorial dimensions have to be investigated in order to have a more profound understanding of this industry.

2.1 MNCs' Newer Organizational Arrangements

MNCs are constantly in pursuit of the best balance between vertical integration and reliance on the market for inputs [4]. Efficiency is one of the driving forces as a way to achieve global competitiveness for labor-intensive products, thus, MNCs have moved to low wage countries. This strategy of flexible centralization is complementing the benefits of scale economies with the advantages of low input costs [5].

The oft-cited strategy is that of General Electric (GE) management's 70-70-70 outsourcing strategy. This strategy mandates that 70% of GE's IT service requirement will be outsourced, out of which, 70% will be given to strategic suppliers, who will in turn execute 70% of the work outside of high wage countries. It is estimated that GE currently sources more than $ 500 million worth of IT services from India and that is about 8 % of the Indian IT services export [2]. As firms continue to transform themselves from a large, vertical corporation several organizational arrangements continue to emerge.

One of the arrangements that has emerged is the network model that adds flexibility and adaptability for the corporation [4]. This transformation is termed "quasi-disintegration", the transformation from vertical integration to increased reliance on sub-contractors [6], or "quasi-integration", the unity of firm with its suppliers, distributors into networks beyond pure market relations [7]. This is one of the trends that has led to the booming of the sub-contracting or outsourcing market. The concept of networks is similar to that of value chain which "divides a company's activities into the technologically and economically distinct activities it performs to do business" [8] and a commodity chain which is "a network of labor and production processes whose end result is a finished commodity" [9].

The metaphor of chain has been employed in different disciplines with slightly different terminology such as value chain, commodity chain, supply chain and filieres [10]. The commodity chain and value chain approaches have numerous similarities between them. As "a firm's value chain is an interdependent system or network of activities, connected by linkages. Linkages occur when the way in which one activity is performed affects the cost or effectiveness of other activities" [11]. In case of a commodity chain "all firms or other units of production receive inputs and send outputs. Their transformation of the inputs that result in outputs locates them within a commodity chain (or quite often within multiple commodity chains)" [12].

Study of the Unites States (US) in late nineteenth and early twentieth centuries has found that the commodity chains were incorporated within the organizational boundaries of vertically integrated corporations. Then the "visible hand" of corporate management served as the governance structure of these corporations [13]. "Under these circumstances, the governance structure, which is essential to the coordination of transnational production systems, is no longer synonymous with a corporate hierarchy" [14]. In the last several decades of the twentieth century the commodity chains have become more internationalized. Some of the links that were internal to the vertically integrated corporation are being outsourced as tasks to be performed by a network of independent firms [14].

"In today's global factory, the production of a single commodity often spans many countries, with each nation performing tasks in which it has a cost advantage. The components of a Ford Escort, for example, are made and assembled in fifteen countries across three continents" [14]. This complex international disaggregation of stages of production and consumption under the organizational structure of densely networked firms or enterprises applies to both manufacturing and services [11,15,16].

The Indian information technology (IT) services firms since the beginning have been part of the external networks of MNCs. MNCs, because of their re-organization of IT services, have increasingly sourced IT services from India. MNC's international network of production of goods and services "combines a lead firm, its subsidiaries and joint ventures, its suppliers and subcontractors, its distribution channels, VARs [Value Added Resellers], as well as its R&D [Research and Development] alliances and a variety of cooperative agreements.... The lead firm outsources not only manufacturing, but also a variety of high-end support services." [17]. This international organization of production and consumption led by the major MNCs is an important reason for the outsourcing of IT services in India.

2.2 Organization of Services in Networks

Services represent two thirds of world gross domestic product (GDP). The production of services is mostly a core economic activity in a country irrespective of its national income. The world exports of commercial services, which excludes government services, was $ 1,570 billion in 2002. The commercial services exports grew at 10.7 percent per year from 1989 to 2000 [15,18]. The trade in commercial services grew faster than trade in goods increasing its share in total world trade by 4 percentage points from 1980-2000. In 2002, services accounted for approximately 20% of total world trade [18]. The atomization, fragmentation and internationalization of production has increased the role of service activities. MNCs have been attracted to the concept of sourcing services not only for cost reductions but also to gain greater flexibility and access to specialized skills [19].

Despite their increasing importance in the world economy, services have been neglected in the commodity chain and network analysis research. In the product commodity chains, the service activities provide links between production segments within international commodity chains. They not only link the overlapping commodity chains but also link larger spheres of production and distribution. As a result of atomization, fragmentation and internationalization of production, service firms are increasingly producing services by internationally coordinated service activities.

Global commodity chain (GCC) research has not investigated the commodity chains where the services play an important role. The focus has been conceptualized as a series of activities where the product input and output dominate. Services have not been examined in GCCs and thus have become mechanical configuration without much theoretical depth.

The GCCs have been examined even less in industries where the predominant activity is services. Service activities in service industries such as financial services, software and health care are increasingly being fragmented and internationalized. In manufacturing industries such as information technology (IT) hardware industry, numerous service activities that are integral to their GCC such as research and development, design, and development have been internationalized [8,20].

The MNCs now manage their product commodity chains as networks of internationally located subsidiaries, affiliates, joint ventures, and sub-contractors. A similar phenomenon is taking place for service activities within the MNC commodity chains. IT services of major MNCs are being sourced from specialized IT services firms with international locations [21]. A specific network's structure is constituted by nodes and their links. The nodes comprise of agents that are linked together with investments. The durability of the capital links are an important element of the network that includes both inter and intra firm links [22]. This study will investigate the nodes and links in the IT services network in India.

A hurdle in conducting research on the IT services industry is the unavailability of data because of absence of proper classifications. For instance, the United States also has not consistently classified the IT services industry. The computer software industry was not classified separately even until 1972 [23]. United Nations (UN) has also acknowledged that there is a wide gap between data needs and availability and narrowing it is bound to be a long term exercise. To resolve this gap, the UN has a taskforce to classify and collect more and better internationally comparable data on services trade in the future [24]. This study had to overcome these serious shortcomings of data unavailability.

3 Methodology

A database of IT services firms in India was developed as part of this study. Data was collected on all the IT services firms listed on the National Association of Software and Service Companies (Nasscom) online directory. Then this data was augmented and reconciled with data from other databases, namely Compustat

Global, Mergent Online and Thompson Research. Finally, data was also collected from firm websites. The data had to be collected from numerous sources because a consolidated and complete database of all IT services is not available. Since the private firms disclose minimal data and MNCs provide negligible data on their subsidiaries, despite sourcing data from numerous databases, the data availability has varied in the database. The database will be continuously updated to ensure better depth and breadth of data and might be employed for other analyses. Currently, the total number of IT services firms in the database is 551. The data was analyzed to study the organizations and the IT services network in India along the structural, relational and territorial dimensions. This method has been adopted in studies of global commodity chains and production networks [14,20].

4 Analysis

4.1 Structural Dimension

Structural dimension studies the different economic agents and their links in the network. The IT services network in India consists mostly of India based private IT services firms, India based public IT services firms, MNC subsidiaries and joint ventures (Table 1). Among India based firms the public firms are older than the private firms. While the India based private firms and MNC subsidiaries were founded in early 1990s the public firms were founded in the late 1980s. Both MNCs and India based public firms prefer stock exchanges and world headquarters in their country of origin. For the MNCs the most popular stock exchange is the NASDAQ while the India based public firms prefer the Mumbai Stock Exchange (BSE). The difference is revenue is stark as a median MNC is more than 60 times bigger than an India based public IT services firm.

Table 1. IT Services Firms in India – Summary

Category	Private (N=145)	Public (N=57)	MNC Subsidiary (N=43)
Median Founding Year	1991	1988	1993
Median Revenues ($M)	-	27.10	1696.12
Median No. of Employees	-	1250	5617
Stock Exchange (Most Popular)	-	BSE	NASDAQ
World Headquarters	India	India	US
Primary Work Location in India	Bangalore	Mumbai	Bangalore
No. of CMM Certified Firms	30	29	8
No. of ISO Certified Firms	49	38	11

Data Sources: Firm websites, Nasscom, Compustat Global, Mergent Online, Thompson Research, and US Securities and Exchange Commission (SEC) filings.

The network (Figure 1) starts with mostly a MNC or sometimes a small and medium enterprise (SME) that decides to source whole or part of its IT services to another firm. The MNC sources it from its own or another MNC subsidiary, an India based firm or a joint venture or, usually, a combination. The SME on the other hand will either employ an India based IT services firm directly or through a sourcing consulting firm. GE's network exemplifies a MNC IT services network in India (Table 2). The network providing IT services to GE has been categorized into inter-firm, intra-firm (subsidiary) and joint venture network. GE's intra-firm provider network encompasses firm subsidiaries or those of different business units delivering IT services. The inter-firm network consists of major Indian IT services providers with a long term relationship with GE mostly as a customer and sometimes even an investor. The joint venture network comprises of IT services firms jointly owned by GE and Indian firms.

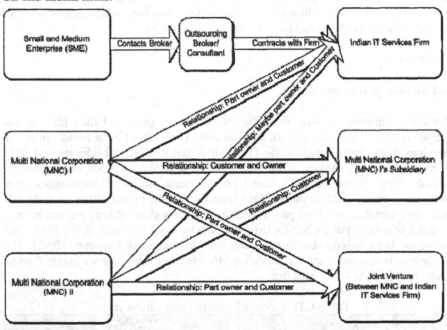

Fig. 1. India's IT Services Network

4.2 Relational Dimension

Relational dimension investigates the governance structure in the network. It studies the strategic drivers and how they exert influence on other economic agents, focusing on power and authority relationships. The IT services network in India is bound together with the help of equity and non-equity forms of ownership and control. Networks are bound together usually through equity holdings, debt holdings, shared directors, and equipment leases. The MNCs are owners of their subsidiaries and the major ones are General Electric (GE) India, IBM Global Services India, Microsoft India and Oracle India. GE is also part equity owner of Patni Computer Services (PCS) and several joint ventures together with other IT service providers (Table 2).

Most of the customers of India's IT services industry are non-Indian MNCs and SMEs. In 2004-05 year, about 74% of the revenues were from export. The customers of the IT services industry is a laundry list of major MNCs. GE is not only a major customer of all its subsidiaries and joint venture firms but also one of the largest customers of PCS. GE constitutes about 20 % and 38% of Satyam and iGATE sales respectively. TCS has also negotiated a $ 100 million outsourcing deal, one of the largest outsourcing deals in the industry, with GE (Table 2). The historical connection with MNCs, which was the basis of the industry, has been maintained in the present network. This connection has been maintained through a record of providing high quality service at a low price. For example, the private, public and MNC IT services firms in India have the highest number of Capability Maturity Model (CMM) certifications in the world (Table 1 and 2).

Table 2. GE's IT Services Provider Network

Network SubType	Entity Providing IT Services	Sample of IT Services Provided	Quality Certifications
Intra-Firm Network	GE Software Solutions: Subsidiary of GE Capital that provides IT services to GE and non-GE companies	Implementation, IT consulting, development, transition, maintenance, and support services	Six Sigma
	GE Global Technology Solutions: Subsidiary for GE Aircraft Engines and GE Appliances	Advanced mainframe software solutions development, client server solutions, e-commerce technology and enterprise resource planning (ERP)	Six Sigma
	Global Technology Operations – India: Subsidiary for GE Medical Systems	Design and development of products and solutions for several computer platforms	ISO 9001 Six Sigma
	John F. Welch Technology Center – India: Subsidiary for Research & Development	Conduct research on IT and e-Business, business-to-business e-commerce market software development	Six Sigma

Network SubType	Entity Providing IT Services	Sample of IT Services Provided	Quality Certifications
Inter-Firm Network	Tata Consultancy Services (TCS): Largest Indian IT service provider. TCS won one of the largest deals in the Indian industry of $ 100 million from GE.	Global development center conducts development on most platforms and also employs object-oriented analysis and design techniques	ISO 9001 People Capability Maturity Model (PCMM) level 4 Capability Maturity Model (CMM) level 5
	Patni Computer Services (PCS): Seventh largest Indian IT service provider. GE is one of the largest customers providing more than $ 108 million of IT services. GE Equity has about a $ 100 million stake in PCS.	Enterprise application solutions, e-business, implementation, and consulting	ISO 9001 CMM level 5 PCMM level 3 Six Sigma
	Satyam Computer Services: Fourth largest Indian IT service provider. GE is one of the largest customers of the firm accounting for 20 % of sales.	Global development center provides consulting, application development, enterprise application integration, data warehousing and customization	ISO 9001 CMM level 5
	iGATE Global Solutions: A mid-size IT service provider. GE is a large customer, especially the employee reinsurance group, which accounts for 38 % of revenues.	Application maintenance and data management	ISO 9001 CMM level 5 Six Sigma
	Nucleus Software: An IT service provider and product firm for GE Capital.	Consulting, software development, support and maintenance services related to its product	CMM level 5
Joint Venture Network	Satyam – GE Software Services (India Design Center): Satyam Computer Services and GE Industrial Systems	Design and develop new products and software solutions for embedded systems, e-commerce, and human machine interface	ISO 9001

Network SubType	Entity Providing IT Services	Sample of IT Services Provided	Quality Certifications
	GE Medical Systems Information Technology: Joint venture between GE Medical Systems and Citadel Health, a niche Indian IT firm.	Develop software products for GE Medical Systems	Six Sigma
	BirlaSoft: GE is a major customer. GE Equity has a 20 % equity stake in the firm.	Develop software solutions at global development center	Six Sigma CMM level 5 ISO 9001

Sources: The table was constructed by integrating data from firm websites, database and Internet searches, Nasscom (2003 and 2005), and Dataquest (www.dqindia.com).

Table 3. IT Services Firms in India – Leading Firms by Firm Type

Firm Type	Examples	World Headquarters/Listed	Worldwide Revenues (2004)
Indian Startup Firms	Infosys	India/NASDAQ	$ 1.50* billion
	HCL Tech.	India/BSE	$ 0.59* billion
Indian Conglomerates	TCS	India/Private	$ 1.64* billion
	Wipro	India/NYSE	$ 1.20* billion
Joint Ventures	Satyam-GE	India/Private	NA
	BirlaSoft	India/Private	$ 0.05** billion
IT MNCs	IBM	US/NYSE	$ 96 billion
	Oracle	US/NASDAQ	$ 10.15 billion
Non-IT MNCs	GE	US/NYSE	$ 152.60 billion
	Citibank	US/NYSE	$ 86.10 billion
Mid-size IT Services Firms	Syntel	US/NASDAQ	$ 0.19 billion
	Covansys	US/NASDAQ	$ 0.37 billion

Notes: BSE: Mumbai Stock Exchange; NA: Not Available; NASDAQ: National Association of Securities Dealers Automated Quotation; NYSE: New York Stock Exchange; *: 2004-05; **: 2001-02; Data Sources: Firm websites, Nasscom, US Securities and Exchange Commission (SEC) filings. Updated from source: [21].

4.3 Territorial Dimension

The territorial dimension studies the spatial dispersion or concentration of production units, location of suppliers, and clients. The average IT employee cost in India of $ 5880 per year is an important factor in the emergence of India as a work location in IT services [1]. The IT services firms have established work locations in the big cities and some locations and their surrounding areas have emerged as favorites, namely Bangalore, Chennai, Hyderabad, New Delhi, and Mumbai (Table 1). Since the cost in these locations has risen drastically, firms are exploring newer locations. Unlike manufacturing the IT services industry does not have several layers of suppliers for the MNCs (Table 2). The Indian IT services firms continue to grow and the top three firms now have revenues of more than $ 1 billion with offices all over the world (Table 3). TCS, the largest Indian IT services firm, is already part of Tata Sons that is a giant Indian conglomerate. As in the past the state continues to assist with tax incentives, establishment of software parks and export processing zones.

5 Brief Conclusions

The quasi-disintegration and internationalization of MNC production activities, the commodification of services, the availability of highly skilled low cost personnel, and Indian IT services firms link with MNCs have aided in the emergence of IT services industry in India. The Indian IT services firms have had a relationship with MNCs since the very beginning. These close links have been strengthened with the MNCs serving as critical customer and sometimes important investors in the Indian IT services firms. The Indian IT services firms on the other hand have gained in reputation and size. It is possible that some of these large firms may become Indian MNCs.

The IT services network is not as layered as compared to a manufacturing network. Presently the service work cannot be packaged more effectively and efficiently with better results, although it is possible that might change. Despite the fact that both MNCs and Indian IT services firms are exploring newer work locations both in India and in other countries, some cities have emerged as hubs for IT services work. The research elucidates that MNCs are key drivers of this complex and inter-dependent network that involve important Indian firms. This is the first study that has investigated the Indian IT services industry as part of the global production network.

References

1. International Data Corporation, *Global Impact Report 2005*, BSA Publication.
2. Nasscom. *Strategic Review Report 2003,* Nasscom Publications, New Delhi, 2003.
3. Nasscom. *Strategic Review Report 2005,* Nasscom Publications, New Delhi.
4. M. Castells. *The Rise of the Network Society.* Revised Blackwell, Oxford (2000).
5. C.A. Bartlett. and S. Ghoshal. *Managing Across Borders: The Transnational Solution.* 2nd Ed., Random House, London (1998).
6. M. Aoki.Information, Incentives, and Bargaining in the Japanese Economy. Cambridge University Press, Cambridge (1988).
7. M. Kenny and R. Florida. *Beyond Mass Production: The Japanese System and Its Transfer to the U.S.,* Oxford University Press, Oxford (1993).
8. J. Dedrick and K.L. Kraemer. Asia's Computer Challenge: Threat or Opportunity for the United States and the World. Oxford University Press, Oxford (1998).
9. T.K. Hopkins and I. Wallerstein. Commodity Chains in the World-Economy Prior to 1800, Review, Vol. 10, No. 1, pp. 157-170 (1986).
10. J. Kydd, R. Pearce, and M. Stockbridge. *The Economic Analysis of Commodity Systems: Environmental Effects, Transaction Costs and the Francophone Filière*

Tradition, presented at the ODA/NRSP Socio-Economics Methodology (SEM) Workshop, ODI: London, 29-30 April (1996).

11. M. Porter. *The Competitive Advantage of Nations*, New York, Free Press (1990).

12. T.K. Hopkins and I. Wallerstein. Commodity Chains in the Capitalist World-Economy Prior to 1800, in *Commodity Chain and Global Capitalism* Ed. Gereffi, G. and Korzeniewicz, M., Praeger, CT (1994.

13. A.D. Chandler, Jr. The Visible Hand, Harvard University Press, Cambridge, MA (1977).

14. G. Gereffi, M. Korzeniewicz, and R.P. Korzeniewicz. Introduction: Commodity Chains, in *Commodity Chain and Global Capitalism* Ed. Gereffi, G. and Korzeniewicz, M., Praeger, CT (1994).

15. P. Dicken. Global Shift: Reshaping the Global Economic Map in the 21st Century, 4th ed., Guilford, New York, NY (2003).

16. R.B. Reich. The Work of Nations: Preparing Ourselves for 21st Century Capitalism, Alfred A. Knopf, New York, NY (1991).

17. D. Ernst. From Partial to Systemic Globalization: International Production Networks in the Electronics Industry. Sloan Foundation Report on *Globalization in the Data Storage Industry*, University of California, San Diego and Berkeley Roundtable on the International Economy (1997).

18. World Trade Organization (WTO), *Measuring Trade in Services*, Economic Research and Statistics Division (2003).

19. T.H. Davenport. The Coming Commoditization of Processes, Harvard Business Review, June, pp. 100-108 (2005).

20. T.S. Poon. *Competition and Cooperation in Taiwan's Information Technology Industry*. Quorum Books, Westport (2002).

21. P. Bharati. India's IT Services Industry: A Comparative Analysis, *IEEE Computer*, Vol. 38, No. 1, pp. 71-75 (2005).

22. C. Karlsson and L. Westin. Patterns of a Network Economy: An Introduction, Johansson, B., Karlsson, C., and Westin, L.(Eds.), *Patterns of a Network Economy*, Springer-Verlag (1994).

23. S.E. Siwek and H.W. Furchtgott-Roth. *International Trade in Computer Software*, Quorum Books, Westport, CT (1993).

24. United Nations, *Manual on Statistics International Trade in Services*, Statistical Publications, Series M 86 (2002).

Work Distribution, Methodology and Technology for ISD and Maintenance
Trends over the last 30 Years

John Krogstie

IDI, NTNU and SINTEF Norway

Abstract. The information systems we see around us today are at first sight very different from those that were developed 30 years ago. On the other hand, it seems that we are still struggling with many of the same problems, such as late projects and unfilled customer demands. In this article we present selected data from survey investigations performed by us in 1993, 1998, and 2003 among Norwegian organisations on how they conduct information systems development and maintenance. The investigations looks on many of the same areas as earlier investigations e.g. by Lientz and Swanson in the late 1970', thus we are able to report on some tendencies of the development in the last 30 years. A major finding is that even if we witness large changes in the implementation technology and methods used, a number of aspects such as overall percentage of time used for maintaining and evolving systems in production compared to time used for development is remarkably stable. The same can be said about the rate of replacement, around 50% of 'new' systems to be developed are replacement systems. On the other hand, since we have more complex infrastructures supporting the information systems, more and more of the resources are used for other tasks such as operations and user-support. Less and less time is available for providing new information systems support in organisation

1 Introduction

Large changes in how we develop information systems and the underlying technology for information systems have been witnessed over the last 30 years. For instance, over this period the prevalent development methods, programming languages and general technological infrastructure have changed dramatically. On the other hand, many of the intrinsic problems and aspects related to information systems support in organisations are similar. Application systems are valuable when they provide information in a manner that enables people and organisations to meet their objectives more effectively [1]. Many have claimed that the large amount of system work that goes into maintenance is a sign on poor use of resources to meet these demands. On the other hand, as stated already in [2], it is one of the essential

Please use the following format when citing this chapter:

Krogstie, J., 2006, in IFIP International Federation for Information Processing, Volume 214, The Past and Future of Information Systems: 1976–2006 and Beyond, eds. Avison, D., Elliot, S., Krogstie, J., Pries-Heje, J., (Boston: Springer), pp. 131–142.

difficulties with application systems that they are under a constant pressure of change. Given the intrinsic evolutionary nature of the sources of system specifications, it should come as no surprise that specifications and the related information system must evolve as well [1].

The goal of both development activities and maintenance activities is to keep the overall information system support of the organisation relevant to the organisation, meaning that it supports the fulfilment of organisational needs. A lot of the activities usually labelled 'maintenance', are in this light value-adding activates, enabling the users of the systems to do new task. On the other hand, a large proportion of the 'new' systems being developed are so-called replacement systems, mostly replacing the existing systems without adding much to what end-users can do with the overall application systems portfolio of the organisation.

Based on this thinking we have earlier developed the concept application portfolio upkeep [1]as a high-level measure that can be used to evaluate to what extent an organisation is able to evolve their application system portfolio efficiently. How application portfolio upkeep is different from maintenance is described further below.

In this paper, we present descriptive results from survey-investigations performed in Norwegian organisations in 1993, 1998, and 2003. These investigations are also comparable to similar investigation by Lientz and Swanson going back to the late 70ties, thus are able to give us a way of tracking the developments over the last 30 years in this area. The statistical significance of some of the main differences is reported in [3], but is not included here for brevity.

1.1 Outline of the Paper

We will first give definitions of some of the main terms used within software development and maintenance, including the terms application portfolio upkeep and application portfolio evolution. The main descriptive results from our investigation are then presented and compared with previous investigations from earlier years. The last section summarises our results and presents ideas for further work.

2 Basic concepts

Maintenance is in the IEEE Glossary divided into three types: corrective, adaptive and perfective [4] inspired by [5]. We here use the IEEE terms with some clarifications:

Maintenance is defined as the process of modifying a software system or component after delivery.

1. *Corrective maintenance* is performed to correct faults in hardware and software.
2. *Adaptive maintenance* is performed to make the computer program usable in a changed environment
3. *Perfective maintenance* is performed to improve the performance, maintainability, or other attributes of a computer program. Perfective

---

[1] This concept was originally termed 'functional maintenance', but we have realized that this term might be misleading,.

maintenance has been divided into *enhancive maintenance* [6] and *non-functional perfective maintenance*. Enhancive maintenance implies changes and additions to the functionality offered to the users by the system. Non-functional perfective maintenance implies improvements to the quality features of the information system and other features being important for the developer and maintainer of the system, such as modifiability. Non-functional perfective maintenance thus includes what is often termed preventive maintenance, but also such things as improving the performance of the system.

In addition to the traditional temporal distinction between development and maintenance, we have introduced the concepts application portfolio evolution and application portfolio upkeep, given the groupings as illustrated in Figure 1.

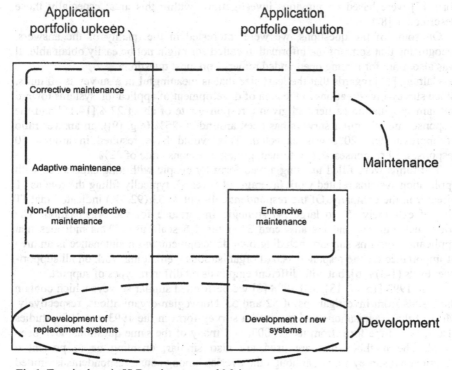

Fig 1. Terminology in IS Development and Maintenance

1. Application portfolio evolution: Development or maintenance where changes in the application increase the functional coverage of the total application systems portfolio of the organisation. This includes:
   - Development of new systems that cover areas, which are not covered earlier by other systems in the organisations
   - Enhancive maintenance.
2. Application portfolio upkeep: Work made to keep up the functional coverage of the information system portfolio of the organisation. This includes:
   - Development of replacement systems.

- Corrective maintenance
- Adaptive maintenance
- Non-functional perfective maintenance

3 Research Method

The survey form used in 2003 was distributed by mail to 247 Norwegian organisations. The organisations were randomly selected from the list of member organisations of Dataforeningen (The Norwegian Computer Society).

The form contained 38 questions, many with sub-questions. The contents of the form [7] were based on previous investigations within this area; especially those described in [8-12].

On some of the questions, we were interested in the quality of the answers, recognising that some of the information called for might not be easily obtainable. It was also room for issuing open-ended remarks on most questions.

Galtung [13] regards that the least size that is meaningful in a survey is 40 units. Since survey-investigations in the area of development of application systems toward the same population earlier had given a response rate of about 22% [14,15] and the response rate of similar surveys has been around 20-25% (e.g. [9]), an answer ratio of approximately 20% was expected. This would have resulted in around 50 responses. 54 responses were returned, giving a response rate of 22%.

The forms were filled in using a web-form by people with long experience with application systems related work (average 14.5 years), typically filling the role as IT director in the company. Of the respondents, 49 out of 53 (92.5%) indicated that IT was of extremely (5) to large (4) strategic importance for the organisation. The additional four respondents answered 3 on the 1-5 scale used. This indicates that application systems support including own development and maintenance is an area of importance for the respondents. All organisations were doing work on all support-line levels (1-3) [16], but with different emphasis on different types of support.

In 1993 [15 17, 18], and 1998 [8] we performed similar surveys which contain the results from investigations of 52 and 53 Norwegian organisations, respectively. Most of the organisations that received a survey-form in the 1993 and 1998 studies also received the form from us in 2003, and many of the same questions have been asked. The methods that are used are also similar, enabling us to present a 'longitudinal survey study', although the overlap among actual respondents is limited to only a few organisations. Because of this and the somewhat low response rate, we will be cautious in our interpretations of the results

3. 1 Other Investigations

We will compare some of the results also with the results of similar investigations in other countries. The most important of these investigations are:

1. The Lientz and Swanson investigation [10]: That investigation was carried out in 1977, with responses from 487 American organisations on 487 application systems.

2. The Nosek and Palvia investigation [11]: A follow-up study to Lientz/Swanson performed in 1990. Their results are based on responses from 52 American organisations.
3. The Swanson and Beath investigation [12]: Reports on case-studies of 12 American companies that in addition to questions given in the Lientz/Swanson study focused on portfolio analysis and the question of replacement systems. These aspects are also a major part of our investigations.

4. Descriptive Results

First, we present some of the overall demographics of the surveys. We focus on 2003 results. Similar results from our previous surveys conducted in 1993 and 1998 are included in parenthesis where the numbers are comparable.

20% (1998-43%) of the organisations had a yearly data processing budget above 10 mill NKr (approx. 1.3 mill USD), and the average number of employees among the responding organisations was 181 (1998-656; 1993-2347). The average number of full-time personnel in the IS-organisations reported on was 9.8 (1998-10.9; 1993-24.3), whereas the average number of full-time application programmer and/or analysts was 4.1 (1998-4.6; 1993-9.5). As we see, the responding companies are generally smaller in our latest survey, whereas they have approximately the same size of IT-departments as in the 1998 survey. The average experience in the local IS-department was 5.4 (1998-6.3; 1993-6.4) years, (average total experience was 8.2 (1998-8.3) years. The average number of full time hired IT consultants was 0.7, which is much lower than what was reported in 1998 (2,7). This reflects the limited activity at the time in the Norwegian consultant-market (and general), where all the major consultant-companies had to lay off hundreds of employees.

4.1 Portfolio Analysis and Replacement Systems

The number of main systems in the organisations ranged between one and 15, with a mean of 4,5 (1998-9.6;1993-10.3) and a median of 3 (1998-4;1993-5) systems. The user population of these systems ranged between 3 and 2005, with a mean of 314 (1998-498; 1993-541) and a median of 55 (1998-150;1993-250). The age distribution of the systems in ours studies and the Swanson/Beath study is provided in Table 1. The average age of the systems was 3.9 years (1998-5,0 ; 1993-4.6; Swanson/Beath-6.6).

Table 1 : Age distribution of systems

Age of systems	2003	1998	1993	Swanson/Beath
0-1	20	7	13	7
1-3	37	19	38	17
3-6	27	33	22	24
6-10	8	23	18	26
> 10	8	18	9	26

An overview of where systems are developed is provided in table 2. As an overall trend, we see that fewer systems are being developed in the IS-organisation, from 82% in Swanson/Beath to 59% in 1993, to just above 20 % in 2003. The amount of systems developed in the user organisation remains low (the peak in 1998 was due to a few organisations with a large number of systems). Similarly we see an increase in systems developed by outside firms, and on the use of packages. Whereas the amount of packages with large adaptations (e.g. ERP systems) appears to be quite stable around 10% over the last 10 years, the number of COTS (packages with small adaptations) is on the rise. The new category we introduced in 1998, component-based development only amounted to 1.0 % (0.4% in 1998) of the total systems.

Table 2: Main place for systems development

Development Category	2003	1998	1993	Swanson/ Beath
Developed by IS-organisation	22,6	26,8	59	82
Developed in user department	1,9	26,6	1	1
Developed by others (e.g. consultants)	35,1	22	12	15
Packages solution, large adaptation	12	9,6	11	NA
Package solutions, small adaptations	27,4	14,6	17	2
Component-based development	1	0,4	NA	NA

The organisations typically supported several technical configurations (mean 1.9, median 2). The average number of different programming languages in use was 2 (median 2). This is similar to the investigation in 1998 and 1993. Table 3 provides an overview of the percentage of systems reported being developed using the different programming languages. As we see, from being dominant ten years ago COBOL is almost not used anymore.

Table 3: Percentages of systems developed using different programming languages

Language/ Investigation	2003	1998	1993	Swanson/ Beath	Nosek/ Palvia	Lientz/ Swans.
COBOL	0,5%	32.6%	49%	63%	51%	51.6%
4GL	13,5%	16.9%	24%		8%	
C	12,5%	15.4%	4%		3%	
C++	23,1%	15.1%				
RPG		12.9%	4%	2%	10%	22.4%
Java	29,8%	2%				
Assembler		0.9%	3%	8%		11.9%
Fortran		0.6%	4%	2%	7%	2.4%
PASCAL		0.3%	2%			
PL/1		0.3%	2%	25%		3.2%
Other	20,2%	2.6%	6%		21%	7.7%

The languages that are used in most organisations and for most systems are now Java (27%) and C++ (24%). Java was just starting to be in widespread use in 1998 and C++ was barely included in 1993. The percentage of organisations reporting to have COBOL applications has decreased from 73% in 1994 to 26% in 1998 to 1% in 2003.

Table 4 summarises the development in database technologies, showing how eventually most installed databases now are relational. Also in 1998, the relational technology was most widespread looking upon the number of organisations using this technology. We also see a rise in the use of object-oriented and other database technology (e.g. for Data Warehouses).

Table 4 : Database Technology

Database Technology	2003	1998
Hierarchical	4,5	16,5
Network	10,7	40,6
Relational	52,9	38,6
Object-oriented	9	1,3
Other	23	3,1

In general, we see that the developments as for implementation technologies follow an expected path, but much slower than one might have expected.

40 new systems were currently being developed, and 23 of these systems (60 %) were regarded as replacement systems. (1998-57%; 1993-48%; S/B-49%). The portfolio of the responding organisations contained 172 systems, meaning that 13% of the current portfolio was being replaced. (1998 – 9%; 1993 – 11%; S/B 10%) . The average age of systems to be replaced was 5.5 years (1998-10.5 years ; 1993-8.5 years). The reasons for the replacements have slightly changed from earlier investigations [3]. The most important reasons for replacement are now a need for standardization and integration with other systems. The burden to maintain is still an important issue in many cases, although of less importance than in earlier investigations. Burden to operate and use is much less important.

4.2 Use of Methodology and Organisational Controls

As for the use of methodology, as many as third of the organisations respond that they have no methodology in place at all. As for the use of methodology within different areas of development and maintenance, the numbers were: Planning (43.5%, 1998-34%), Analysis (23,9%, 1998-30,2%), Requirements specification (56.5%, 1998-50,9%), Design (45.7%, 1998-39,6%), Implementation/Coding (52.2%,1998-43,3%), Testing (54.3%, 1998-34%), Conversion and rollout (32.6%,1998-26,4%), Operations (37%,1998-32,1%), Maintenance (28.3%,1998-30,2%), Project management (34.8%,1998-41,5%).

As for the use of comprehensive system development tools, 53.7% (1998-13.2%; 1993-27.1%) use such tools for development, and 39% (1998-11.3%;1993-10.6%) use such tools for maintenance. The tools are primarily used in planning, requirement specification, design and implementation. The average experience with the tools was 4.2 (1998-3.1; 1993-2.8) years, and the organisations have only on average 2 (1998-2;1993-2) systems supported by the tools. This shows that the use of advanced system development tools still makes a limited although increasing impact on the overall application systems support of organisations.

With 'organisational controls' we mean procedures and functions that are intended to control different aspects of the maintenance process. Use of organisational controls concerning maintenance has been reported in several studies [8, 10, 11, 12, 15].

The use of organisational controls and a comparison with previous investigations are given in Table 5. The majority of the organisations document user requests, classify change requests and re-test changes in their systems as in the previous investigations. A marked improvement in the use of cost-justifications can be seen. On the other hand, a dramatic worsening of the use of periodic implementations of errors and new functionality can also be seen. The use of organisational controls have in other studies shown to be efficient for improving the amount of value added time of maintenance by increasing the percentage enhancive maintenance [19].

Table 5: Comparisons on use of organisational controls

Control[2]	2003	1998	1993	Nosek/ Palvia	Lientz/ Swans.
e. Changes are re-tested	75%	59%	79%	54%	59%
b. Classification of CR	64%	59%	60%	N/A	N/A
d. Changes documented	57%	51%	67%	83%	77%
c. Requests cost-justified	55%	36%	54%	37%	33%
h. Users kept informed	51%	51%	79%	N/A	N/A
a. User requests logged	49%	59%	77%	89%	79%
i. Equal routines for all	40%	40%	58%	N/A	N/A
j. Periodic formal audits	38%	17%	68%	39%	32%
g. Acceptance testing of doc.	34%	28%	43%	N/A	N/A
l. Personnel charge-back	19%	13%	31%	25%	31%
k. Equipment charge-back	17%	15%	40%	23%	34%
f. Changes are batched	13%	52%	40%	28%	33%

Organisational controls are typically used to assure adhering to software maintenance success factors [20]. An assumption concerning use of organisational controls is that there always is a potential for improvement of the IS-system portfolio. Usually the amount of change requests exceeds the capacity of the IS-organisation. Based on this it seems reasonable to prioritise change requests and perform cost-benefit analysis. Among the responding organisations, however, 45% did not perform analysis of consequences related to changes and requests were not cost-justified.

4.3 Distribution of Work

Work on application systems was in the survey divided into the six categories presented in the section 2. The same categories were also used in 1993 and 1998. We also asked for the time used for user-support and for systems operations and other tasks which took up the additional time for the work in the IS departments.

Table 6 shows the distribution of work in previous investigations, listing the percentage of maintenance work relative to development work, the study reported, and the year of the study. Based on this we find that in most investigations, between 50% and 60% of the effort is done to enhance systems in operation (maintenance) when disregarding other work than development and maintenance. An exception from this was our previous study in 1998.

Table 6: Result on maintenance from previous investigations on maintenance

Maintenance	Investigation	Year
49	Arfa et al [21]	1990
53	Lientz and Swanson [10]	1980
56	Jørgensen [22]	1994
58	Nosek and Palvia [11]	1990
58	Yip [23]	1995
59	Krogstie [15]	1993
63	Martinussen [24]	1996
72	Holgeid [8]	1998

Table 7 summarises the descriptive results on the distribution of work in the categories in our investigation, comparing to previous investigations.

Table 7: Distribution of the work done by IS-departments

Category	2003	1998	1993	Lientz/ Swanson
Corrective maintenance	8.7	12,7	10,4	10,6
Adaptive maintenance	7.2	8,2	4	11,5
Enhancive maintenance	12.5	15,2	20,4	20,5
Non-functional perfective maintenance	7.5	5,4	5,2	6,4
Total amount of maintenance	**35.9**	**41,4**	**40**	**48,8**
Replacement	9.7	7,7	11,2	NA
New development	12.2	9,5	18,4	NA
Total amount of development	**21.9**	**17,1**	**29,6**	**43,3**
Technical operation	23.1	23	NA	NA
User support	16.8	18,6	NA	NA
Other	2.3	0	30.4	7,9

In 2003, 35.9% of the total work among the responding organisations is maintenance activities, and 21.9% is development activities. When disregarding other work than development and maintenance of application systems, the percentages are as follows: maintenance activities: 65.8%, development activities: 34.1%. This is a smaller percentage maintenance than in 1998, but still more than in 1993 where the corresponding percentages were: maintenance activities: 58.6%, development activities: 41.4%. In organisations were developing and maintaining IS systems accounts for more than 50% of total effort, development activities accounts for 30.0 % of the total work. 61% of development and maintenance work was application portfolio upkeep, and 39% was application portfolio evolution. This is almost the same as in 1998, which in turn was a dramatic change from the situation in 1993 where application portfolio upkeep- and application portfolio evolution respectively amounted to 44% and 56% of the work. Further comparisons of descriptive results between different studies are presented in Table 8. The first column lists the category, whereas the other columns list the numbers from our investigation, the one in 1998, the one in 1993, the Lientz/Swanson investigation and the Nosek/Palvia investigation. The first set of number compare the numbers for development, maintenance and other work. The amount of *other work* reported in our investigations is much larger than in the American investigations. Therefore, in the second set of figures, we compare the data without considering other work. For the categories application portfolio evolution and application portfolio upkeep, we only have numbers from our own investigations.

Table 8: Comparisons of maintenance figures with previous investigations

Category	2003	1998	1993	Lientz/ Swanson	Nosek/ Palvia
Percentage of all work					
Development	21	17	30	43	35
Maintenance	35	41	40	49	58
Other work	44	42	30	8	7
Disregarding other work than development and maintenance					
Development	34	27	41	47	38
Maintenance	66	73	59	53	62
Functional effort, disregarding other work than development and maintenance					
Application portfolio evolution	39	38	56	N/A	N/A
Application portfolio upkeep	61	62	44	N/A	N/A

5 Conclusion and Further Work

Looking at the overall trends, there are a number of differences in the underlying technology, which is as expected. This is very clearly witnessed in the distribution of programming languages used, where procedurally languages like COBOL have to a large extend been suppressed by object-oriented languages like Java and C++. This has happened at a smaller pace than one might have expected, applications exist for a number of years in organisations before they are being replaced, even if it appears that the replacement time is decreasing. On the other hand, overall percentage of time uses for maintaining and evolving systems in production compared to time used for development is remarkably stable. The same can be said about the rate of replacement, around 50% of 'new' systems to be developed are actually replacement systems. Since more complex infrastructures are supporting the information systems, more and more of the resources is used for other tasks such as operations and user-support, less and less time is available for providing new information systems support in organisation

Several of our results have spurred new areas that could be interesting to follow up in further investigations, either in the form of further surveys, or more likely by developing several detailed case studies. To come up with better empirical data on to what extent the application systems support in an organisation is efficient, would take another type of investigation, surveying the whole portfolio of the individual organisation, and getting more detailed data on the amount of the work that is looked upon as giving the end-user improved support, and how efficient this improved support was provided. This should include the views of the users of the application systems portfolio in addition to those of the IS-managers and developers.

A long-term plan is to do a similar investigation in 2008, following up our five-year cycle.

References

1. B. Boehm, K. Sullivan, Software economics: status and prospect. Information and Software Technology 41(14) (1999) 937-946.
2. F. P. Brooks, No silver bullet. Essence and accidents of software engineering, IEEE Computer 20 (4) (1987) 10-19.
3. J. Krogstie, A. Jahr, D. I. K. Sjøberg. A Longitudinal Study of Development and Maintenance in Norway: Report from the 2003 Investigation, accepted in Information and Software Technology, 2006
4. IEEE Standard Glossary of Software Engineering Terminology, 1991
5. E.B. Swanson, The dimensions of maintenance, Proceedings of the Second International Conference on Software Engineering, San Francisco, USA, August 1976, pp. 492-497.
6. Chapin, N. Software Maintenance Types – A Fresh View. Proceedings of the International Conference on Software Maintenance (ICSM'2000) pp 247-252 2000
7. A. Jahr Development and Maintenance of IT-systems in Norwegian Organizations, Master Thesis IFI, UIO 2005
8. K. K. Holgeid, J. Krogstie, and D. I. K. Sjøberg, A study of development and maintenance in Norway: Assessing the efficiency of information systems support using functional maintenance. Information and Software Technology, 2000. 42: p. 687-700.
9. B.P. Lientz, E.B. Swanson, G.E. Tompkins, Characteristics of application software maintenance, Communications of the ACM, 21 (6) (1978) 466-471.
10. B.P. Lientz, E.B. Swanson, Software Maintenance Management, Addison Wesley, 1980.
11. J.T. Nosek, P. Palvia, Software maintenance management: Changes in the last decade, Journal of Software Maintenance, 2 (1990) 157-174.
12. E.B. Swanson, C. M. Beath, Maintaining Information Systems in Organizations, Wiley Series in Information Systems, John Wiley & Sons, 1989.
13. J. Galtung, Theory and Method of Social Research, Universitetsforlaget, Oslo, Norway 1967.
14. L. Bergersen, Prosjektadministrasjon i systemutvikling: Aktiviteter i planleggingsfasen som påvirker suksess (In Norwegian), PhD thesis, ORAL, NTH, Trondheim, Norway 1990.
15. J. Krogstie, A. Sølvberg, Software maintenance in Norway: A survey investigation, in: H. Muller and M. Georges (Eds.) Proceedings of the International

Conference on Software Maintenance (ICSM'94), IEEE Computer Society Press, Victoria, Canada, September 19-23 1994, pp. 304-313.

16. M. Kajko-Mattsson, Ahnlund, C. and Lundberg, E. CM^3 : Service Level Agreement. Proceedings of the 20th IEEE International Conference on Software Maintenance (ICSM'04) 2004

17. Krogstie, J., Use of methods and CASE-tools in Norway: Results from a survey. Journal of Automated Software Engineering, 1996. 3: p. 347--367.

18. J. Krogstie. On the distinction between functional development and functional maintenance, Journal of Software Maintenance, 7 (1995) 383-403.

19. J. Krogstie, Process improvement as organizational development: A case study on the introduction and improvement of information system processes in a Norwegian organization. in Proceedings from NOKOBIT'2000. 2000. Bodø, Norway

20. H. M. Sneed and P. Brössler. Critical Factors in Software Maintenance: A Case Study Proceedings of the 19th IEEE International conference on Software Maintenance (ICSM'03) (2003)

21. L. B. Arfa, A. Mili and L. Sekhri   Software maintenance management in Tunisia: A statistical study Proceedings of ICSM 1990 pages 124-129, IEEE 1990

22. M. Jørgensen, Empirical Studies of Software Maintenance, PhD Thesis University of Oslo, 1994, Research Report 188, ISBN 82-7368-098-3.

23. S.W.L. Yip, Software Maintenance in Hong Kong, in G. Caldiera, K. Bennett (Eds.) Proceedings of the International Conference on Software Maintenance (ICSM'95), IEEE Computer Society Press, Nice, France, October 17-20, 1995 pp. 88-97.

24. J.P. Martiniussen, Vedlikehold av programvare – Hypoteser testet i et større programvarehus, (In Norwegian), M. Sc. Thesis, Department of Informatics, University of Oslo, 1996.

An Analysis of IFIP TC 8 WG 8.6
In Search of a
Common Theoretical Denominator

Helle Zinner Henriksen, Karlheinz Kautz
Department of Informatics, Copenhagen Business School,
Howitzvej 60, 2000 Frederiksberg, Denmark
hzh.inf@cbs.dk, khk.inf@cbs.dk

Abstract. The IFIP TC 8 WG 8.6 focuses on the transfer and diffusion of information technology. Since the working group was established in 1993 there have been a number of events where members of the group have produced contributions analyzing transfer and diffusion of IT in different settings and from different perspectives. In this paper we report the result of an analysis of the theoretical perspectives the contributors have applied in the studies. Our analysis suggests that even though there is an even distribution of factor and process oriented studies reported in proceedings the theoretical denominator for the long standing members of WG 8.6 is the process oriented approach to the study of transfer and diffusion of IT.

1 Introduction

In 2003 the IFIP TC 8 WG 8.6 celebrated its 10th anniversary. On that occasion a review of the proceedings from the events during the period 1993-2003 was presented. This presentation was compiled to a contribution appearing in the proceedings of the WG 8.6 conference in 2005 [1]. The comprehensive review of the 113 papers appearing in the seven volumes of proceedings from the first ten years provided insights in the multiplicity of the study of "Transfer and Diffusion of Information Technology", which is the thematic label of IFIP TC 8 WG 8.6. Among other issues the review demonstrated which terms from the transfer and diffusion vocabulary had been used, which types of technologies were studied over the ten-year period, what the unit of analysis had been, what types of methods researchers applied in the studies, the nature of exploration in the studies, and the type of theoretical framework used in the analysis of diffusion and transfer of information technology.

The latter theme related to the use of theoretical frameworks in the studies gave food for thought with respect to the issue of whether or not the researchers involved

Please use the following format when citing this chapter:

Henriksen, H.Z., Kautz, K., 2006, in IFIP International Federation for Information Processing, Volume 214, The Past and Future of Information Systems: 1976–2006 and Beyond, eds. Avison, D., Elliot, S., Krogstie, J., Pries-Heje, J., (Boston: Springer), pp. 143–152.

in the WG 8.6 have developed a common theoretical foundation. The overall mission statement of IFIP and also the specific statement for WG 8.6 explicitly state as an objective to foster and develop suitable and robust frameworks, models or theories and it is our understanding that one of the purposes of bringing academics and practitioners together at the IFIP events is to support this type of activity for example through the presentation of papers included in the proceedings.

The objective of this paper is to outline which academic frameworks for transfer and diffusion of information technologies have been applied in the studies presented in the proceedings of the past events in WG 8.6. Without doubt Rogers [2] has been of the most influential researchers in the general field of diffusion of innovations, a claim which has also been supported and extended for IT diffusion research by members of WG 8.6 [3]. Thus, before becoming familiar with the results of the review of the proceedings it was our assumption that Rogers' prominent framework on diffusion of innovations would be one of the core theoretical frameworks and also the most cited source in the work of WG 8.6. However, it turned out that few of the reported studies had actually directly applied Rogers' framework in their work, but many studies referred to Rogers. The limited frequency of using Rogers' framework could therefore not be explained with the fact that the contributors were not familiar with the framework. This insight has inspired us to pursue this issue further in the present paper and to provide an overview of which other frameworks have then been used to conceptualize and analyze diffusion and transfer of information technologies.

It has been argued that the works of Rogers represent a positivistic approach to the study of the diffusion and transfer of technological innovations[4]. One assumption is therefore that the reason for not applying Rogers is that contributors to WG 8.6 prefer more interpretive approaches to the study of the transfer and diffusion of technological innovations. One consequence of this assumption is that apart from identifying which theories and frameworks are applied in the working group the analysis also aims at looking for possible patterns with respect to the methodological approaches of the studies presented in the proceedings. It is not our ambition to determine if one framework has better explanatory power than another. Nor is it to judge its relevance. Instead our goal is to provide an overview mapping of those frameworks, models, theories which contributors of the WG 8.6 events have found useful for explaining transfer and diffusion of information technologies.

The remainder of the paper is structured as follows: Section 2 outlines the conclusions on the usage of Rogers' work as explanatory framework from the WG 8.6 anniversary review as a motivation for the present study. Section 3 provides some reflections on differences between models, frameworks, theories and theory building. The section also presents our classification scheme and our method of deriving data from the contributions in the proceedings. Section 4 is dedicated to a discussion of benefits of making the type of exercise the study provides and some concluding remarks and directions for future work.

2 Background

As mentioned earlier Rogers [2] is considered a most influential researcher in the field of diffusion of innovations. In the WG 8.6 proceedings from 2001, McMaster [5] opened the discussion whether or not Rogers' work on diffusion of innovations was actually the most quoted theoretical contribution by researchers in the WG 8.6. Based on his analysis of the proceedings from three previous conferences McMaster concluded that it was not the case. Furthermore, based on proceedings from seven conferences [1] observed that Rogers' seminal book which by that time has been published in five editions was not as widely used by the researchers contributing to the seven volumes of the proceedings of IFIP WG 8.6 as one would expect. Rogers was identified as the single most cited author, but a closer look at the references to Rogers indicated that a citation is not identical with application of the theory. The review by [1] identified that roughly a third of all articles (31 out of 108, 29%) showed a neutral attitude towards Rogers in the sense that reference is made to Rogers without specifically making any value judgment about whether or not the framework is helpful for the particular study. Twelve articles are critical to Rogers (11%), typically drawing attention to the limitations of his factor oriented approach when studying diffusion of innovations. Ten articles (9%) are directly based on his work. This counting punctuates the myth that Rogers' framework is often used in the studies of diffusion of innovations.

Even though Rogers is often cited this is not synonymous with direct use of his theory in the analysis of adoption and diffusion of innovations. It could as well be a matter of simply citing Rogers as a proponent of the study of diffusion of innovations or quoting him as an example of a positivistic or factor oriented approach to the study of the diffusion of innovations.

Another conclusion Kautz et al. [1] reached with respect to the limited use of Rogers as explanatory framework was that contributions to the WG 8.6 in their majority focus on adoption on the organizational level whereas Rogers predominantly deals with adoption by individuals: hence Rogers' framework is not suitable for the analysis. This insight triggered our interest in investigating which other frameworks or models were used by the contributing researchers. The next section presents alternatives to Rogers' framework which have been applied in the WG 8.6 contributions. However, before getting that far a few comments on the terms framework, model and theory are provided.

3 Frameworks, Models and Theories

In the work of WG 8.6 we do not distinguish strictly between the terms frameworks, models or theories. What the difference between them is and what defines the three terms would justify an in-depth discussion in itself (see e.g. [6]). The group of researchers in WG 8.6 represent multidisciplinary traditions – especially with researchers from the IS field being strongly represented – and the distinctions between frameworks, models and theories are not always used rigorously by academic contributors. In addition, contributing practitioners do not always greatly appreciate the "academic terminological pedantry".

A number of researchers have produced comprehensive reviews of the study of diffusion of innovations [7-9]. The reviews have provided different classification schemes with respect to characteristics of the innovation [10] and impact of innovation [4,11]. Common for these reviews is that they have not focused specifically on the methodological approach of the studies. In his review of the study of innovations Wolfe [4] suggested that depending on the nature of the study researchers should choose their methodological approach. Wolfe distinguished between factor and variance theory.

Members of WG 8.6 have also contributed to reviews on diffusion of innovations. McMaster and Kautz [3] provided a review on the history of the concept of diffusion. Tracing the term back about five hundred years they noted that imbedded in the concept is a master-slave connotation. Larsen [12] has also contributed to the collection of reviews of diffusion of innovations and its content and scope. Larsen suggested that in order to align the further study with the technological development the WG 8.6 should "focus on societal implications, business potential, stakeholder awareness, marketing and solution development requirements of new IS/IT products." Common for the above-mentioned studies is a recommendation of considering both positivistic and interpretivistic school(s) of thought in the study of diffusion of innovations. However, without favoring any approach or strictly defining the characteristics of the two.

Markus and Robey [13] have provided an account on that particular issue. They suggested that researchers should distinguish between variance and process theory, the latter representing interpretative approaches to the study of diffusion of innovations and variance theory representing a more positivistic approach to studying the subject.

One of the strengths of the interpretive approach is the critical approach to the myth of objectivity of scientific research. It is accepted that there are no objective causal relations which can be observed and communicated and it is accepted there is no truth which is just waiting to be explained by the researcher(s) [14]. The positivistic reductionism is in other words dismissed and phenomenology and hermeneutics are among other interpretivistic approaches used to make sense of the world as it is viewed in the lenses of the researcher.

In the present study we apply Markus and Robey's [13] broad methodological classification. To identify which theoretical frameworks for studying diffusion and transfer of IT contributions published in the seven volumes of WG 8.6 proceedings were read and categorized based on the broad distinction between process research oriented studies and factor research oriented studies. Our classification of the contributions with respect to use of framework, theory or model is mainly based on what the researchers argue they apply. In those cases where no indication of use of a specific framework, theory or model is given, our classification is based on an analysis of the text including an examination of references. Our presentation of contributions representing different theoretical frameworks does not include the total number of contributions appearing in the proceedings. Instead we select and provide exemplars for the identified approaches.

3.1   Process Research Oriented Studies

Contributions falling in the category of process research oriented studies mainly include studies applying Walsham's interpretative framework [14]. Actor-Network-Theory [15,16], and Soft Systems Methodology [17]. A number of studies also combine factor oriented frameworks with process oriented frameworks. These studies often argue that the factor oriented frameworks are insufficient in explaining the processes of adoption, diffusion and implementation hence it is necessary to add elements from an interpretative school.

In his book "Interpreting Information Systems in Organisations" Walsham outlines his framework constructed around the elements content, context, and social and political processes. He derives these elements from contextualism [18] and structuralism [19]. Kautz and Henriksen [20], Muzzi and Kautz [21], and Nilsson, Grisot and Mathiassen [22] make explicit reference to Walsham's interpretative framework. Jayasuriya, Rawstorne, Caputi [23] apply Walsham in a more diverse way. They use Walsham's framework to test Rogers' stage-model. The authors explicitly mention that they apply contextualism in their study. Bøving and Bødker [24] also combine Rogers' model with an interpretative framework. They combine Rogers with a "participative approach".

Actor-Network-Theory (ANT) is another analytical approach which has been applied by a number of researchers. Contrary to Walsham's interpretative framework for IS in organizations ANT is less clear in its premises for studying the phenomenon of diffusion of innovations. Actors, actants, translation, enrolment and inscription are among the key concepts that constitute an ANT analysis. Hedström [25] applies a pure ANT perspective in her study. This is also the case with McMaster [3] in his study of how the concept of diffusion has developed over time. Lines, Andersen, and Monteiro [26] apply ANT and neo-institutional theory in their study of uptake of IT in hospitals in a Norwegian county.

A number of contributions which focus on diffusion of software development practices use Soft Systems Methodology (SSM) [17]. Through thorough case studies typically of single organizations the researchers provide interpretations of practices and reasons for the outcome of these practices. Examples of this type of contribution include Levine and Syzdek [27] and East and Metcalfe [28] who focus in particular on the use of rich pictures.

Common for all the studies in the category of process research oriented studies is that they are based on case studies. Modeling, experiments and quantitative tests are not used as research methods. In our second category, factor research oriented studies, there is a broader variety in research methods but the theoretical foundation is not as clear cut as in the process research oriented studies.

3.2   Factor Research Oriented Studies

As demonstrated in Section 2 Rogers' framework on diffusion of innovations does play a role in the contributions. Regardless of not being used as often as we expected Rogers is the single most cited author of a diffusion framework in the WG 8.6. When applying Rogers it is most often in connection with a factor oriented study. Among those contributions directly applying Rogers in their analysis of adoption, diffusion and implementation of innovations are Lyytinen and Damsgaard [29]. However, Lyytinen and Damsgaard analyze the framework and conclude that it is not suitable for analyzing diffusion of complex networked information technologies. Stuart, Russo, Sypher, Simons and Hallberg [30] combine Rogers with general IS adoption literature (which generally rests on Rogers' framework). Mitsufuji [31] applies Rogers, but combines his analysis with the Bass [32] model. This contribution is among the few contributions using econometrics to analyze the phenomenon of diffusion of innovations.

The majority of factor oriented studies apply contributions from the IS literature in their studies. Often cited contributions from the IS literature are [33-38]. The IS literature which focuses on adoption, transfer and diffusion of IT includes factors related to technological, organizational and environmental attributes which are then tested quantitatively or qualitatively as explanatory factors for adoption – and often also non-adoption – of a given IT innovation. The studies used as inspiration in the WG 8.6 contributions are mainly focused on the organizational or inter-organizational context. [39-41] are all examples of WG 8.6 contributions inspired by IS studies.

Some of the studies included in WG 8.6 proceedings do not give IT itself any particular attention. Instead, transaction cost theory has been used to support their arguments [42-43]. These contributions are however the exception from the rule of a very technology centric lens in the WG 8.6.

Having this in mind it is surprising that very few apply the TAM model [44] or the TRA model in their study of adoption and diffusion of technological innovations among individuals given that these models are specifically designed to embrace uptake of IT innovations -contrary to Rogers' model which does not distinguish between uptake of mobile phones, hybrid seed, or contraceptives. Sandhu and Corbitt [45] applied the TAM model in their study of e-commerce adoption and Moore and Benbasat used the TRA model in their study of end-users adoption of IT in organizations.

4 A Look Back to Look Forward

As stated in the introduction, the objective of this paper is to outline which academic frameworks for transfer and diffusion of information technologies that have been applied in the studies presented in the proceedings of the past events in WG 8.6.

Our analysis of the use of frameworks, theories and models supporting the study of transfer and diffusion of technological innovations shows a varied picture of how contributors to the proceedings approach the phenomenon. Variation is found at the different conferences: when the WG 8.6 event was held in Copenhagen, Denmark in 2003 the proceedings mainly consisted of process oriented studies whereas the proceedings from the event in Sydney, Australia in 2001 were dominated by factor oriented studies. However, when analyzing the seven volumes of proceedings as a whole the share of contributions reporting process oriented studies and factor oriented studies is more or less even.

The factor oriented studies of the adoption and diffusion of innovations are mostly not based on Rogers' framework. Instead other explanatory factors than those Rogers lists in his framework are operationalized. Well-established factor oriented diffusion-frameworks such as the Bass-model [32] or TAM [44] are also only rarely applied in the search for variables explaining adoption and diffusion patterns. Instead, the contributions are inspired by IS adoption studies mainly focusing on attributes of the particular (technological) innovation under examination and attributes of more general (organizational) conditions, e.g. managerial support, organizational size, slack and structure.

With respect to the interpretative frameworks applied there seems to be a more consistent pattern compared to the factor oriented contributions. The frequency of studies applying ANT, SSM, and Walsham's interpretative framework is relatively high compared to the more scattered picture of the use of factor oriented frameworks.

Based on our analysis of the contributions it is observed that contributions falling into the category of factor oriented studies are often authored by "single event" contributors or newcomers to the working group. The long standing members of WG 8.6 are on the other hand more inclined to stick to the same theoretical foundation which they apply in different settings over time and write new accounts of their work for the different events over the years. For some reason the theoretical foundation applied by the long standing members often falls into the category of process oriented studies. Given that a number of the long standing members appear in most of the volumes of the proceedings a more consistent picture appears with respect to the process oriented frameworks, models and theories.

It can therefore be argued that even though there is a more or less even distribution of factor oriented studies and process oriented studies in the proceedings of the WG 8.6 events, the common theoretical denominator in WG 8.6 is rooted in the process oriented schools of theories for understanding the transfer, diffusion and adoption of information technologies.

The majority of the longstanding members of WG 8.6 provide process research oriented studies within an interpretative approach. Studies based on this approach are certainly also applicable and necessary in the future, and refinements of the existing frameworks and theories are needed to further improve our understanding of complex phenomena such as transfer, adoption and diffusion. This is true especially in light of the continuous stream of IT innovations and their potential adoption by new user groups and in geographical and cultural areas of what is traditionally called the 'Western World'.

However, while sustaining methodological and theoretical pluralism, future work of the WG 8.6 ultimately has to tackle the question whether particular approaches or theoretical models are more appropriate for particular aspects of the transfer adoption and diffusion of IT innovations. The apparent focus of the group on organizations and the organizational level as expressed by its established members should in the future – beyond their sporadic appearances – also allow for researchers who like to study transfer, adoption and diffusion of IT and IT related phenomena either on the individual, sectoral, societal, regional or global level and who favor different research approaches, independently of whether they are more factor or more process based to join the group on a more permanent basis.

References

1. K. Kautz, H.Z. Henriksen, T. Breer-Mortensen, and H.H. Poulsen. Information Technology Diffusion Research: An Interim Balance. Proceedings of the IFIP TC8 WG 8.6 conference, Atlanta, US. (2005).

2. E.M. Rogers. Diffusion of Innovations. Free Press, New York. (1962).

3. T. McMaster and K. Kautz. A Short History of Diffusion. In The Adoption and Diffusion of IT in an Environment of Critical Change. D. Bunker, D. Wilson and S. Elliot (eds.), Pearson Publishing Service, pp. 10-22. (2002).

4. R.A. Wolfe. Organizational innovation: Review, critique and suggested research directions. Journal of Management Studies, 31(3), 405-431. (1994).

5. T. McMaster. The illusion of diffusion in information systems research. Diffusing Software Product and Process Innovations. Proceedings at IFIP TC8 W.G 8.6, fourth working conference, April 7-10 2001, Banff, Canada., 67-85. (2001).

6. K.E. Weick. Theory construction as disciplined reflexivity: Tradeoffs in the 90s. Academy of Management Review, 24(4), 797-806. (1999).

7. G.W. Downs and L.B. Mohr. Conceptual issues in the study of innovation. Administrative Science Quarterly, 21(December), 700-714. (1976).

8. R.G. Fichman. Information technology diffusion: A review of empirical research. Proceedings at the Thirteenth International Conference on Information Systems, Dallas, 195-206. (1992).

9. S. Gopalakrishnan and F. Damanpour. A review of innovation research in economics, sociology and technology management. OMEGA, International Journal of Management Science, 25(1), 15-28. (1997).

10. L.G. Tornatzky and K.J. Klein. Innovation characteristics and innovation adoption-implementation: A meta-analysis of findings. IEEE Transactions on Engineering Management, 29(1), 28-45. (1982).

11. M.B. Prescott and S.A. Conger. Information technology innovations: A classification by it locus of impact and research approach. DATA BASE Advances, 26(2 & 3), 20-41. (1995).

12. T. Larsen. The Phenomenon of Diffusion. In Diffusing Software Product and Process Innovations, Proceedings at IFIP TC8 W.G 8.6, fourth working conference, April 7-10 2001, Banff, Canada, pp. 35-50. (2001).

13. L.M. Markus and D. Robey. Information Technology and Organizational Change - Causal Structure in Theory and Research. Management Science 34(5), pp. 83-598. (1988).

14. G. Walsham. Interpreting information systems in organizations. Chichester: John Wiley & Sons. (1993).

15. B. Latour. We have never been modern. Cambridge, Mass.: Havard University Press. (1993).

16. B. Latour. Pandora's Hope: Essays on the reality of science studies. Cambridge, Mass.: Havard University Press. (1999).

17. P. Checkland. Soft Systems Methodology: A 30-year Retrospective. New York: John Wiley & Sons. (1999).

18. D. Webb and A. Pettigrew. The temporal development of strategy: Patterns in the UK insurance industry . Organization Science, 10(5), pp. 601-621. (1999).

19. A. Giddens. The constitution of society -outline on the theory of structuration. Cambridge: Polity Press. (1984).

20. K. Kautz and H.Z. Henriksen. Brilliant Idea? Bit it didn't do the Trick: The Role of a Designed Project in the Adoption and Diffusion Porcess of Inter-Organizational Information Systems. In The Adoption and Diffusion of IT in an Environment of Critical Change. D. Bunker, D. Wilson and S. Elliot (eds.), Pearson Publishing Service, pp. 160-174. (2002).

21. C. Muzzi and K. Kautz. Information and Communication Technologies Diffusion in Industrial Districts. In Networked Information Technologies - Diffusion and Adoption, J. Damsgaard and H. Z. Henriksen (eds.), Kluwer Academic Publishers, pp. 19-38. (2003).

22. A. Nilsson, M. Grisot, and L. Mathiassen. Translations in Network Configurations. In Networked Information Technologies - Diffusion and Adoption, J..Damsgaard and H. Z. Henriksen (eds.), Kluwer Academic Publishers. (2003).

23. R. Jayasuria, P. Rawstorne, and P. Caputi. Understanding the Adoption of IT in a Mandatory Situation: Does the Staged Model of Organizational Innovation Fit Reality? In The Adoption and Diffusion of IT in an Environment of Critical Change. D. Bunker, D. Wilson and S. Elliot (eds.), Pearson, pp. 114-127. (2002).

24. K.B. Bøving and K. Bødker. Where is the Innovation? In Networked Information Technologies - Diffusion and Adoption, J. Damsgaard and H. Z. Henriksen (eds.), Kluwer Academic Publishers, pp. 39-52. (2003).

25. K. Hedström. The Socio-political Construction of CareSys. In Networked Information Technologies - Diffusion and Adoption, J. Damsgaard and H. Z. Henriksen (eds.), Kluwer Academic Publishers, pp. 1-18. (2003).

26. K. Lines, K.V. Andersen, and E. Monteiro. MIS and the Dynamics of Legitamacy in Health Care. In Networked Information Technologies - Diffusion and Adoption, J. Damsgaard and H. Z. Henriksen (eds.), Kluwer Academic Publishers, pp. 95-114. (2002).

27. L. Levine and G. Syzdek. Across the divide: Two Organisations Form a Virtual Team and Codevelop a Product. In Diffusing Software Product and Process Innovations. Proceedings at IFIP TC8 W.G 8.6, fourth working conference, April 7-10 2001, Banff, Canada., pp. 147-172. (2001).

28. C. East and M. Metcalfe. Drawing Concerns: A Structured Rich Picturing Approach. In The Adoption and Diffusion of IT in an Environment of Critical Change. D. Bunker, D. Wilson and S. Elliot (eds.), Pearson Publishing Service, pp. 90-101. (2002).

29. K. Lyytinen and J. Damsgaard. What's Wrong with the Diffusion of Innovation Theory? In Diffusing Software Product and Process Innovations. Proceedings at IFIP TC8 W.G 8.6, fourth working conference, April 7-10 2001, Banff, Canada., pp. 173-190. (2001).

30. W.D. Stuart, T.C. Russo, H.E. Sypher, T.E. Simons, and L.K. Hallberg. Influences of Sources of Communication of Adoption of a Communication Technology. In Diffusing Software Product and Process Innovations. Proceedings at IFIP TC8 W.G 8.6, fourth working conference, April 7-10 2001, Banff, Canada., pp.191-204. (2001).

31. T. Mitsufuji. A Perspective of the Innovation-Diffusion Process from the Self-Organizing System. In Diffusing Software Product and Process Innovations.

Proceedings at IFIP TC8 W.G 8.6, fourth working conference, April 7-10 2001, Banff, Canada., pp. 51-66. (2001).

32. F.M. Bass. New product growth for model consumer durables. Management Science, 15(5), 215-227. (1969).

33. P.Y.K. Chau and K.Y. Tam. Factors affecting the adoption of open systems: An exploratory study. MISQ, March, 1-21. (1997).

34. R.B. Cooper and R.W. Zmud. Information technology implementation research: A technological diffusion approach. Management Science, 36(2), 123-139. (1990).

35. F. Damanpour and S. Gopalakrishnan. Theories of organizational structure and innovation adoption: The role of environmental change. Journal of Engineering and Technology Management, 15, 1-24. (1998).

36. P. Hart and C. Saunders. Power and trust: Critical factors in the adoption and use of electronic data interchange. Organization Science, 8(1), 23-42. (1997).

37. C.L. Iacovou, I. Benbasat, and A.S. Dexter. Electronic data interchange and small organizations: Adoption and impact of technology. MISQ, December., 465-485. (1995).

38. G. Premkumar, K. Ramamurthy, and B. Nilakanta. Implementation of electronic data interchange: An innovation diffusion perspective. Journal of Management Information Systems, 11(2), 157-177. (1994).

39. M. Themistocleous and Z. Irani. A Model for Adopting Enterprise Application Integration Technology. In The Adoption and Diffusion of IT in an Environment of Critical Change. D. Bunker, D. Wilson and S. Elliot (eds.), Pearson Publishing Service, pp. 61-75. (2002).

40. I. Anderson and K. Nielsson. Diagnosing Diffusion Practices Within a Software Organization. In Diffusing Software Product and Process Innovations. Proceedings at IFIP TC8 W.G 8.6, fourth working conference, April 7-10 2001, Banff, Canada., pp. 111-130. (2001).

41. J. Heikkila, H. Vahtera, and P. Reijonen. Taking Organizational Implementation Seriously: The Case of IOS Implementation. In Networked Information Technologies - Diffusion and Adoption, J. Damsgaard and H. Z. Henriksen (eds.), Kluwer Academic Publishers, pp. 181-198. (2003).

42. H.Z. Henriksen. In Search of an Efficient EDIcebreaker. In Diffusing Software Product and Process Innovations, Proceedings at IFIP TC8 W.G 8.6, fourth working conference, April 7-10 2001, Banff, Canada, pp. 211-292. (2001).

43. K. Reimers and M. Li. Should Buyers Try to Shape IT-markets through Non-market (Collective) Action? In Networked Information Technologies - Diffusion and Adoption, J..Damsgaard and H. Z. Henriksen (eds.), Kluwer Academic Publishers, pp. 131-152. (2003).

44. F.D. Davis Perceived usefulness, perceived ease of use, and user acceptance of information technology. MIS Quarterly, 13(3), 319-339. (1989).

45. K. Sandhu and B. Corbitt. Exploring and Understanding of Web-Based E-Service End-User Adoption. In The Adoption and Diffusion of IT in an Environment of Critical Change. D. Bunker, D. Wilson and S. Elliot (eds.), Pearson Publishing Service, pp. 46-60. (2002).

Promoting Learning Practices: Moving Towards Innovation

Chiara Frigerio[1], Federico Rajola[1] and Alessia Santuccio[2]

1 Catholic University, Business and Administration Department, L.go
Gemelli 1, 20123 Milan, Italy (chiara.frigerio,federico.rajola)@unicatt.it
2 IULM University, Economics and Marketing Department, via Carlo Bo
1, 20143 Milan, and Catholic University, Business and Administration
Department, L.go Gemelli 1, 20123 Milan, Italy
alessia.santuccio@unicatt.it

Abstract. As many authors have stated, the importance of organizational learning is fundamental in order to gain competitive advantage and survive in a turbulent environment. Many learning models have been studied in recent years. They have been used to analyze practices or aspects of learning in many industries. This paper aims to develop a particular framework in order to understand the determinants for organizational learning, depending on the firm's general approach towards information and knowledge management. The theoretical framework is derived from Blackler and McDonald's study, which focused on organizational learning approaches, and from Duncan and Weiss's work, which studied attitudes towards knowledge management. This is applied to a particular context characterized by a high level of bureaucracy: the Italian banking industry. In particular, the study is conducted on a sample of 54 banks. The empirical analysis is carried out through questionnaires and interviews. Data is analyzed using statistical analysis. Results are shown and empirical implications are discussed, also in order to explain the reasons for the current situation.

1   Introduction

Taking Simon [1] as a starting point, who first introduced the concept of organizational learning, this topic has been thoroughly explored over the last few years. Learning practices allow the organization to spread knowledge between members and thus react to external instability [2, 3] in order to achieve some kind of success [4]. Organizational learning, in particular, has been defined as the process through which action is improved thanks to a better understanding of context variables [5]. According to Lanzara [6], there can be no organizational learning as long as individual knowledge is not widespread and shared between members.

Please use the following format when citing this chapter:

Frigerio, C., Rajola, F., Santuccio, A., 2006, in IFIP International Federation for Information Processing, Volume 214, The Past and Future of Information Systems: 1976–2006 and Beyond, eds. Avison, D., Elliot, S., Krogstie, J., Pries-Heje, J., (Boston: Springer), pp. 153–164.

Learning is never individual, but always comes from comparisons between members [7]. It is supported by dialogue and communication; collaboration and co-operation; networks of ideas; incentives [8]. This strategy has to be realized at all levels within the organization. This means that even if organizational processes are complex, companies need to maintain learning practices, giving adequate incentives to their members [9]. According to Argyris' [2] definition of learning practices, the concept of organizational learning is also related to that of knowledge. Not many authors, however, have analyzed in any great detail the relationship between the two [10, 11]. In fact, the learning loop implies the creation of organizational knowledge, which comes from individuals' shared knowledge. Organizational learning begins from the sharing of individual knowledge, which needs to be spread throughout the organization and easily reached to be subsequently re-used [12].

Analyzing two proposed theoretical models, one concerning organizational learning and the other focusing on the concept of knowledge, this paper formulates a distinct framework. The aim is to explore the following research questions:

1. what are the determinants for organizational learning, depending on the firm's general approach towards information and knowledge management?

2. How can a hierarchical organization move towards innovation through the organizational learning approach?

The paper is organized as follows. Considering the explanation of the theoretical framework, it explains how this is applied to the sample. The results of the empirical study are shown and statistical analysis is presented. The implications are then discussed and some suggestions for future research are offered.

2   Theoretical Framework

2.1   Organizational Learning Perspective

To study the organizational learning perspective, the paper's approach is based on Blackler and McDonald's study [13], who – in order to investigate the organizational learning cycle - distinguish between four dimensions of learning, which are all present in every organization [13]. This distinction is based on two variables which analyze the complexity of learning practices. Firstly, they consider the (in)stability between organizational groups or networks of members who collaborate, ending up with a distinction between emergent and established ones. Secondly, they focus on the degree of routine which characterizes the relationships between members, distinguishing between emergent and established activities, as showed in figure 1.

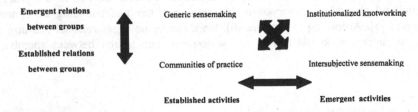

Fig. 1. Blacker and McDonald's dynamics of organizational learning

According to Cohen and Sproull [14], the distinction between established and emergent activities comes from the level of complexity in conducting them. McCall [15] considers the level of variety and diversity of work required to conduct the activity. Engestrom et al. [16] define an activity as emergent when there is not yet a centre of control for it, when technology or processes or the people involved in them change. An emergent activity always needs new contributions and it is typical of an unpredictable environment. On the other hand, the variable of group stability is classified as established or emergent depending on people's ability to collaborate in a situation of uncertainty [14]. According to Raeithel [17], it depends on the level of familiarity between individuals. Usually in established groups a common aim is created, such as in a community of practice [18].

Adopting Engestrom's view [16], this paper investigates the distinction between emergent or consolidated activities in terms of the presence or absence of a structured learning cycle. When some activity is new, it is not formalized yet; employees manage the activity without following procedures, but by using a non-structured approach. The activity requires many contributions in order to be improved and also many tools to explain the knowledge about it. So if an organization has more formalized and automated activities, it is considered as characterized by established activities and vice-versa. The paper assumes there is a structured learning cycle when knowledge on activities is firstly formalized and then spread using technological tools. This implies that the structured learning cycle depends on the correlation value of the following two variables:

- level of formalized knowledge in order to conduct the activity;
- degree of automation, which considers the presence and use of technological tools in order to support knowledge sharing and collective learning.

With reference to Cohen and Sproull's [14] and Pautzke's [19] papers, the more the organization allows informal meetings and moments of collaboration, the greater the possibility that knowledge can be shared. If communication between individuals or groups is recurrent and there is a high level of informal coordination (both at top management and staff level), this paper supposes that new relationships and potential new knowledge can emerge within the organization to react to the instability and reach some kind of innovation. The paper's approach considers the relationships as emergent valuating the correlation value of the following three variables:

- frequency of moments dedicated to collaboration;
- level of coordination accomplished through team work (unstructured forms of collaboration), both at business unit and top management level;
- creation of communities of practice and informal teams at all hierarchical levels and the presence of incentives.

2.2   Knowledge Management Perspective

As regards the concept of knowledge, this paper refers to Duncan and Weiss's [20] work. The current paper considers their distinctions: reinforcing or innovating through the creation of a new organizational knowledge base. Those aims can be accomplished through organizational or technological tools, as the literature states. As far as the organizational aspects are concerned, Nahapiet and Goshal [21] state that the creation of new knowledge is facilitated by the presence of a strong social capital. The importance of a culture of co-operation, collaboration, based on people's autonomy and fair incentives is stated by many authors such as Virkkunen and Kuutti [22]. In addition, Von Krogh et al. [23] analyze the obstacles that lie in the path of knowledge sharing. Also, theories of networks and social interaction explain the importance of promoting physical and virtual relations between individuals in order to create new knowledge [23, 24]. As well as this, more contributions on this topic come from theories on socialization [25]. The significance of combinative capabilities is offered by [26] or [27] as well. Also the importance of shared experiences and knowledge re-use is explained in Swan et al.'s work [28] and Gray's [29]. Considering the technological perspective, many authors classify technologies which can support a knowledge management approach, new knowledge creation and learning practices. Videoconferences, document management or collaboration tools are mentioned as useful tools [30, 31]. With reference to evidence in literature, the paper distinguishes between reinforcing and innovating the knowledge base by statistically analyzing the following:

- technological and organizational tools of KM;
- culture and incentives.

Considering these two perspectives on, respectively, organizational learning and knowledge management, the paper's theoretical framework is the following:

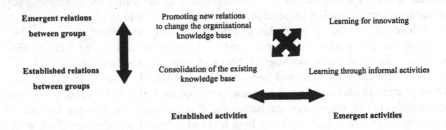

Fig. 2. Organizational learning and knowledge: an integrative approach

The aim of the paper is to demonstrate the differences in organizational practices and technological tools which explain the differences in knowledge sharing and learning between different clusters.

3   Research Methodology

The study is conducted on the banking industry. The reason for choosing this particular industry is the rapid changes that banks are experiencing, which need to be supported by learning practices, in order to react to the uncertainty of change (normative changes, the need to address customer satisfaction and follow market trends, international competition etc.). Moreover, to answer the second research question, questionnaires are completed and interviews conducted. Of 100 questionnaires distributed, 54% were completed and returned to be analyzed.

Considering the dimension variable, based both on the amount of intermediate funds – according to Bank of Italy directives - and on the number of employees, the sample is composed as follows:

- 38.9% (21 units) small banks;
- 33.3% (18 units) medium banks;
- 27.8% (15 units) large banks.

Quantitative data is collected thanks to structured questionnaires, filled in by KM managers (where possible), organizational and/or IT managers. Questionnaires are divided into two parts. The first one regards the bank's description; the second part concerns more specifically the current situation of learning practices, which are studied both from the organizational and technological point of view (practices and tools which support learning processes). People who were interviewed through questionnaires could answer the statements by choosing from a range between 1 and 7 (the answer is based on the Likert scale). The sample is classified using a cluster method. For each cluster a certain number of correlations are included, in order to understand the distinctiveness of each group. 6 interviews were also carried out (a couple for each size). They allow us to collect qualitative data in order to understand better the reasons for implementing some choices instead of others and extract tacit information and knowledge on the firm's processes of learning.

Data collection starts in November 2003 and finishes in July 2004.

4   Findings and Discussion

4.1   Clustering the Sample's Relations and Activities

The initial classification of the sample, based on Blackler and McDonald's study, is conducted by investigating those variables proposed in paragraph 2.1 through cluster analysis. In particular, to find out whether a bank has more established than emergent activities, the degree of formalization and automation is considered for each activity (payments, risk management and auditing, marketing etc.) and their means are calculated for each bank. The institution is characterized for established activities if the means of formalization and automation are, at the same time, greater than 4 (on a 1 to 7 scale). The same statistical analysis is conducted as regards the relationship variable, evaluating the average of the three variables proposed in the theoretical framework: the moments of collaboration, informal coordination and presence of incentives to the creation of informal teams.

In figure 3 cluster analysis output is presented, showing the number of banks which belong to each cluster. The results show that the majority of the banks have more established than emergent relationships and activities. Indeed, the banking industry has always been known for its high level of control, rigid procedures, formalized processes and hierarchical structure. This is due to the kind of activity it carries out: banks are risk adverse. Consequently, they strictly follow the rules. Over the last years there have been very few examples of investments made towards the creation of informal teams or communities in order to promote creativity, learning and knowledge exchange and when they can be found they only concern specific projects, such as Basel 2.

Table 1. Cluster analysis results

Relationship	Emergent	12 (cluster 4)	6 (cluster 2)
	Established	18 (cluster 3)	18 (cluster 1)
		Established	Emergent
		Activity	

At this point, a list of variables is considered through correlation analysis and the statistical significance is illustrated for each one of them (Table 2). The aim is to find out if they are relevant in order to explain differences in the way the four clusters go through the learning process, considering the organization's general approach towards information and knowledge management.

Table 2. Variable statistical significance

Variable	p	Significance
Dimensional class	>0.05	Low
Current situation of knowledge management systems	<0.01	Medium
Hierarchical level of knowledge management systems implementation	<0.01	Medium
Employment and dismissal rates	>0.05	No
Job rotation	>0.05	No
Responsible or sponsor of learning projects	<0.01	Medium
Use of technological tools	<0.001	High
Use of virtual spaces to support long distance learning and knowledge sharing	<0.001	High
Incentives to knowledge sharing and learning practices	<0.01	Medium
Kind of decisions supported by learning practices and knowledge management systems	<0.001	High

The dimension variable does not explain the variability between clusters. Anyway, while cluster 1 is mainly composed of large banks, clusters 2, 3 and 4 are made up of, respectively, small-medium, small and medium-sized banks. Generally, all these clusters consider learning practices important in order to maintain a competitive advantage. There is a divergence, however, in the way they promote them and some variables do not explain the clusters' differences in learning practices, such as employment and dismissal rates. What makes the difference between clusters is the dissimilarity in tools that emergent and established activities use to promote learning. While banks with prevalent emergent activities are based on both paper and electronic communication, established ones communicate mainly by electronic means. This evidence can be explained in terms of knowledge formalization and the use of it to promote learning practices at a distance too. Knowledge of consolidated activity is made explicit and formalized, while - regarding emergent activities - new concepts are continually in evolution. These are not strongly formalized and distributed through electronic tools yet. The low importance placed on electronic tools is explained also by the significance of knowledge management. In cluster 2 great importance is given to opportunity for collaboration, while investments in technology are not high. This can be explained looking at the main cluster's characteristics, which is characterized by emergent relationships between groups and emergent activities. The main focus is on the people variable, in order to promote innovation. Investments cannot be high because of the predominantly small size of the banks which are involved. In cluster 1, processes and technology are both considered equally important. These mainly large banks formalize knowledge and distribute it using technology. Investments in IT are consistent because of the size – these banks can afford them and also permit a higher level of communication and reduce bureaucracy-connected risks. This also regards cluster 4, characterized by banks which are not small. Finally, banks in cluster 3 give importance to people working together to promote organizational learning, but also to processes, while IT investments are not high because of the small size. Also while clusters characterized by established activities give importance to learning practices at business unit and top management level, cluster 2 focuses mainly on business unit level. Cluster 4 is the only one which implements a learning culture also at branch level, even if these banks place moderate importance on learning as a tool of innovation. This cluster differs also because of the kind of decisions the learning cycle supports. While in clusters 1, 3 and 4 the learning process supports daily and operational decisions, in cluster 2 it also supports the strategic ones. As concerns the presence of a learning project sponsor, the difference between clusters mainly depends on the way banks interpret the learning process and what they focus on. Only in cluster 3 this responsibility is given to the human resources managers, since these banks interpret the learning approach as the management of people. Generally, in all clusters the persons responsible and sponsor for learning projects are the CIO (especially in cluster 4), CEO or heads of departments. The main reasons for spreading organizational learning practices between members differ depending on the aim of learning. In clusters with established activities, the aims of a learning approach are the efficiency and effectiveness of process management, better formalized knowledge, competence sharing and a better process of communication. On the other hand, clusters characterized by emergent activities implement learning practices firstly, in order to introduce some innovation, and secondly to improve communication between members or groups and efficiency in process management. Cluster 2 shows an interest in reducing the time taken to reach the market, supported by flexible organizational learning.

In order to support an effective approach toward learning, management commitment seems to be the most common incentive between clusters. Banks, generally, do not adopt strategies such as bonuses, benefits, or career improvements. What is evident is a lack in promoting formal learning. Porter and Lawler's [32] theory of motivation suggests the mixing of different incentives, to promote learning in a better way by aligning the individual and organizational interests. As regards the use of technological tools, clusters with emergent relationships are based on collaboration tools. Generally, all clusters present repositories on the web (usually intranet and portals) to spread knowledge. E-mails and videoconferences are the most widespread mechanisms of learning, while it is not the same as regards brainstorming and forums.

The empirical study also shows whether there are obstacles in the learning practices. In cluster 1, there is the perception that learning is a waste of time and useless. In many cases personal knowledge is considered as a source of power [33], useful mainly to build up one's personal career. In cluster 2, which has a more innovative approach towards learning, the main obstacle is the kind of relationships that exists between members. Even if these banks are characterized by emergent relationships, the ones which already exist are not flexible enough. This depends on the way of conducting banking activities, which do not require a highly flexible relationship between members. Cluster 3 complains that there is poor competence in the use of technological tools, but also considers learning – as cluster 1 does – a waste of time. Cluster 4 criticizes lack of skills to support the learning cycle.

4.2   The Main Approaches towards Organizational Learning

Considering the determinants of learning proposed for each cluster, this paper takes 4 main approaches towards learning inside the banking industry, which differ from each other in the way activities and relations are managed, but also for the current situation of knowledge management tools to support it. The differences between approaches are presented in table 3 and discussed.

Cluster 1 adopts what here is called informal learning. This cluster is characterized by mainly large banks. The most important aim seems to be the management of bureaucracy in order to drive the organization towards flexibility. The main obstacle is the evidence that people do not want to share their knowledge. There is also evidence that people are poorly managed: few incentives are present and the culture is still too bureaucratic; this may be because of the large size. The focus is on processes and large investments are made in technology. On the other hand, cluster 4 promotes a learning approach based on the creation of new relationships. Activities are consolidated and well formalized, which means that knowledge is made explicit. The focus is on competence sharing and communication through technological tools, such as collaboration tools. A big obstacle, however, is present, which is the lack of support in order to promote learning. Cluster 3 is characterized by a focus on coordination, which seems to be achieved perhaps because of the fact that the banks are not large. The main limitation is the particular attention this cluster pays to established relationships, while an innovative approach should also promote new ones. Because of the poor investments made in IT and the lack of IT competence, the learning process is found mainly in skill sharing and communication. Virtual learning techniques are not so widespread. Finally cluster 2 is considered the most innovative one as regards learning practices; it still involves a minority of the analyzed sample. The main aim consists of reducing the time it takes to reach the market, which can be achieved only if activities are carried out in a flexible way. New relations and activities are always created or modified to allow for the alignment with changes. To do so, opportunities for collaboration are created to promote the sharing of ideas between members and groups, also using technological tools such as collaboration tools. But obstacles are also present. Banks have to focus on the kind of relationships that exist between members, which in the banking industry have always been characterized by rigidity. A change in this is underway. The commitment appears to be intense. It promotes a learning culture which is essential in order to have innovation.

Table 3. Main differences between clusters

	Established activity	Emergent activity
Emergent relationship	12 banks (cluster 4) Medium sized banks High percentage of formalization of activities Positive attitude towards making knowledge explicit and competence sharing Communication promotion High use of technological tools to support collaboration and learning Lack of support (people with the right skills) to promote learning ⇩ *Promoting new relations* *to change the organizational knowledge base*	6 banks (cluster 2) Small/medium sized banks Focus on time to market, supported by rapid learning approaches and knowledge sharing Creation of collaboration opportunities High investments in technology Management commitment to support learning ⇩ *Learning for innovation*
Established relationship	18 banks (cluster 3) Medium sized banks Focus on coordination Little investment in technology Physical and not virtual knowledge-sharing and organizational learning ⇩ *Consolidation of the existing knowledge base*	18 banks (cluster 1) Large sized banks Management of bureaucracy Bureaucratic culture Few incentives towards knowledge-sharing and learning practices Focus on processes and technology ⇩ *Learning through informal activities*

If the number of banks in each cluster is considered, the evidence is that there are still too many organizations characterized by a bureaucratic approach in the way they manage business. In order to promote more flexibility in learning, and so move toward cluster 2, banks need to consider all the other clusters' approaches. Innovative learning needs to consolidate the existent knowledge to create a new one (cluster 3). But this is only possible by promoting new relationships between employees (cluster 4) and also focusing on informality of action, to reduce the bureaucracy-connected risks (cluster 1). The banking industry is expected to become more flexible, to favor the exchange of knowledge between members and groups, and to increment learning practices. This is possible by acting on culture, trying to reduce the "not invented here" syndrome, which represents a big barrier to the diffusion of collective learning practices. As Shein [34] says, emergent learning strongly depends on the historical context, on the organization's culture and beliefs.

5   Conclusion and Future Research

As concerns the determinants for organizational learning, the paper has shown those variables which differ between banks, depending on the specific attitude toward information and knowledge management they develop. In particular, the main differences refer to the following variables: the presence of technological tools which support knowledge management, the culture, incentives used toward knowledge sharing and individual learning, informal cooperation, opportunities for collaboration, the presence of virtual areas for long distance learning and the kind of hierarchical decisions the organizational learning approach supports. As regards the second question under research, the hierarchical organization's move towards innovation through the learning attitude consists of a couple of steps. The first one is the need to promote new relationships between members or groups in order to change the organizational knowledge base. In this way a flexible approach is adopted, which allows the organization to give importance to new ideas, to anticipate external changes and adapt to environmental instability. On the other hand is the need to promote new activities. This paper underlines the importance of an initial informality in the way new activities are approached. In fact, a reduction in the formalization of activities allows the organization to reduce bureaucracy and acquire some degree of flexibility, which is the starting point for innovation purposes.

Some of the limitations in the research must be mentioned. The paper's theoretical framework has been useful in order to classify the sample of banks using the cluster analysis. The main limitation refers to the variables choice. Certain indicators have been used, while others have been rejected because of the impossibility to analyze all of them at the same time.

Finally, this paper proposes a particular theoretical framework in order to connect knowledge management and learning methodologies, but it focuses on a particular industry, which is characterized by its high level of rigidity. This is the reason for suggesting a further analysis and comparison of these results with those conducted on learning practices in other industries. The expectation would be to discover, for example, a different way of learning which is widespread, for example, in hi-tech industries. In fact, their reason for being is based on knowledge sharing practices and learning practices. It would be interesting to analyze whether the banking industry can reach the degree of flexibility that characterizes other industries.

References

1. H. A. Simon, *Administrative behaviour* (The Free Press, New York, 1976).
2. C. Argyris, Action science and organizational learning, *Journal of Managerial Psychology* 10(6), 20-26 (1995).
3. E. H. Schein, How can organizations learn faster? The challenge of entering the green room, *Sloan Management Review* 34, 85-92 (1993).

4. P. M. Senge, *The fifth discipline: the art and practice of the learning organization* (Currency Doubleday, New York, 1990).

5. C. M. Fiol, M. A. Lyles, Organizational learning, *Academy of Management Review* 10(4), 803-813 (1985).

6. G. Lanzara, Le mappe cognitive degli attori organizzativi, *Rivista Trimestrale di Scienza dell'Amministrazione* 4, (1990).

7. M. Easterby-Smith, M. Crossan, D. Nicolini, Organizational learning: debates past, present and future, *Journal of Management Studies* 6(37), 783-796 (2000).

8. K.E Watkins, V.J. Marsick, *Sculpting the learning organization: lessons in the art and science of systemic change* (Jossey-Bass, San Francisco, 1993).

9. M. Glynn, F. Milliken, T. Lant, in: Advances in managerial cognition and organizational information processing, edited by C. Stubbart et al. (CT: JAI Press, Greenwich, 1994), pp. 48-83.

10. C. Argyris, D. Shon, *Organizational learning: a theory of action perspective* (Reading, MA: Addison-Wesley, 1978).

11. R. Lipshitz, M. Popper, S. Oz, Building learning organizations: the design and implementation of organizational learning mechanisms, *Journal of Applied Behavioral Science* 32, 292–305 (1996).

12. I. Nonaka, H. Tacheuki, *The knowledge creating company* (Oxford University Press, New York, 1995).

13. F. Blackler, S. McDonald, Power, mastery and organizational learning, *Journal of Management Studies* 37(6), 833-851 (2000).

14. M. Cohen, L. Sproull, *Organizational learning* (Sage, London, 1996).

15. M. W. Jr. McCall, in: Perspectives on behaviour in organizations, edited by J. R. Heckman et al. (McGraw Hill, New York, 1977), pp. 375-386.

16. Y. Engestrom, R. Engestrom, T. Vahaaho, in: Activity theory and social practice: cultural-historical approaches, edited by S. Chaiklin et al. (Aarhus University Press, Aarhus, 1999), pp. 342-367.

17. A. Raeithel, in: Cognition and communication at work, edited by Y. Engestrom at al. (Cambridge University Press, Cambridge, 1996), pp. 319-339.

18. E. Wenger, W. Snyder, Communities of practice: the organizational frontier, *Harvard Business Review* 78(1), 139-145 (2000).

19. G. Pautzke, *Die evolution der organisatorischen Wissensbasis* (Herrsching: B. Kirsch, Munchen, 1989).

20. R. Duncan, A. Weiss in: Research in organizational behaviour, edited by L. Cummings and B. Staw (JAI Press, Greenwich, 1979), pp. 75-123.

21. J. Nahapiet, S. Goshal, Social capital, intellectual capital and the organizational advantage, *Academy of Management Review* 23, 242-266 (1998).

22. J. Virkkunen, K. Kuutti, Understanding organizational learning by focusing on activity systems, *Accounting Management and Information Technologies* 10, 291-319 (2000).

23. G. Von Krogh, K. Ichijo and I. Nonaka, *Enabling Knowledge Creation* (Oxford University Press, Oxford, 2001).

24. B. Latour, S. Woolgar, *Laboratory Life: The Construction of Scientific Facts* (Thousand Oaks: CA: SAGE, 1979).

25. I. Nonaka, A dynamic theory of organizational knowledge creation, *Organization Science* 5(1), 14-37 (1994).

26. B. Kogut, U. Zander, Knowledge of the firm, combinative capabilities and the replication of technology, *Organizational Science* 3, 383-397 (1992).

27. R. M. Grant, Prospering in dynamically competitive environment: organizational capabilities as knowledge integration, *Organization Science* **7**(4), 375-387 (1996).

28. J. Swan, H. Scarbrough, M. Robertson, The construction of communities of practice in the management of innovation, *Management Learning* **33**, 477-496 (2003).

29. P. H. Gray, The effects of knowledge management systems on emergent teams: towards a research model, *Journal of Strategic Information Systems* **9**, 175-191 (2000).

30. U. Borghoff, R. Pareschi, *Information Technology for knowledge management* (Springer-Verlag, New York, 1998).

31. R. L. Ruggles, *Knowledge management tools*, (Butterworth-Heiniemann, Boston, 1997).

32. L. Porter, E. Lawler, *Managerial attitude and performance* (Homewood, Illinois, 1968).

33. W. C. Kim, R. Mauborgne, Fair process: managing in the knowledge economy, *Harvard Business Review* **7/8**, 65–75 (1997).

34. E. Shein, *Organizational culture and leadership* (Jossey-Bass, San Francisco, 1992).

1.5 Million Years of Information Systems:
From Hunters-Gatherers to the Domestication of the Networked Computer

Ellen Christiaanse

ESADE Business School, Universitat Ramon Llull & Universiteit van Amsterdam
Business School, Avenida Pedralbes 60, Barcelona, Spain

"The comparative evolutionary success of humans by developing their specific individual, social and ecological regimes, their cultures, is ultimately grounded in the increasing capacity to communicate with one another. This has allowed us to coordinate our ideas and behaviour on a greater scale and in more effective ways than any other species known to have lived on this planet"   (Spier 1996, p.35)

Abstract This paper develops the argument that information systems have not only existed for the last 50 years (as most accounts of ICT argue) or since the 1700 century (as some more accurate readings would propose), but they are indeed as old as mankind. It provides a historical account of how information and communication systems have greatly interacted with some major transformations in human society, in addition to demonstrating the implications of the most recent changes in the last 10 years with the Internet. It builds on literature which distinguishes 3 major phases in the history of mankind and provides accounts of the role of information and communication systems in each of these phases. The main argument is that the *"domestication of information systems"* is better understood when previous regime transformations and their dynamics are taken into account and investigated. Implications of these developments in relation to innovation and learning are provided.

1. Introduction

Information and Communication systems, their design and use and the role of information have been studied by biologists, economists, ecologists, linguistics and

Please use the following format when citing this chapter:

Christiaanse, E., 2006, in IFIP International Federation for Information Processing, Volume 214, The Past and Future of Information Systems: 1976–2006 and Beyond, eds. Avison, D., Elliot, S., Krogstie, J., Pries-Heje, J., (Boston: Springer), pp. 165–176.

historians to explain human and animal behaviour. Nothing would work in the absence of information [1]. Hauser argues that basically 3 reasons underlie all communication among animals: 1) mating, 2) socialization and 3) survival. Whereas we humans have developed more or less sophisticated and increasingly electronic means for these 3 basic reasons, animals have not been as creative. The last decade it was claimed that we humans are going through a communication revolution or that we are entering an Information age [2,3]. However, we argue that our information age is not the first information age in history. Humans have always needed and communicated information and the field of information systems did not start in 1976 as the IFIP call for papers might suggest. For all organisms, including humans, communication and information systems provide a vehicle for conveying information and for expressing to others what has been perceived [4]. We argue with Headrick [4] that the information age has no beginning, for it is as old as mankind. We live in such an age but it is certainly not the first information age nor is the PC the first information system we have built.

This paper intends to deliberately take a broad perspective and investigate the role of information and communication systems and their impact on humans and the societies they live in. It is our objective in this paper to give a historical account of how information and communication systems have greatly interacted with some major transformations in human society. A second objective is to show the implications of the most recent changes in the last 10 years with the Internet.

This paper is organized as follows: the next sections will first discuss the role of information systems in regime transformations. To introduce the concept of regimes and their role in human history we need to introduce the construct by which Spier [5] has conceptualized the structure of human ecology. In a subsequent section we argue that a fourth regime transformation can be distinguished, related to the *"domestication of information systems"* which is better understood when previous regime transformations and their dynamics are considered and investigated. We argue that each of the previous regime transformations have had information and communication systems implications. We will discuss each of these periods from a multi-disciplinary perspective. Although not discussed explicitly by many world historians, they each implicitly refer to the communication and information systems' implications of their findings. The objective of this section is to make these arguments more explicit and analyze them profoundly. The final section of this paper discusses the implications of the patterns associated with communication and information systems and will shed new light on understanding of the role of communication and information systems in the past and future.

2. Information and Communication Systems In History

We believe no profound understanding of the impact of information and communication systems can be obtained when limiting our study to the last 20-30 years, the years of the "invention" and proliferation of the computer and the Internet. It is our firm belief that the rise of the network society [3], the information society [2,6], the information age [7] has firm roots in previous ages. Sociologists and historians as well as information systems researchers have traced the roots of our present information age. However most of these accounts go back to, at most the industrial revolution [2,8].

A notable exception is a book by the historian Headrick who claims that in the age of reason (1700-1850) information systems of all kinds were flourishing. He makes the important distinction between the use of the specific technology and the information systems applying that technology. The purpose of his book is to argue that the current information revolution is a result of a cultural change that began roughly three centuries ago, a change as important as the political and industrial revolutions for which the 18th and 19th centuries are so well known. Increasing interest in information of all sorts, led to information systems, which are the basis for today's information age. Systems of nomenclature, classification (plants and chemicals) measurement and the visual display of information (graphs, maps) are examples of information systems provided by Headrick. He argues that "Most historians attributed great significance to certain machines: the printing press, telegraph, the computer, but between the printing revolution and the 19th century lies a period that was less significant for its information handling machines but just as fertile in new information systems" [1]. To my knowledge he is one of the few writers that go back to the seventeen hundreds for the origins of our information age. Most authors stop at the industrial revolution when looking at factors to explain or predict the changes that are occurring in our present day societies and organization of economic activities.

We argue that the way societies and groups of people have organized themselves has always been closely related to the way they communicated and transmitted and gathered information. This argument however has been made before and is not new. The fundamental questions of why people have organized themselves in specific network configurations and how communication infrastructures and information ecologies have evolved and adapted or driven certain configurations, remain underdeveloped. Access to resources such as food and shelter were often the driving force behind settlements and the development of groups and nations [9] but the access and specific role of information and communication systems has not received sufficient multi-disciplinary attention.

3. Structuration using the Notion of Regimes

To provide an historical account of how information and communication systems have greatly interacted with some major transformations in human society we base our arguments on the concept of "regime transformations" developed by Spier [5]. When introducing the term regime, an important issue to address first is that Spier's timescale is slightly larger than we as information system scientists are used to, in

---

1 We follow Headrick's views of information systems as being much broader than communication systems. Communication systems in his view are systems like telegraphic and postal systems while information systems are systems that organize, transform, display, store or communicate information. In his view communication systems are a subset of information systems ([4]p. 181)

our very young field of barely 30 years or 2-3 generations of researchers[2]. As is common among world historians [5,9-12] phenomena are viewed from the origins of mankind or often even on cosmic scales. As a result, even the inhabitants of (post)modern societies by and large have the physiological make-up of gatherers and hunters."

The word "regime" comes from the Latin "regimen", which means both "guidance" and "rule". Spier [5] prefers the word 'regime' to terms such as system, order, pattern, constellation, configuration, field, etc. since in his eyes 'regime' is the only term that can be utilized without hindrance, as he sees regimes as structuring elements for all cosmic, planetary and human history. I will use the term regime in line with Spier's definition and "a more or less regular but ultimately unstable pattern that has a certain temporal permanence" p.14. Spier's main argument is that the history of humanity can be structured referring to the three great ecological regime transformations which have taken place so far:

1) the domestication of fire (1.5 million years ago),

2) the domestication of plants and animals (8000-10000 years ago) and

3) the industrialization on the basis of engines driven by inanimate energy (late 1700 s).

While information systems researchers hardly ever go back more than 40 years, sociologists investigating the information society usually go back to the origins of the transformation of the agrarian into the industrial age. Only very few historians go back more than 200-300 years in their analysis to understand information and communication systems. As a result communication science as a field often starts with the invention of technologies like the telegraph, radio and TV . Not much truly multidisciplinary research has been done on the topic. An exception being a recent integrative work by Hauser discussing the evolution of communication from a multi-disciplinary perspective (biology, linguistics, cognitive psychology) which does go back to the origins of communication among living species but as a biologist, he spends more time in his book on communication among other animals than primates.

The domestication of fire, animals and plants has interacted with and affected the way the human web has organized itself but has never influenced mankind as profoundly as the impact that new forms of ubiquitous computing and the domestication of information and communication systems have had. We argue that the roots of the domestication of information and communication systems are in the previous regime transformations and that a profound understanding of their impact can only be achieved by analyzing what these changes were and why some of these changes took place in certain societies but not in others. Each of these regime transformations had a significant impact on the way humans interacted and lived together. We will briefly discuss Spier's regimes in turn. We argue that there has been an information and communication regime playing a role in mankind in each of these periods. In the discussion below of the regime transformations and their drivers and interaction, we will complement Spier's arguments where possible with those of other authors with information and communication systems implications.

---

2 On February 13th 2005 the question : How old is the field of Information Systems? was put on ISWorld asking whether the field started with the first course in IS, its first PhD student graduated or its first significant journal publication.

3.1 The First Great Ecological Regime Transformation: The Domestication of Fire

Spier bases his description of his first regime transformation on the argument that the possession of fire control may have been of decisive importance in an elimination contest that would have taken place both within and among the various hominid subgroups, as a result of which only the fire-possessing victors survived [5, p. 46]. Control of fire indeed became so valuable that only those groups that learned the full spectrum of fire's uses survived [11]. The human fire regime had further consequences on an ecological, social and communicative level. Spier argues that while people tended to flee rather that fight, [5, p. 51] people steered away from social conflicts as long as there was enough free land available.

Information and Communication Systems during the first regime transformation

During the gatherer –hunter social regime, technical skills appear to have developed slowly. The same seems to apply to social organization. For a long time, humanity formed one single, very loosely connected network which shared many characteristics and exhibited only limited local variations [11]. In comparison with later periods, communication in the form of messages and material exchanges progressed slowly, while local cultural developments followed suit. Consequently, inventions could easily spread everywhere before any group developed a decisive cultural advantage [5, p.50]. Symbolic meanings, capable both of exceedingly rapid evolution and also of coordinating the behaviour of infinite numbers of individuals [11], have coordinated actions of humans over the last thousands of years. Language and dance and ritual were important breakthroughs that allowed humans with these new kinds of communication, to form larger and larger yet still cohesive and coordinated groups. Not much is known about how a " perpetual web of social interactions within small bands of humans permitted and rewarded incremental improvements in the speed, scope and accuracy of communication [11].

3.2 The Second Great Ecological Regime Transformation: The Transformation to an Agrarian Regime.

The domestication³ of plants and animals around 8000-10000 years ago had significant implications on the ways in which humans organized themselves. Why did the same crop have to be domesticated in several different parts of the world and why are there such huge differences in the spread of crops between continents? Diamond's "tilted axis theory" [9] links the spread of food production techniques to the diffusion of other technologies and inventions. He argues that through indirect links of food production systems and their consequences with other innovations like wheels and writing which were used to facilitate the transportation of food and its administration (goods inventories, record keeping) [9] certain innovations were

---

3 Spier defines domestication as " human efforts to actively influence the reproductive chances of other species" In English it refers to both home and country.

communicated and spread around the world in distinct patterns related to the efficiency of the communication systems used.

The evolving agrarian social regime was very different from the hunters and gatherers [11]: "Since the early plant cultivators became tied to the land they had come to depend on, they also became more tightly bound to one another, processes of social differentiation accelerated. This had consequences for the social structures of these people. In addition the way they gathered information and communicated changed significantly. The first human webs of our distant ancestors were formed through the rise of speech, migration, and primitive agricultural groupings. The development of settled farming injected new kinds of information into the human web. Apprentice farmers exchanged and communicated skills, knowledge and breeding stock with their neighbouring communities".

Information and Communication Systems during the second regime transformation

Spier argues that "the effort to reign over the forces of fire may have stimulated the need for more intense social interaction, and thus contributed to a growing ability to communicate and think in abstract terms" [5, p. 49]. Sedentary agriculture lead to complex societies and more advanced communication and information systems. People designed more complex information systems and communicated more intensively through ever expanding human webs [11], resulting in a need for more advanced communication and information systems. He concludes that: "much later, the agrarian regime would prove to be a major precondition for the industrialization of society, likewise the fire regime was a necessary precondition for the agrarian regime. It was hard to imagine that any sedentary agrarian life would have been possible for long without control over fire of various kinds". Information and communication systems are interactive and need to be supported by the societies and the environment in which they have been adopted by or invented.

The effect of information and communication networks is defined by the volume and variety of the information being pooled and the efficiency and speed at which information is shared [10]. The size of the information network or the number of communities and individuals that can share information has changed significantly since humans were gatherers and hunters. In any given network the number of links between nodes (n) is $n \times (n-1)/2$. "The number of possible connections (and thereby the potential information synergy of the entire network) increases faster than the number of nodes and the difference between the two rates, increases as the number of nodes increases [10,11]. Increased population density tends to stimulate innovation and as networks expand in size, their potential intellectual synergy increases much faster: larger and denser populations equal faster technological advance [12]. In our view the effects of the internet are interesting in this regard as the internet obviously does not affect population density but it does increase the number of possible connections. An important question is whether this will trigger a period of significant increase of information sharing and innovation and thus change the knowledge ecology of the inhabitants of this globe.

According to [10]: "the variety of the information being pooled may be as important as the sheer volume. Neighbouring communities living similar lifestyles maybe able to help each other to finetune technologies and skills but they are unlikely to introduce radically new ideas. Fundamentally new forms of information are likely to be shared only where two communities living different lifestyles come into significant contact. Indeed when dissimilar groups belong to the same information networks we are most likely to find processes of collective learning leading to significant changes in technologies and lifestyles. It is important to describe the size and variety of information networks – the regions over which information can be exchanged. " p. 183

3.3   The Third Great Ecological Regime Transformation: The Transition Towards An Industrial Regime

The Industrial Revolution may be defined as the application of power-driven machinery to manufacturing. "The third large ecological regime transformation, industrialization on the basis of the large-scale use of engines driven by fossil fuels, lay at the root of this remarkable discontinuity. Because it happened so very recently and left such a great many traces, the emergence of the industrialization process is known with a precision unattainable for the preceding two great ecological regime transformations. On an ever growing scale and at an ever increasing rate the world was turned into a provider of natural resources for industry and into a market for its products" Spier [5]. In other words, social regime development stimulated improvements of the human ecological regime [5, p.37-38].

Information and Communication Systems during the third regime transformation

Improvements in infrastructure (transportation, communication technologies) in the late 1800s led to massive vertical integration because allocation of resources within the firm became cheaper than the cost of using the market. The way the telegraph and telephone contributed as communication systems to support the industrialization of societies has been very significant[4] [2]. The rapidly growing and intensifying means of long-distance communication would not have been possible either without an economy increasingly based on inanimate fuels: " The coupling of ever refined techniques of information processing to machines driven by inanimate fuels can be related to the rapidly growing and intensifying communication networks of various kinds. [5, p. 78]

Diamond [9] relates the development of certain technologies to the way societies organized themselves and communities communicated: " No hunter-gatherer society ever developed states, writing, metal technology, or standing armies. Those developments depended on food production (agriculture and herding), which arose

---

4   Interesting in this regard is the argument by [8] that we have faced several control crises in periods were communication systems could not keep up with the speed of for example transportation or complex energy generating systems. He provides examples of train collisions due to the fact that the scheduling and location information was exchanged slower than the speed by which the trains traveled leading to significant numbers of accidents in the late 1800s.

independently in different parts of Eurasia by 8000 BC. The resulting dense populations, food storage, social stratification, and political centralization led in Eurasia to chiefdoms (5500 BC), metal tools (4000 BC), states (3700 BC), and writing (3200 BC). Multiplied over succeeding millennia, that huge head start let Eurasians eventually to sail and conquer peoples of other continents."

The development of communication systems and information systems in all periods discussed above is heavily related to the way humans organized themselves. An important tool humans have to alter their environment has always been innovations in technology and so to coordinate their actions collectively they have always used communication and information systems. In summary, the industrialization of society could not have taken place without a long history of specific political, economic, socio-cultural, technical and scientific developments, most notably the first and second great ecological regime transformations as well as some of the social regime transformations associated with them, such as the formation of a regime of competing states and the associated drive for economic and military inventions. Like the domestication of plants and animals and, undoubtedly, gathering and hunting, too, industrialization is an ongoing process.

3.4 The Fourth Regime Transformation: The Domestication of the Computer

Humans had designed increasingly complex production, transportation and other systems in the industrial revolution that required increasingly more computation and calculation. As a result various attempts to build calculating machines had been done mechanically (Babbage's Engines) and later electrically (punch card machines and the Mark 1). However, we start our 4th regime transformation from the moment that these calculating machines became available to individuals with microprocessors that contained memory, logic, and control circuits , an entire CPU on a single chip and allowed for home-use personal computers or PCs, like the Apple (II in 1977 and Mac in 1984) and IBM PC in 1981. Fourth generation language software products like Lotus 1-2-3, dBase, Microsoft Word, and many others and Graphical User Interfaces (GUI) for PCs arrived in the early 1980s with the clunky MS Windows debuting in 1983. Windows would not take off until version 3 was released in 1990. We refer to this period in the 1980s as the domestication of the computer, when PC's started to enter the home and workplaces of ordinary citizens. Once these PC's were networked a real communication transformation began. Kelly writing about 10 years of the Internet marvels: " In the years roughly coincidental with the Netscape IPO, humans began animating inert objects with tiny slivers of intelligence, connecting them into a global field, and linking their own minds into a single thing. This will be recognized as the largest, most complex, and most surprising event on the planet. Weaving nerves out of glass and radio waves, our species began wiring up all regions, all processes, all facts and notions into a grand network. From this embryonic neural net was born a collaborative interface for our civilization, a sensing, cognitive device with power that exceeded any previous invention. The Machine provided a new way of thinking (perfect search, total recall) and a new mind for an old species. It was the Beginning."

As we have seen above in all periods, the transmission and exchange of information about technological innovations and thus for the survival of groups was crucial. Innovations like fire control, hunting techniques, food production systems but also of guns, germs and steel spread around the world in distinctive patterns interacting with the social structures of their societies. Some innovations were slow (the wheel), some fast (the steam engine) depending on the communication systems in place at the time and in the society of the invention. The spread of innovations was always tightly linked to the communication and information systems available to distribute and share the new knowledge obtained [9,10]. The new wired information and communication we humans have had access to over the last 10 years obviously surpasses any communication system we have had before: "With a significant number of people connected, the scope of the Web today is hard to fathom. The total number of Web pages, including those that are dynamically created upon request and document files available through links, exceeds 600 billion. That's 100 pages per person alive. How could we create so much, so fast, so well? In fewer than 4,000 days, we have encoded half a trillion versions of our collective story and put them in front of 1 billion people, or one-sixth of the world's population. That remarkable achievement was not in anyone's 10-year plan."

This information and communication system brought great changes in the organization, transmission, display, storage and communication of information. Making instant sharing with unlimited numbers of people possible, this technology provides us with the opportunity to have access to anything that has ever been written, designed, sung, drawn or painted and instantly share it and build upon it. The world wide web has only been around for ten years but has allowed the human web to expand, interact and communicate more intensively and with more impact on societies then any period before. The domestication of the networked pc is our latest transformation which only really started 10 years ago (on the cosmic scales of world historians an invisible dot).

4. Conclusions and Suggestions for Further Research

Up to 500 years ago three different world zones were moving through similar trajectories at different speeds governed by different synergies of informational exchange [10]. I argue that only during the last 500 years have we slowly moved to a single global system of information exchange with collective learning at the human species level. The exact implications of collective learning through the ever more dense global communication since the internet, will remain unknown for a while, but other periods of intense communication (e.g. 18th century) led to quick transmission of innovations across cultures. With significantly increased volume and variety of the information being pooled and increased efficiency and speed at which information is shared, in the last 10 years since the world started to communicate through hypertext, I expect to see major implications for collective learning and collective knowledge exchange. While one of the central problems of all individuals of any species is finding food whilst avoiding becoming food [11], ecology is concerned with the relations between organisms and their environment and the survival mechanisms that species adopted. Information and communication systems have been key to the survival of the human species and to the supremacy of one group over another in our history. As discussed earlier, Christian [10] is very explicit about the role of information and communication for innovation. He argues for the general principle that the size, diversity, and efficiency of information networks should be an important large-scale determinant of rates of ecological innovation (p. 184). Examining the size and variety of information networks in different parts in the world, together with the varying efficiency with which information is pooled within those networks, he considers this of key importance to the understanding of communication systems for the spread of innovation. I argue that innovations for mankind have been closely linked to the communication systems that transmitted and facilitated adoption by other groups or nations. Humans made use of information systems and these played a role in gaining control and influence over other groups across the world and societies. In earlier days obviously to define the size of a region within which information was exchanged to a large extent defined the spread of certain innovations. To define the size of a region within which information is exchanged is one thing but within that region the speed and regularity of exchanges may vary greatly. The ecological and natural environment in combination with food production techniques to a large extent defined which direction innovations were spreading [9].

Based on Christian [10] who states that the efficiency of information exchanges reflect above all, the nature and regularity of contacts and exchanges between different communities which may be shaped by social conventions, geographical factors and technologies of communication and transportation (p. 184) I argue that the size, diversity and efficiency of information networks should be an important large scale determinant of rates of ecological innovation. Tracking the changing synergy of processes of collective learning, by examining the size and variety of information networks in different parts of the world, as well as the varying efficiency with which information was pooled within those networks, might be an important indicator for innovation. (p.184). In the Paleolithic era, the existence of small groups that had limited contact with each other meant that exchanges of ecological information worked sluggishly. In a single lifetime, each individual was unlikely to encounter more than a few hundred individuals and most of that lifetime would have been spent in the company of no more then ten to thirty individuals who belonged to the same family. The amount of information that could have been exchanged in these networks was clearly limited."

I argue that because these information and communication systems increase the efficiency and speed at which information is shared will stimulate ecologically significant learning and innovation at the human species level. Information systems facilitated processes of collective learning and associated changes accelerated by the accumulation of ecologically significant knowledge. As McNeill and McNeill note, agriculture and the wheel were invented in a number of places, but the steam engine only had to be invented once. While hunter-gatherers used information systems to gain control over fire, we use information systems to gain control over each other.

For a long time, humanity formed one single, very loosely connected web-like network that shared many characteristics and exhibited only limited local variations. In comparison with later periods, communication in the form of messages and material exchanges progressed very slowly, while local cultural developments followed suit. Consequently, inventions could easily spread everywhere before any group developed a decisive cultural advantage. The development of our current information and communication infrastructure will significantly change this. Collective learning at the human species level will significantly increase and the spread of innovations in the years to come will be much faster and more efficient than in previous times. Only by understanding these changes in a larger historic perspective and understanding how humans have communicated in the past and how this affected their social structures and lives, can we begin to understand the changes that information and communication technologies will bring. The domestication of the personal, networked and increasingly mobile computer will have a greater impact than any other type of domestication has ever had before. Capturing and sharing content is what humans have done since the dawn of mankind but doing this through networked computers is significantly different. The domestication of the networked computer should be seen as another major regime transformation.

Further research should investigate the interplay between information and communication systems and the effects on innovation of capturing and disseminating content instantly in a global context. The fact that we are no longer living in isolated communities without information exchange but are functioning in "an online global human web" where discoveries, innovations, patents, scientific publications and paradigms shifts can be shared instantly with all online, humans on our planet will reduce the "re-inventing of the wheel phenomenon" and provide us with the ability to build upon each others innovations. An important aspect of this development is obviously the potentially increased effects of the "digital divide".   Research questions to be addressed by future research could involve: Does learning at the human species level increase as a result of the fact that the number of possible connections (and thereby the potential information synergy of the entire network) increases faster than the number of nodes, and that the difference between the two rates will increase as the number of nodes increases as McNeill and McNeill 2003 predict? How will certain groups in our global society be able to retain control over crucial information systems and therefore survive while others will not?

History though seems to have come full circle: many of us roam around cyberspace as gatherers and hunters, picking up whatever information item we encounter on our way. Even though we know what we came for and started off purposeful searches, the web in its present shape, keeps distracting us and providing us with information items that we are not really looking for. We end up back again as nomads and gatherers, surfing endlessly to where we think we might find the information of our interest and of our survival.

References

1. M.D. Hauser. The Evolution of Communication. Cambridge MA, MIT Press. (1996).
2. F. Webster. Theories of the Information Society. London, Routledge. (2002).
3. M. Castells. The Rise of the Network Society. Malden, Blackwell Publishing. (2000).
4. D.R. Headrick. When information Came of Age: Technologies of Knowledge in the Age of Reason and Revolution, 1700-1850. New York, Oxford University Press. (2000).

176   Ellen Christiaanse

5. F. Spier. The Structure of Big History. Amsterdam, Amsterdam University Press. (1996).
6. R. Mansell and W. E. Steinmueller Mobilizing the Information Society: Strategies for Growth and Opportunity. Oxford, Oxford University Press. (2000).
7. A.D. Chandler and J. W. Cortada, Eds. A Nation Transformed by Information: How Information Has Shaped the United States from Colonial Times to the Present. Oxford, Oxford University Press. (2000).
8. J.R. Beniger. The Control Revolution: Technological and Economic Origins of the Information Society. Cambridge MA, Harvard University Press. (1986).
9. J. Diamond. Guns, Germs and Steel: The Fates of Human Societies. New York, Norton & Company. (1997).
10. D. Christian. Maps of Time. Berkeley, University of California Press. (2004).
11. J.R. McNeill and W. McNeill The Human Web: A Bird's Eye View of World History. New York, Norton & Company. (2003).
12. R. Wright. Nonzero: The logic of Human Destiny. New York, Random House. (2000).

Fulfilling the Needs of a Metadata Creator and Analyst

An Investigation of RDF Browsing and Visualization Tools

Shah Khusro, A. Min Tjoa
Institute for Software Technology and Interactive Systems
Vienna University of Technology, Vienna, Austria.
{khusro, tjoa,}@ifs.tuwien.ac.at

Abstract. The realization of Semantic Web vision is based on the creation and use of semantic web content which needs software tools both for semantic web developers and end users. Over the past few years, semantic web software tools like ontology editors and triple storage systems have emerged and are growing in maturity with time. While working on a large triple dataset during the course of a research aiming at a life-long "semantic" repository of personal information, besides other semantic web tools, we used several RDF browsing and visualization tools for analyzing our data. This analysis included ensuring the correctness of the data, conformance of instance data to the ontology, finding patterns and trails in the data, cross-checking and evaluating inferred data, etc. We found that many of the features needed by a metadata creator and analyst are missing from these tools. This paper presents an investigation of the tools that are used for browsing and visualizing RDF datasets. It first identifies the browsing and visualization features required by a semantic web developer and a metadata creator and analyst and then based on those features evaluates the most common RDF browsing and visualization tools available till date. We conclude this paper with recommendations for requirements to be fulfilled for future semantic web browsing and visualization.

1 Introduction and Background

The current web despite all its benefits assumes human presence for the interpretation of its content. The Semantic Web [1] is an extension of the current web, based on the idea of exchanging information with explicit, formal and machine-accessible description of meaning. Semantic Web technologies like RDF [2], Topic Maps [3, 4], and Ontologies are used for making the semantics of information explicit and thus machine-processable. Despite the fact that RDF and other Semantic Web technologies make the semantics of information explicit, but this machine-

Please use the following format when citing this chapter:

Khusro, S., Tjoa, A.M., 2006, in IFIP International Federation for Information Processing, Volume 214, The Past and Future of Information Systems: 1976–2006 and Beyond, eds. Avison, D., Elliot, S., Krogstie, J., Pries-Heje, J., (Boston: Springer), pp. 177–188.

oriented content representation does not lend itself for presentation in a human-readable way. Over the past few years several applications have attempted to solve this problem by using different representation paradigms. These tools attempt to provide support to Semantic Web users, developers and metadata analysts with varying degrees of abstraction and usability [5].

At the Institute of Software Technology and Interactive Systems, Vienna University of Technology, Vienna, Austria, we are working on a research project called SemanticLife [6] which aims at a life-long "semantic" repository of personal information. Our system is based on semantic web technologies like OWL and RDF. In our research we have been using several semantic web tools for different tasks like ontology engineering and RDF storage. We are making use of several ontologies, some existing and others developed for our own domain. We also used several RDF browsing and visualization tools which are briefly introduced in section 4. Though we see a considerable growth in the development and maturity of semantic web tools but still there is a long way to achieve a position that the relational database theory and tools enjoy. While working with these tools and several ontologies and instance data from different sources with sometime unknown structure, we strongly felt the need for a better RDF browsing and visualization tool.

This paper gives a survey of existing RDF browsing and visualization tools and concludes with recommendations for a future tool which could prove more useful and effective for a metadata creator and analyst. Section 2 identifies the needs of a metadata creator and analyst. Section 3 presents the evaluation framework that we have employed for our comparison. Section 4 gives a brief description of RDF browsing and visualization tools selected for our survey. Section 5 provides the comparison of the basic and more technical features of the tools. Section 6 lists some recommendations for a future tool and Sections 7 finally concludes this paper.

2   The Needs of a Metadata Creator and Analyst

Producer and Consumer of semantic web data are the two important roles of people and most of the research and development emphasis is on their support. The aim of this paper is to identify another role related to the Producer and his/her needs; that of a metadata creator and analyst. Semantic web developers and people working with metadata always need to have their data visualized in different ways. Their browsing and visualization needs are different from those of the end users; some are listed below [7]:

- To produce good-quality RDF and to cover the limited expertise in defining ontologies, creating and converting existing XML-based metadata into RDF.
- To rapidly test and visualize a dataset and to understand if there are mistakes in the model as well as spelling mistakes in the namespaces and URIs.
- To get a mental model of an unfamiliar dataset and the related ontologies.
- To have a sense of the density of connectivity of a particular dataset.
- To identify potential mappings between resources and ontologies.

- To discover the parts of a dataset having special graph-theoretical properties and therefore might 'stand out' as having some latent meaning that might get otherwise unnoticed.
- To have the ability to drill down from global view to local information at the resource level.

Semantic web development tools like ontology editors, triple storage systems, and semantic web toolkits seldom address these needs. Tools targeted towards the end user allow browsing the semantic web content if available and otherwise extract it from existing documents. Triple storage systems also provide some browsing and visualization features like Sesame Explore Mode and Kowari web interface, but do not show more than a list of triples. Moreover, ontology editors also provide some browsing and visualization features but they mostly show and edit the ontology structure rather than intelligent browsing of the ontology instances [8].

3   Evaluation Framework of RDF Browsing and Visualization Tools

A general evaluation framework used to compare RDF browsing and visualization tools comprises of the following four criteria:

3.1   Supported RDF Representation Formats

Import/Export Formats

An RDF graph can be serialized in several different formats including RDF/XML, Notation-3, N-Triples, and TriX. The most known serialization format is RDF/XML which is an XML representation of RDF graph in terms of XML Information Set and Namespaces. N3 is a shorthand non-XML serialization of RDF, designed with human-readability in mind. N-Triples is a line-based, plain text format and was designed to be a fixed subset of N3, hence all tools which currently work with N3 can seamlessly work with it too. TriX (Triples in XML) is a serialization for named graphs and is an attempt to provide a highly normalized and consistent XML representation of RDF model.

For an RDF tool to be effective and useful it should support as many of these formats as possible. As "common understanding" and "shared knowledge" lie at the heart of semantic web, this enables a metadata creator and analyst to use existing ontologies and data encoded in any format and also to map between different formats.

Accessing Data in a Triple Store

In the previous years, several RDF storage systems have emerged and continue in growth and use. Besides local and remote files, the metadata may exist in these triple stores. For local and remote access these systems define interfaces mainly based on RMI, HTTP, and SOAP. Like any other RDF tool, a browsing and visualization tool having the facility of accessing local and remote triple store data will make it more flexible and useful.

Integration of Inference Capabilities
Ideally, an RDF visualization tool should allow a range of inference engines or reasoners to be plugged into it. Such engines are used to derive additional RDF assertions which are entailed from some base RDF together with any optional ontology information and the axioms and rules associated with the reasoner. This inferred data may be utilized by the visualization tool for providing an integrated interface for browsing the data. The global part of this integrated interface may group resources based on their type and the class hierarchies. The local interface may utilize inferred information such as resource and class labels and comments for a more user friendly view of the data.

Merging Input Files
RDF data is usually dispersed across different files and data sources, and instance data is usually created separate from the ontology. A tool is more useful and effective if it can read data from several data sources to merge and show a unified display.

3.2   Display Features

Display Interface
Browsing a document repository is simple as it usually consists of a small number of large chunks of information, with few explicit relationships. The situation is exactly opposite with RDF data which consists of many small chunks of information with many explicit relationships among them. An RDF browsing tool may provide a *Global* view of these many relationships, or a *Local* view to concentrate on a single piece of information, or an *Integrated* view to combine these two [9].

An analyst usually needs to identify emerging structures within the relationships in an RDF dataset. This is achieved by a Global interfaces which emphasizes global structure by providing large scale views of RDF data. An RDF browser that generates graph-based views of RDF statements gives some information about the underlying structure, in particular with some grouping performed by its layout algorithm. More advance interfaces may use grouping, ordering, or prioritizing information to provide global views. Data in global interfaces may be grouped based on the user search or resource types and concept hierarchies obtained through inference.

In contrast to global interfaces, a Local view provides richer details for a particular information item. Users and analysts usually need information at this level of specificity. Local interfaces can have hyperlinks to each other, providing users with navigation through the entire repository. Sesame's Explore Mode [10] and Kowari's [11] Web Interface provide a browser like interface to RDF. Selecting a URI in this interface shows all RDF statements with that URI as subject, predicate, or object, thus making RDF browsable. But the current view is always limited to the immediate vicinity of the current resource and no underlying structure is visible [9].

A more useful approach is the Integrated view in which these two approaches are combined. Usually a global view is presented at the beginning from where the data can be explored at different levels of detail. Automation of this view is quite difficult and a general technique for this is a question that needs to be answered.

Sharing Presentation Knowledge

The two major issues in displaying RDF data are the specification of content selection and the content formatting and styling which are addressed by each tool in a different and ad hoc way. This makes it difficult to share and reuse this presentation knowledge across applications. The need to use a shared display vocabulary for presenting RDF content and sharing presentation knowledge has been recognized in the Semantic Web community. Fresnel [12] is an attempt to address this issue and its core modules are currently implemented in various types of applications [13,14].

Presentation Paradigm

Displaying RDF data in a user-friendly manner is a problem addressed by various types of applications using different representation paradigms. Some tools represent RDF models as node-link diagrams explicitly showing their graph structure [14,15]. Other tools use nested box layouts or table-like layouts for displaying properties of RDF resources with varying levels of details [13]. Another approach combines these paradigms and extends them with specialized user interface widgets [16].

Editing Features

These may vary from simple triple editing to more advanced features like resource linking and annotation. Usually other systems like ontology editors are used for this purpose but a browsing tool with these features available proves more effective.

Graph Statistics

This is an important feature always needed by metadata analysts and is required to be implemented by a browsing tool. These vary from general graph statistics to more advanced features like in-degree, out-degree, clustering coefficient and other graph theoretical properties.

3.3 Scalability Issues

Maximum Dataset Size

One of the most import features to measure the scalability of a tool is the size of input RDF file or the maximum number of statements in a model or nodes in a graph. For demonstration purposes the size of input data is usually very small (within a megabyte or a graph with less than a thousand nodes). But a working RDF dataset may be in hundreds of megabytes with millions of statements which, if a tool is unable to load, will compel the analyst to split it up and thus lose its global view. Hence a more effective tool should allow a user to work with much bigger models.

Visual Scalability

Sometime a tool can load a very large dataset but is unable to render it in a way that a user can make sense out of it. Tools that provide a graph based view usually have limited visual scalability but the inclusion of visual cues and search and query options make the situation better. A text-based tool is usually better in visual scalability and heavily depends on grouping and ordering of data to produce the global interface. Visual scalability is lost if a text-based tool cannot visualize global structures and there is little difference between global and local views.

Extension Mechanism

A static tool with no extension mechanism may be useful for sometime but becomes useless as the changing trends and emerging technologies are not accommodated. Plugins are a general concept that allows extra functionally to be dropped into a tool, usually by simply adding files to a directory. Plugins are very loosely coupled to the base tool, and can thus be added very easily without modifying the tool itself. Plugin architecture provides an organized way for independent groups of people to add new behavior to an application without having to modify it.

3.4   Search, Query and Filtering

Selection and Filtering

This gives a user the ability to select sections of an RDF graph based on some criteria. This selection may be based on global or local filters. Global filters like *rdf:type*, *rdfs:domain*, and *rdfs:range* are applied to the whole graph independent of its domain. Local filters are domain-specific and include namespaces, specific properties and classes, and generally resources and URI's. Selection and Filtering allows the not-so-technical user to browse and analyze the model.

Support for RDF Query Language

Usually more fine-grained control over data selection and filtering is needed which is provided by an RDF query language. Several RDF query languages have been developed each with its own features and expressiveness but SPARQL [17] has been recently adopted as the standard RDF query language. To use this feature, though the analyst should be aware of the query language syntax but it also gives him a total control over the data.

Full Text Graph Search and Full Text Document Search

Sometime the exact name of a resource or the exact contents of a literal are not known in advance or the resources or literals with a common text pattern need to be filtered out. Full text graph search if available enables a user to search for keywords and text patterns inside resource names and literals contents. Sometime the URI references in an RDF model point to text-based documents stored locally or available on remote systems. Such a search, if available, checks the contents of these documents for any match.

4   Description of RDF Browsing and Visualization Tools

4.1   Drive RDF Browser and W3C's RDF Validation Service

Though a very simple and primitive tool, Drive RDF Browser [18] is an effective tool for validating and browsing small RDF datasets. On one page in the form of HTML, Drive displays separately all nodes, edges, literals, namespaces, triples, graph summary, and errors and warnings, if any. Similar to Drive is the W3C RDF Validation Service [19] which provides a hyperlinked list of triples with errors and warnings, if any, and optionally a graph-based view of the validated statements.

4.2   Ontopia Omnigator

Omnigator [20] is a generic application built on top of the Ontopia Navigator Framework that allows users to load and browse any conforming topic map. Designed primarily as a teaching aid to help newcomers understand the topic map concepts, it is now an extremely useful tool for debugging topic maps and for building demo applications. Some of the features in the Omnigator 8 include plug-ins for performing querying, filtering, full text search, the ability to display class hierarchies (in both text and graphics modes), better stylesheets, RDF to Topic Map mapping, and an improved statistics printer.

4.3   SIMILE RDF Browsing Tools (Welkin, Longwell, Knowle)

The SIMILE project, jointly developed by the W3C, HP, and MIT, is working to make it easier to browse diverse collections of metadata and, more generally, to find the way around in the Semantic Web. SIMILE's domain specific and end-user friendly Longwell [13] and domain independent and RDF-savvy friendly Welkin [7] and Knowle [13] are proving very useful in different application areas. Suitable for end-users, Longwell is a faceted browser that displays only the metadata fields that are configured to be 'facets' and hides the presence of the underlying RDF model. Knowle which is shipped as part of the Longwell distribution is a node-focused graph navigation browser that is targeted at people who want to see or debug the underlying RDF model. Longwell and Knowle work together to provide a user-friendly Web-based front-end to RDF. As Longwell requires a thorough understanding of the structure of the data being examined and it is hard to get a global overview of an RDF model, thus Welkin was created by the SIMILE team to summarize and to give a quick mental model of the data being manipulated. Designed for metadata analysts, Welkin is a graph based tool that provides global view and cluster characteristics of its data.

4.4   IsaViz

IsaViz [14] is a visual environment for browsing and authoring RDF models represented as graphs. It allows smooth zooming and navigation in the graph; creation and editing of graphs by drawing ellipses, boxes, and arcs, and has support for several import and export RDF formats. Since version 2.0, IsaViz can render RDF graphs using GSS (Graph Stylesheets), a stylesheet language derived from CSS and SVG for styling RDF models represented as node-link diagrams and version 3 will have support for Fresnel display vocabulary.

4.5 RDF Gravity

RDF Gravity [15] from Salzburg Research is a graph visualization tool for RDF/OWL datasets of moderate sizes. Though only a graph visualization tool, RDF Gravity has a rich set of features that can satisfy several of the needs of a metadata creator and analyst. These include graph visualization and navigation features, local, global and custom filters, full text search, and RDQL [21] queries.

4.6 SWOOP and Protégé

SWOOP [22] and Protégé [23] are ontology development toolkits that provide an integrated environment to build and edit ontologies, check for errors and inconsistencies, browse multiple ontologies, and share and reuse existing data by establishing mappings among different ontological entities. Both are based on plugin design with some very useful plugins. Protégé is a desktop application whereas SWOOP is hypermedia inspired web based tool, and is more light weight. SWOOP and Protégé though basically ontology development tools can be used for visualizing small RDF datasets but their visualization capabilities are limited and we are not including them in our survey.

4.7 Fresnel Display Vocabulary

Fresnel [12] is an RDF vocabulary which aims to model information about how to present Semantic Web content (i.e., what content to show, and how to show it) as presentation knowledge that can be exchanged and reused between browsers and other applications. Fresnel presentation knowledge is based on two fundamental concepts: *lenses* which specify the properties and ordering of RDF resources to be displayed, and *formats* which indicate how to format the content selected by lenses. Content selection is supported by using URIs, SPARQL, or its own language called Fresnel Selector Language [24]. The upcoming versions of Longwell and IsaViz will support Fresnel and some other tools claim to support its core features.

5 Comparison of RDF Browsing and Visualization Tools

Following is a comparison of the tools against the evaluation framework adopted in section 3. These tools were briefly introduced in section 4 and here their more technical features are evaluated from the view point of a metadata creator and analyst.

RDF is an abstract model and it can be realized in several concrete serializations like RDF/XML, N3, and N-Triple. RDF data may also reside in in-memory databases and remote triple stores. During our investigation we found that all of the tools have support for RDF/XML as its import/export format and most of the tools also support other common formats like N3 and N-Triples. Originally a Topic Map browser, Omnigator has import/export support only for RDF/XML which provides the facility of mapping between RDF and Topic Maps, though the results are not always promising. Longwell can access data in several triple storage systems but needs several configurations steps. Omnigator can also access data available on its native Ontopia Knowledge Server. IsaViz can browse and edit data in a Sesame triple store by using a plugin. All of the tools support reading data from several RDF files, merge the resulting graphs, and provide a unified display. Longwell utilizes its built-in inference mechanism for providing a more friendly display but none of the tools have the option of integrating an external inference engine. Longwell is not domain independent and the dataset needs to be prepared before browsing. Table 1 provides a summary of these features.

Table 1. Triple data format related features of RDF browsing and visualization tools

	Import Format	Export Format	Triple Store Access	File Merging	Inference Support
RDF Gravity	RDF/XML	RDF/XML	No	Yes	No
Drive RDF	RDF/XML	RDF/XML, HTML	No	Yes	No
Longwell	RDF/XML, N3, N-Triple	RDF/XML, N3, N-Triple	Jena, Joseki, 3Store, Kowari, Sesame	Yes	Built-in
Welkin	Turtle/N3, RDF/XML	RDF/XML,	No	Yes	No
IsaViz	RDF/XML, N3, N-Triple	RDF/XML, N3, N-Triple, SVG, PNG	Through Plugin for Sesame	Yes	No
Omnigator	XTM, LTM, HyTM, RDF	XTM, HTM, HyTM, CXTM, RDF	OKS only	Yes	No

Table 2 shows an overview of the display features of the RDF browsing and visualization tools. Text-based representation, in general, cannot nicely depict the structure of a large amount of data but is very effective for data mining, i.e., posing targeted queries once the required structure is known. Moreover, text-based displays are not effective for data "understanding", i.e., making sense of a large dataset of unknown global structure. Gravity, Welkin, and IsaViz provide graph-based displays consisting of node-link diagrams whereas Drive, Longwell, and Omnigator are text-based. Omnigator can also display a graph output by using its Vizigator plugin. Only Longwell and Omnigator provide an integrated interface consisting of a global view and the details of a selected item. All of the graphical browsers provide a general global view of the data with no grouping and clustering of similar items. Gravity and IsaViz use several visual cues (shape, color, size, and shading) together to visualize similar items. The development releases (alpha versions) of Longwell and IsaViz have support for Fresnel Display Vocabulary. Graph statistics are not available in Gravity, IsaViz and Longwell; Omnigator provides some useful statistics on the graph, whereas Welkin is capable of showing more advanced graph-theoretical properties. Graph editing features are only available in IsaViz which is basically an RDF graphical editor and browser. Other editors like Protégé can also be used for browsing RDF datasets but these display information in a hierarchical way which makes it difficult to grasp the inherent graph structure.

For scalability tests, besides our own datasets we used data from SIMILE project and Open Directory Project. Table 3 lists our results. We found that most of the tools can work only with a few megabytes of RDF data or a model consisting of a thousand statements at the most. Longwell and Omnigator can work with larger datasets scaling up to several thousand statements. A graphical tool may load a larger file but its visual scalability is very limited as compared to a text-based tool. Graph display in Gravity is improved by visual cues and by selection and filtering. The output of IsaViz, though not better than Gravity, is much better than Welkin mainly because of its zoomable user interface. Omnigator has plugin architecture and can be extended very easily. Longwell also provides the facility of extension.

Table 2. Display features of RDF browsing and visualization tools

	Display Interface	Presentation Paradigm	Graph Editing	Support for Fresnel Voc.	Graph Statistics
RDF Gravity	Global	Graph	No	No	No
Drive RDF	Local	HTML	Very Poor	No	Simple
Longwell	Integrated	HTML	No	Yes (2.0)	No
Welkin	Global	Graph	No	No	More Advanced
IsaViz	Global	Graph	Yes	Yes (3.0)	No
Omnigator	Integrated	HTML, Graphical support	Yes	No	Advanced

Table 3. RDF browsing tools' scalability factors

	Max. Dataset Size	Visual Scalability	Extension Mechanism
RDF Gravity	Limited (<1000 statements or Approx. 1 MB of RDF)	Limited	No
Drive RDF	Limited (<1000 statements or Approx. 2 MB of RDF)	Poor for relatively large graphs	No
Longwell	High (>500,000 statements)	High	Yes
Welkin	Limited (<1000 statements or Approx. 1 MB of RDF)	Limited	No
IsaViz	Limited (<1000 statements or Approx. 1 MB of RDF)	Limited	No
Omnigator	High (up to 100,000 TAOs)	Fairly high in text mode	Plugins

Table 4 is a listing of searching, querying, and filtering facilities available in the RDF visualization tools that we investigated. Selection and filtering features available in Longwell and Omnigator are based on ontological concepts like classes, properties, resource types, etc. A Gravity user can apply local and global filters and can hide selected graph elements. Similarly, IsaViz also provides simple selection and activation/deactivation of nodes, links, and regions. For fine-grained control RDF gravity provides support for RDQL and Omnigator supports its own topic map query language, tolog. Full text search of graph elements is available in almost all of the tools and none can create full text indexes of the documents annotated by the underlying RDF model.

Table 4. Search, query, and filtering facilities in RDF browsing and visualization tools

	Selection & Filtering	RDF Query Language	Full Text Graph Search	Full Text Document Search
RDF Gravity	Yes	Yes (RDQL)	Yes	No
Drive RDF	No	No	No	No
Longwell	Yes	No	Yes	No
Welkin	Yes	No	Yes	No
IsaViz	Simple	No	Yes	No
Omnigator	Yes	Yes (tolog)	Yes	No

6   Recommendations

The following recommendations for future effective and useful tools can be deduced from our investigation:

- Import/export support for common RDF serialization formats like RDF/XML, N3, N-Triple, TriX, etc. and extendable to other upcoming formats
- Support for reading from multiple data sources to provide a unified display
- Possibility of connecting to a triple store over common protocols
- Support for both graphical and textual display of information
- The option of simple and more advanced graph statistics
- An integrated display interface consisting of both local and global views
- Built-in support for basic reasoning and possibility of plugging in external inference engines
- Global and local filters for simple selection and browsing
- Support for SPARQL RDF query language
- Full text graph and annotated documents search
- Use of visual cues for highlighting similar items
- Support for Fresnel Display Vocabulary
- Support for data in the range of millions of triples
- Tool extension by a plugin mechanism

The maximum support for these features in the future releases of semantic web browsers or development toolkits will enable metadata creators and analysts to better perform their tasks.

7   Conclusions

In this paper we presented and compared a set of tools for the browsing and visualization of Semantic Web data expressed in RDF from the point of view of a metadata creator and analyst. All of tools that we investigated provide source validation, have support for RDF/XML as its import/export format, have the facility of merging different RDF files, and have limited scalability in terms of maximum number of triples that could be loaded.

All graphical tools have very limited visual scalability and most of them use a single display representation, and very few have promised to provide support in their coming releases for Fresnel display vocabulary. Moreover, most of the tools have searching and filtering facilities but at different levels of granularity, few have the option of Full text search, none has support for SPARQL, and none can build full text indexes for RDF annotated documents. Few tools provide the facility of accessing data in triple stores and none of the tools allows the integration of external inference engines.

Like in other semantic web tools, we found Java as the pre-dominant implementation language, Jena as semantic web development toolkit, Lucene as full text search engine, and Velocity as template engine.

References

1. T. Berners-Lee, J. Hendler, and O. Lassila. The Semantic Web. In: *Scientific American*, May, 2001.
2. W3C: Resource description framework (RDF): Concepts and Abstract Syntax (2004), http://www.w3.org/TR/rdf-concepts/
3. M. Biezunski and S. Newcomb (Editors): ISO/IEC 13250 Topic Maps.1999. See http://www.y12.doe.gov/sgml/sc34/document/0129.pdf
4. S. Pepper and G. Moore. XML topic maps (XTM) 1.0. Xtm specification. http://www.topicmaps.org/xtm/1.0/. (2001)
5. D. Quan and D. Karger. How to Make a Semantic Web Browser. In: Proceedings of the *13th International Conference on World Wide Web. pp* 255–265 (2004).
6. M. Ahmed et al. SemanticLife – A Framework for Managing Information of a Human Lifetime. In: *The Sixth International Conference on Information Integration and Web-based Applications and Services*, 27-29th September, (2004)
7. SIMILE: Welkin (2004-2005) http://simile.mit.edu/welkin/
8. R. Albertoni, A. Bertone, and M. De Martino. Semantic Web and Information Visualization. In: *1st Italian Semantic Web Workshop*, 10th December 2004, Ancona, Italy
9. L. Rutledge, J. van Ossenbruggen, and L. Hardman. Making RDF Presentable: Selection, Structure and Surfability for the Semantic Web. In: Proceedings of the *14th international conference on World Wide Web*. (2005)
10. J. Broekstra, A. Kampman, and F. Harmelen. Sesame: A Generic Architecture for Storing and Querying RDF and RDF Schema. In: *International Semantic Web Conference 2002*: 54-68
11. Kowari Metastore: http://www.kowari.org/
12. C. Bizer, R. Lee, E. Pietriga. Fresnel - Display Vocabulary for RDF (2005). http://www.w3.org/2005/04/fresnel-info/manual-20050726/
13. SIMILE: Longwell RDF Browser (2003-2005) http://simile.mit.edu/longwell/
14. W3C: IsaViz: A Visual Authoring Tool for RDF (2001-2005) http://www.w3.org/2001/11/IsaViz/
15. S. Goyal S and W. Rupert. RDF Gravity (RDF Graph Visualization Tool). Salzburg Research, Austria. http://semweb.salzburgresearch.at/apps/rdf-gravity/
16. Mc.Schraefel and D. Smith. The Evolving mSpace Plateform: Leveraging the Semantic Web on the Trail of the Memex. In: *16th ACM Conference on Hypertext and Hypermedia.* (2005).
17. E. Prud'hommeaux and A. Seaborne (2005) SPARQL Query Language for RDF http://www.w3.org/TR/rdf-sparql-query/.
18. R. Singh. Drive: An RDF Parser for .NET. (2002) http://www.driverdf.org/
19. E. Prud'hommeaux and R. Lee. W3C RDF Validation Service. http://www.w3.org/RDF/Validator/
20. Ontopia Omnigator: http:///www.ontopia.net/omnigator/
21. A. Seaborne. RDQL – RDF Data Query Language, part of the Jena RDF Toolkit, HPLabs Semantic Web activity, http://hpl.hp.com/semweb/ , W3C Working Draft, http://www.w3.org/Submission/2004/SUBM-RDQL-20040109 (2005)
22. A. Kalyanpur, B. Parsia, and J. Hendler. A Tool for Working with Web Ontologies. In: Proceedings of *Extreme Markup Languages* (2004).
23. J. Gennari et al. The evolution of Protégé-2000: An environment for knowledge-based systems development. In: *International Journal of Human-Computer Studies*, 58(1):89–123. (2003)
24. E. Pietriga (2005) Fresnel Selector Language for RDF http://www.w3.org/2005/04/fresnel-info/fsl-20050726/.

LUPA: A Workflow Engine

Emely Arráiz[1], Ernesto Hernández-Novich[1] and Roger Soler[1]

Universidad Simón Bolívar, Caracas, Venezuela
arraiz@ldc.usb.ve, emhn@ldc.usb.ve, soler@ldc.usb.ve

Abstract. Workflow Management Systems depend on a Workflow Enactment Service having several interfaces to establish communication with external applications, manage persistent information and exchange it with similarly capable systems. The study of business processes has shown multiple workflow patterns that have been modelled and implemented in several engines. The Workflow Management Council has combined commercial and academic efforts towards a standard structure for engines and information exchange regarding workflow processes. LUPA is a Workflow Engine designed around the Workflow Management Council Reference Model that implements basic workflow patterns with a graphical syntax, establishing their semantics on Interpreted Petri Nets with extensions. It provides a new Cancellation workflow pattern, that has also been used to provide an Iteration pattern with guaranteed termination.

1 Introduction

The Unified Language for Administrative Processes (LUPA) focuses on the programming and communicating tasks associated with the transaction management needed to fulfill business processes of an organization. It precisely models de Routes and Rules that information must follow in order to comply with the organizational policy.

LUPA's syntactic specification consists of Process Expressions built over a small set of operations that allow writing formulas which describe the Routes. It has operational semantics expressed with Interpreted Petri Nets covering the networked Process structure along with an Environment containing the associated information. A Cancellation operator is particularly interesting, it being able to model two transactions operating in parallel, keeping only the operations of the first one that finishes.

A simple interpreter component has been implemented following the formal syntactic and semantic specifications, leading to a prototype that is able to instantiate, execute and control processes defined under this schema. The prototype has been built following the WFMC recommendation regarding the Workflow System Reference Model.

This paper has been structured in sections. Section 2 gives an introduction regarding processes, process expressions and some of the associated graphs.

Please use the following format when citing this chapter:

Arráiz, E., Hernández-Novich, E., Soler, R., 2006, in IFIP International Federation for Information Processing, Volume 214, The Past and Future of Information Systems: 1976–2006 and Beyond, eds. Avison, D., Elliot, S., Krogstie, J., Pries-Heje, J., (Boston: Springer), pp. 189–200.

Section 3 defines the semantic for the process expressions, along with its operational semantics. Section 4 presents a brief review of Workflow concepts. Section 5 shows how LUPA fits into the Worflow Reference Model and Section 6 briefly comments on related and similar work both commercial and academic, while Section 7 briefly explains LUPA's implementation model. Finally, conclusions and further directions are presented in Section 8 .

2 Process Expressions

Each transaction has an associated process formed by the set of tasks the organization completes in order to effectively complete such transaction, and by the order and precedence in which those tasks have to be undertaken [1].

The set of tasks that make up the process has a "natural" graph structure given by the "programming". The idea of effective completion is seen as the fact that the transaction finishes and all its associated events have taken place. Therefore, a Process is understood as both the tasks and its programming. Being able to define the state of a process, seen as the set of tasks that are taken place at any given time along the process flow, becomes interesting. This notion can be modeled as the marking of the Petri Nets [2].

The Process Expressions (PE) are defined inductively as:

- T the finite set of simple tasks.
- EP the process expressions.
- pr_j predicates.
- $Clock$, a process that measures time.

Table 1. Process Expressions

If $t_i \in T$	then	1. t_i	$\in EP$ (simple task)
If $Z, Q \in EP$ then			
		2. $Z \bowtie Q$	$\in EP$ (sequence)
		3. $Z \oplus Q$	$\in EP$ (conjunction)
		4. $Z \varnothing Q$	$\in EP$ (disjunction)
		5. $Z \oslash Q$	$\in EP$ (cancellation)
		6. $Z^{\oplus_r, Clock}$	$\in EP$ (iteration)

Each process expression has an associated graph, with a general form G(E) shown in Figure 1.

The transaction (a document) enters the net through the place **i** , is handled by the transition E, where the transaction is properly "processed", exiting the net through the place **o** afterwards.

All associated graphs have a single input place **i** and a single output place **o**.

Since we are working with bipartite graphs, the lexicon is similar to the one used when talking about Petri Nets.

Fig. 1. Generic Graph

We have the following cases with their associated graphs:

1. Simple Task: Process $E = t_i$ (t_i being the simple task which is atomic). This process E ends as soon as task t_i ends.
2. Sequence: Process $E = Z \bowtie Q$, stating that process Z is processed until it finished and its followed by process Q until it finishes. Process E ends when Q ends. Figure 2 shows its associated graph $G(E) = G(Z \bowtie Q)$. Where t is a "dummy process" that helps preserve process' Z output independent from process' Q input. That is, process t only copies its input to its output.

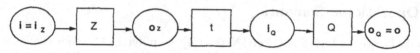

Fig. 2. Sequence

3. Conjunction: Process $E = Z \oplus Q$, stating that both processes Z y Q execute in parallel until both have ended thus ending process E.
4. Disjunction: Process $E = Z \oslash Q$, stating that one and only one of Z or Q will execute depending on predicate's pr truth value. Process E ends when the process chosen to execute ends.
5. Cancellation: Process $E = Z \oslash Q$, stating that both processes Z y Q execute in parallel. When one of them finishes, process E will also finish. It also has the effect of cancelling (rolling-back) all the tasks completed by the other process. Figure 3 shows its associated graph $G(E) = G(Z \oslash Q)$. Where $\oslash$ is a "control place" that copies the input to both input places i_Z and i_Q, while $\oslash^*$ is another "control place" which will determine which sub-process finished first (be that Z or Q), handing its output to place o, while remembering to cancel (rollback) the output of the sub-process finishing last.

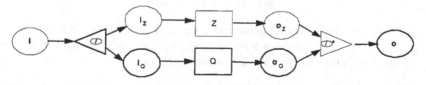

Fig. 3. Cancellation

The Cancellation operator ($\oslash$) is useful to start processes in parallel when only the results of one of them is needed, but which one will end first is not known or doesn't matter for the correct outcome of the process.

6. Iteration: Process $E = Z^{\oslash, Clock}$, stating that process E will be repeatedly executed until predicate's pr truth value is false, or until the amount of time controlled by $Clock$ has passed. Figure 4 shows its associated graph.

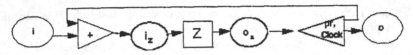

Fig. 4. Iteration

3 Operational Semantic

Unlike [3], we use Interpreted Petri Nets as [4], simplifying of standard definition and adapting them, thus partially using its potential. Our nets fall into Category 3 according to the Petri Net classification in [5].

Using Interpreted Petri Nets allows us to have and Environment carrying all the information needed for the transaction in process, and a classical Petri Net which establishes when to transform or create information on the Environment.

Definition 1 (Interpreted Petri Nets (IPN)) *An Interpreted Petri Net consists of a classical Petri Net $< P, T, A >$, an Environment $Env = < D, OP, PR >$, and two functions φ and ψ that link Net and Environment together by completing operations. Thus $IPN = << P, T, A >, Env, \varphi, \psi >$.*

1. $D = D_{form} + D_{control}$, the disjoint union of the Environment states, the "form" and "control".
2. $OP = \{op_1, op_2, \cdots, op_s\}$, a set of operators

$$op_i : D \to D$$

3. $PR = \{pr_1, pr_2, \cdots, pr_k\}$, a set of predicates over D

$$pr_i : D \to \{true, false\}$$

4. $\varphi : P \to OP$, defining an operator op_i for each place of the Net.
5. $\psi : T \to PR \times OP$, defining a pair $<predicate, operator>$ for each transition of the Net, being the specific task to complete there.

An *IPN* works like a classical Petri Net, except that before firing a transition its associated predicate must have a true truth value when applied on the Environment, thus allowing the application of the operator.

The function φ will generally be the identity function, except for the place **i** which stands "isolated", that is $\varphi : (P - \{\mathbf{i}\}) \rightarrow \mathcal{I}$

A precise construction of φ for each input place **i**, is given for each case, being particularly important for cases 5 and 6.

3.1 Operational Semantics for Process Expressions

These semantics are given by the Interpreted Petri Net associated with the expression, constructed inductively according to the particular case. Being IPN_E the Interpreted Petri Net associated to the Process Expression E, that is: $IPN_E =<< P_E, T_E, A_E >, Env, \varphi_E, \psi_E >>$ where the Environment $Env =< D, OP, PR >$ is general while constructing the net. For all cases it must be true that: $P_Z \cap P_Q = \emptyset$ and $T_Z \cap T_Q = \emptyset$. We use the lambda notation [6] to specify each case. Case 5, the Cancellation operator, is specified as follows (all the specifications and the mathematical properties of the IPN are in [7]):

Case 5 Let $E = Z \oslash Q$.
restricted to:

$$(P_Z \cup P_Q) \cap \{\mathbf{i}, \mathbf{o}, \mathbf{b}, u, v, r, s\} = \emptyset$$
$$(T_Z \cup T_Q) \cap \{t_1, t_2, t_3, t_4, t_5\} = \emptyset$$
$$(\varphi_Z(P_Z) \cup \psi_Z(T_Z) \downarrow 1 \cup \psi_Z(T_Z) \downarrow 2) \perp (\varphi_Q(P_Q) \cup (\psi_Q(T_Q) \downarrow 1 \cup \psi_Q(T_Q) \downarrow 2)$$
$$\lambda d.M_{k1} \perp \lambda d.M_{k2}$$

and IPN_E:

$$
\begin{aligned}
P_E \quad &= P_Z \cup P_Q \cup \{\mathbf{i}, \mathbf{o}, \mathbf{b}, u, v, r, s\} \\
T_E \quad &= T_Z \cup T_Q \cup \{t1, t_2, t_3, t_4, t_5\} \\
A_E \quad &= A_Z \cup A_Q \cup \{< \mathbf{i}, t_1 >, < t_1, s >, < t_1, u >, < t_1, i_Z >, \\
&\quad < t_1, i_Q >, < u, t_2 >, < u, t_3 >, < v, t_4 >, < v, t_5 >, < o_Q, t_3 >, \\
&\quad < o_Z, t_2 >, < t_4, \mathbf{o} >, < s, t_4 >, < t_4, u >, < t_4, r >, < t_2, v >, \\
&\quad < t_3, v >, < r, t_5 >, < t_5, \mathbf{b} >\} \\
\varphi_E(\mathbf{i}) \quad &= \lambda d.(\varphi_Q(i_Q) \circ \varphi_Z(i_Z) \circ M_{k1} \circ M_{k2}) \\
\varphi_E(P_E - \{\mathbf{i}\}) &= \mathcal{I} \\
\psi_E(t_1) \downarrow 1 \quad &= \lambda d.d \downarrow k1 \quad \text{(unique codomain index of } M_{k1}) \\
\psi_E(t_1) \downarrow 2 \quad &= \lambda d.(\overline{M_{k1}} \circ Copy(D_{form})) \\
\psi_E(T_Z) \quad &\equiv \psi_Z(T_Z) \text{ (i.e. } \forall t \in T_Z, \ \psi_E(t) = \psi_Z(t), \\
&\quad \text{working over } D_{form} + D_{control}) \\
\psi_E(T_Q) \quad &\equiv \psi_Q(T_Q) \text{ (i.e. } \forall t \in T_Q, \ \psi_E(t) = \psi_Q(t), \\
&\quad \text{working over a copy of } D_{form} \text{ and the unique } D_{control}) \\
\psi_E(t_2) \downarrow 1 \quad &= \psi_E(t_3) \downarrow 1 = \psi_E(t_4) \downarrow 1 = \psi_E(t_5) \downarrow 1 = \lambda d.true \\
\psi_E(t_2) \downarrow 2 \quad &= \lambda d. \begin{cases} (\overline{M_{k2}} \circ Keep(Z))(d) & \text{si } (d \downarrow k2) \text{ in } D_{control} \\ (M_{k2} \circ Destroy(Z))(d) & \text{if not} \end{cases} \\
\psi_E(t_3) \downarrow 2 \quad &= \lambda d. \begin{cases} (\overline{M_{k2}} \circ Keep(Q))(d) & \text{if}(d \downarrow k2) \text{ in } D_{control} \\ (M_{k2} \circ Destroy(Q))(d) & \text{if not} \end{cases} \\
\psi_E(t_4) \downarrow 2 \quad &= \mathcal{I} \\
\psi_E(t_5) \downarrow 2 \quad &= \lambda d.M_{k1}
\end{aligned}
$$

This case will have one of the following execution flows, starting from an initial marking μ_0:

$$S \in \{<< i, t_1, < Z, t_2, t_4, \{o\} > \| < Q, t_3, t_5, \{b\} >>>, \\ << i, t_1, < Q, t_3, t_4, \{o\} > \| < Z, t_2, t_5, \{b\} >>>\}$$

The set of output places is $P_o = \{o, b\}$.

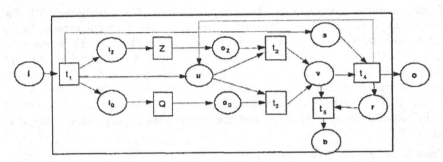

Fig. 5. Cancellation Operator underlying Petri-Net

Place i has a special φ component built (two M_{kj} for each cancellation operator ($\oslash$)). Each "memory" M_{kj} will keep track of specific conditions. M_{k1} makes sure that the cancellation operator remains blocked until both processes have finished, the last one being properly cancelled (rolled-back); while M_{k2} signals which process has to be cancelled. The output place b becomes a sink for all the tokens kept in the net by transitions that must be cancelled (rolled-back). Function $Keep$ does permanently modify the form part of the Environment, whereas function $Destroy$ discards any changes that were made by the process finishing last and thus being cancelled.

The iteration operator has been built as a specialized cancellation operator in such a way that all iterations will finish, either by completion or by the Clock timing out.

4 Workflow System and the Reference Model

The Workflow Management Coalition (WFMC) defines Workflow as the total or partial systematic automation of Business Processes during which documents, information or tasks are exchanged among participants, determined by a set of rules [8, 9]. It also defines a Workflow Management System as a set of software components used to support the definition, administration and execution of Workflow Processes [8, 9].

Research by the WFMC [10] have shown the feasibility of establishing a general model for Workflow Management System's implementation that fits the majority of existing solutions, as well as a basis for interoperability among them.

Since all Workflow Systems have a number of generic components interacting in predefined ways, the general model was built after identifying the main functional components of those systems as well as the interfaces between them. Several levels of functional capabilities have been established for each interface, thus specifying each one's minimal requirements.

In practice, the reference model of a Workflow System centers around at least one Workflow Engine [11] in charge of storing, activating and interpreting instances of processes as modeled by the organization. In fact, several engines can act simultaneously in a cooperative fashion, becoming a Workflow Enactment Service. It must provide interfaces that ease interaction with Process Definition Tools, External Support Tools such as Human or Cybernetic Agents, Control and Administration Tools, while helping exchange information with other Engines.

The Workflow Engine works on Process Definitions, which are nothing more than a Business Process presented in a way that eases its automatic manipulation either for analysis or application. This representation is just a network of activities and its relations, with several criteria allowing starting a finishing processes, while keeping process' relevant information at hand, who is involved and which applications are needed in order to complete it. There's a hierarchical relationship among process definitions, and the concept of a sub-process gives organizations the opportunity of reusing automation efforts, by solving simpler processes first and then tackle complex ones in a *"bottom-up"* fashion. Figure 6 shows the high-level Reference Model with its components and interfaces.

A simple *Workflow Enactment Service* was implemented, providing a runtime environment in which processes are instantiated and activated. A LUPA-based Workflow Engine handles interpretation and activation of the needed tasks, as described in the particular process definition, interacting with external resources in order to complete them.

5 LUPA and the Reference Model

While studying the LUPA proposed model and the many refinements of both "high-level" and "low-level" representations, LUPA's roles in the Reference Model were clearly identified.

5.1 LUPA as a Pre-Processor

The Workflow Enactment Service receives a process definition from a process design tool, and transforms it into an internal in-core representation which helps interpret it. During this conversion process [1] all the syntactic and semantic conditions are verified following LUPA's specification, checking if the process can be effectively constructed and executed, whether it has been defined directly or indirectly by means of combination of simpler existing processes. Once converted to the internal representation, the process is available for activation on

---

[1] A sort of "compilation" from a process "source form" closer to the designer, to an "executable form" closer to the engine that will execute it.

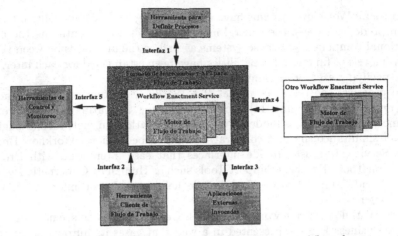

Fig. 6. Workflow Reference Model. Components and Interfaces.

any authorized user's request, or even moved to another Engine with a compatible intermediate representation. Our reference implementation has shown that LUPA fulfills these roles because:

- It receives a "high level" representation in terms of the graphical LUPA syntax. Even though during this work we did not develop a process designing application based on LUPA's graphical syntax, the XML process definition given as input to the engine is based on LUPA's regular expressions, showing not only it's feasibility but also suggesting an usable representation.
- It is able to convert this input definition into a more efficient one for execution purposes. During this conversion process, all the conditions required by LUPA's semantics are enforced and only properly conditioned definitions are accepted.
- It is able to turn this internal efficient representation into a textual "low level" one that helps ensure the persistence of it inside the work area of the Workflow Enactment Service. That is, if the service is stopped for whatever reason, the available process definitions and the executing instances will be stored in a persistent and consistent repository that allows resuming operations in the same Workflow Enactment Service, or in any other one to which they can be transported as long as its based on LUPA.

5.2 LUPA as an Interpreter

The Workflow Enactment Service takes a previously processed low level definition from its repository, and activates it as many times as necessary to handle specific cases. This activation and consequent workflow, must keep Control Information and Case Relevant Information, changing them according to the concrete operations associated with each task to be performed. At any given time there will be many types of processes, each one having several instances, all of them executing simultaneously; knowing which tasks are pending, how far has any case advanced, suspending and resuming, finding out whether or not a process has finished, an even terminating o moving instances are some of the needed capabilites on such a system. Our reference implementation has shown that LUPA fulfills these roles because:

- The "low level" in core representation is based on a direct representation of the LUPA Net, with or without markings, be it active or not, sharing all the control (φ) and operation (ψ) functions in a single representation. A single representation of the flow structure (a single net) and a single set of operations, can model an abstract definition or as many instances as needed by means of the Petri Net Color extension to the LUPA Net and the Environments. The execution ability that models the operational semantic of the LUPA Nets as Interpreted Petri Nets is able to work on the appropriately colored marks and environment as needed by each case.
- The "low level" exchange representation is built from the "low level" in core representation, being able to select either the process definition (network and functions, without environment), a single instance (network, functions, and a single color marking and environment) or all instances.
- The "low level" in core representations are easily exchanged over a text-based protocol service, allowing for simple starting, stopping, checkpointing, cancelling and other simple operations over the available processes including exporting to other LUPA-based engines.

5.3 LUPA as an External Application Integrator

The Workflow Enactment Services must help the bidirectional exchange of information between the Workflow Engine and any external application needed to complete the tasks for each transaction. If the task must be completed by a human agent, it must be able to notify her of "pending tasks"; if the task must be completed by a cybernetic agent, it must be able to initiate execution possibly sending data and check its completion possibly retrieving processed data. At any given time there may be several ongoing external interactions, and knowing which ones are pending and checking for their current status must be easy. Our reference implementation has shown that LUPA fulfills these roles because:

- The Environment's representation provides a simple mechanism for procedural manipulation through a simple class interface. This eases writing operations (ψ) that exploit all the power and flexibility of Perl [12].
- The Environment's representation provides a simple mechanism for exporting and importing equivalent XML documents [13, 14] to external applications.
- The invocation of external applications is clearly split in such a way that the start of execution is separated from checking if it has finished. This allows for exporting process information prior to executing the external applications, and importing of results when finished. It also allows external applications to be executed asynchronously, while the Engine continues processing other tasks.

6 Related Work

An in depth analysis of thirteen commercial WorkFlow systems can be found in [15], while [16] does a similar analysis over ten WorkFlow languages proposed by academic communities. A large number of open source and free software initiatives [17] have worked on the process automation problem, providing different tools and systems. This project belongs on that list, but being different insofar as having a graphical syntax and a formal mathematical basis and expressive power of Petri Nets that combine with the Interpreted Petri Net techniques in order to link the workflow net, the case-specific and workflow-related information, and the operations over them. Only YAWL [18] has a similar approach, except that they use web-services and XML.

7 Modelling and Implementation

The interpreter for the language defined by LUPA's syntax and semantics has been modeled as closely as possible so as to be able to apply all the theory, analysis and verification tools available for Petri Nets [19]. It also has been built around the WFMC's Workflow Reference Model by following all the recommendations and basing it on open standards for information exchange.

The Execution Environments have been built as symbol tables, with total or partial exporting abilities to an XML representation. This eases portability and manipulation for the persistence infrastructure and external application interaction.

The Operators and Predicates have been modelled as functions in the native programming language chosen, with explicit information regarding domain and co-domain needed to perform the integrity checks while combining simple processes to build complex ones. Operators may be asked to perform asynchronous tasks, therefore their execution has been broken up in two phases: startup and test for finish. Introspective features provided by the programming language have been used to export the actual executable code for this functions (even if they were dynamically built at runtime) to an XML representation for persistence and interoperability purposes. Functions φ and ψ have been modelled in a similar fashion.

LUPA Nets have been modelled as Petri Nets, building the operational semantics using the aforementioned models for Environments and Functions and utility libraries provided by the programming language, in particular the ability to build closures. Each process operator has been implemented in such a way that it builds new LUPA nets as long as it is possible based on the restrictions imposed by each construction case. The network structure can be exported to an XML representation for persistence and interoperability purposes.

The programming language of choice is Perl. It allowed object-oriented techniques and functional programming techniques simultaneously, thus making the programming as close as possible to the mathematical model. Perl's own abilities and the availability of several utility libraries allowed for the quick and easy development of a working prototype that is as compact and elegant as the formal structures it represents.

The Environment with the Petri Net and its markings, become an exact representation of the process status, and by using the color extension on Petri Nets, of all instances. The mechanisms in place for inspecting and exporting this structures provide clear and direct means of finding out completed, enabled and active tasks of any business process modeled with LUPA.

8 Conclusions and Further Directions

This work has formally defined the LUPA language as a way to model business processes.

It has the advantage of being highly expressive and adequate, by means of its fundamental flow patterns, including the cancellation and an iteration that guarantees termination.

The Petri Nets were chosen as the semantic model for process expressions because of their easily understandable and simple functionality, and the availability of analysis and graphical presentation tools [20].

Having developed a working Workflow Engine [19] shows that the LUPA language is useful and effective at its purpose. Having developed it using free software tools [21] enabled us to easily build a basic infrastructure following the Workflow Reference Model.

The reference implementation is highly portable. Choosing Perl as a programming language and libraries that are platform independent, ensure that the engine runs on GNU/Linux (development platform), any Unix, Win32, MacOS and even VMS, since Perl has been ported to all of them. The programming style also guarantees portability of all the programs without modification nor conditional execution. Selecting XML [13, 14] to build the low level representation of the many structures, combined with the introspective abilities of Perl to export source code out of its executables and dynamically generated data structures, makes then interchangeable across platforms and eases writing additional tools for analysis and verification.

References

1. R. Endl G. Knolmayer and M. Pfahrer. Modeling processes and workflows by business rules. *Lecture Notes in Computer Science*, 1806:16–29, 2000.
2. J. Peterson. Petri nets. *ACM Computing Surveys*, pages 223–252, Sept 1977.
3. W.M.P. van der Aalst. Workflow verification: Finding control-flow errors using petri-net-based techniques. *Lecture Notes in Computer Science, 1806*, pages 161–183, 2000.
4. G. W. Brams. *Réseaux de Petri: Théorie et pratique*. Texte de l' Agence de l' Informatique. Masson, 1983.

5. L. Bernardinello and F. De Cindio. A survey of basic models and modular net classes. *Advances in Petri Nets*, pages 304–351, 1992.

6. A. Church. *The Calculi of Lambda Convertion*. Princenton University Press, 1941.

7. E. Arráiz. Las expresiones de procesos y su semántica a través de las redes de petri interpretadas. Technical Report, Universidad Simón Bolivar, 2004.

8. Workflow Management Coalition. The workflow reference model. Disponible en URL:http://www.wfmc.org/standards/docs/tc003v11.pdf, 1995.

9. Workflow Management Coalition. Terminology & glossary. Disponible en URL:http://www.wfmc.org/standards/docs/TC-1011_term_glossary_v3.pdf, 1999.

10. The Workflow Management Coalition. Workflow management coalition terminology and glossary. Disponible en URL:http://www.wfmc.org, 1999.

11. S. Jablonski. Workflow management between formal theory and pragmatic approaches. *Lecture Notes in Computer Science, Volumen 1806*, 2000.

12. T. Christiansen L. Wall and J. Orwant. *Programming Perl, 3rd Edition*. O'Reilly & Associates, 2000.

13. World Wide Web Consortium (W3C). Extensible markup language (xml). Disponible en URL:http://www.w3.org/XML.

14. World Wide Web Consortium (W3C). Extensible markup language (xml) 1.1. Disponible en URL: http://www.w3.org/TR/2004/REC-xml11-20040204/, 2004.

15. B. Kiepuszewiski & A.P. Barros W.M.P. van der Aalst, A.H.M. ter Hofstede. Workflow patterns. 2003.

16. W.M.P. van der Aalst & A.H.M. ter Hofstede. Yawl: Yet another workflow language. *QUT Technical Report, FIT-TR-2003-04*, 2003.

17. C. E. Perez. Open source workflow engines written in java. 2004.

18. M. Dumas & A.H.M. ter Hofstede W.M.P. van der Aalst, L. Aldred. Implementation of the yawl system. *Lecture Notes in Computer Science, 3084*, 2004.

19. E. Hernández-Novich. Mirando procesos con lupa: Un motor de flujo de trabajo. Tésis de Maestría en Ciencias de la Computación, USB, 2005.

20. CNP group. Petri nets world. Disponible en URL:http://www.daini.au.dk/PetriNets, 2002.

21. D. A. Wheeler. Why open source software/free software(oss/fs)? look at the numbers! Disponible en URL:http://www.dwheeler.com/oss_fs_why.html, 2004.

Data Modeling Dealing With Uncertainty in Fuzzy Logic

Angélica Urrutia[1], José Galindo[2], Leoncio Jimenéz[1], and Mario Piattini[3]

1 Dpto. de Computación e Informática, Universidad Católica del Maule, Chile,
aurrutia, ljimenez@ucm.cl

2 Dpto. Lenguajes y Ciencias de la Computación, Universidad de Málaga, España, jgg@lcc.uma.es

3 Escuela Superior de Informática, Universidad de Castilla-La Mancha, Mario.Piattin@uclm.es

Abstract. This paper shows models of data description that incorporate uncertainty like models of data extension EER, IFO among others. These database modeling tools are compared with the pattern FuzzyEER proposed by us, which is an extension of the EER model in order to manage uncertainty with fuzzy logic in fuzzy databases. Finally, a table shows the components of EER tool with the representation of all the revised models.

1 Introduction

On occasions the term "imprecision" embraces several meanings between which we should differentiate. For example, the information we have may be incomplete or "fuzzy" (diffuse, vague), or we may not know if it is certain or not (uncertainty), or perhaps we are totally ignorant of the information (unknown), we may know that that information cannot be applied to a specific entity (undefined), or we may not even know if the data can be applied or not to the entity in question ("total ignorance" or value "null") [1]. Each of these terms will depend on the context in which they are applied.

The management of uncertainty in database systems is a very important problem [2] as the information is often vague. Motro states that fuzzy information is content-dependent, and he classifies it as follows:

- Uncertainty: It not possible to determine whether the information is true or false. For example, "John may be 38 years old".
- Imprecision: The information available is not specific enough. For example, "John may be between 37 and 43 years old", — disjunction — "John is 34

Please use the following format when citing this chapter:

Urrutia, A., Galindo, J., Jimenéz, L., Piattini, M., 2006, in IFIP International Federation for Information Processing, Volume 214, The Past and Future of Information Systems: 1976–2006 and Beyond, eds. Avison, D., Elliot, S., Krogstie, J., Pries-Heje, J., (Boston: Springer), pp. 201–217.

or 43 years old", — negative — "John is not 37 years old", or even unknown.

- Vagueness: The model includes elements (predicates or quantifiers) which are inherently vague, for example, "John is in his early years", or "John is at the end of his youth". However, once these concepts have been defined, this case would match the previous one (imprecision).
- Inconsistency: It contains two or more pieces of information, which cannot be true at the same time. For example, "John is 37 and 43 years old, or he is 35 years old"; this is a special case of disjunction.
- Ambiguity: Some elements of the model lack a complete semantics (or a complete meaning). For example, "It is not clear whether they are annual or monthly salaries".

Zadeh as described in [3] introduces the fuzzy logic, in order to deal with this type of data. Traditional logic, because it is bi-valued, can only operate with concepts like: yes or no, black or white, true or false, 0 or 1, which allowed just for a very limited knowledge representation. Although there are other logics which take more truth values, namely multi-valued logics, fuzzy logic is one extension which takes endless truth levels (or degrees), associating the concept of membership degree or truth degree in an interval [0,1] within the fuzzy logic theory.

Fuzzy databases have also been widely studied [1,4], with little attention being paid to the problem of conceptual modeling [5]. This does not mean that there are no publications, however, but that they are sparse and with no standard. Therefore, there have also been advances in modeling uncertainty in database systems [6-9] including object-oriented database models [9].

At the same time, the extension of the ER model for the treatment of fuzzy data (with vagueness) has been studied in various publications [4,7,10-15], but none of these refer to the possibility of expressing constraints by using the tools by fuzzy sets theory. In [8] a summary of some of these models can be found.

On the other hand, the main methodologies of databases design [8,16-19] have not paid attention to the modeling of data with uncertainty, although the intent of uncertainty modeling of the real world is rarely absent.

Based on these concepts, in this paper we will discuss different approaches, by various authors, related to the uncertainty conceptual modeling problem in database models. Closing the modeling stage, in sections 2, 3, 4, 5, 7 we present a Fuzzy Enhanced Entity-Relationship model, also known as FuzzyEER, a tool for fuzzy database modeling with many advantages with respect to the modeling tools presented in this section 6: fuzzy values in the attributes, degree in each value of an attribute, degree in a group of values of diverse attributes, as well as, fuzzy entities, fuzzy relationships, fuzzy aggregation, fuzzy constraints. In section 8 includes a comparison of FuzzyEER and some other fuzzy models.

2 The Zvieli and Chen Approach

In [15] is the first great approach in ER modeling. They allow fuzzy attributes in entities and relationships and introduced three levels of fuzziness in the ER model:

1. At the first level, entity sets, relationships and attribute sets may be fuzzy, namely, they have a membership degree to the model. For example, in Figure 1 the fuzzy entity "Company" has a 0.9 membership degree, the relationship "To Accept" has a 0.7 membership degree and the fuzzy attribute "Electronic mail" has a 0.8 membership degree.

2. The second level is related to the fuzzy occurrences of entities and relationships. For example, an entity Young_Employees must be fuzzy, because its instances, its employees, belong to the entity with different membership degrees.

3. The third level concerns the fuzzy values of attributes of special entities and relationships. For example, attribute Quality of a basketball player may be fuzzy (bad, good, very good...).

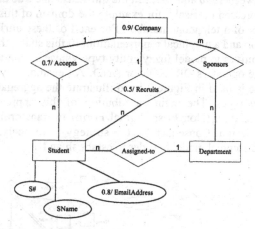

Fig. 1. Example with membership degrees to the model in some sets (entities, relationships or attributes): The first level of the Zvieli and Chen approach [3].

The first level may be useful, but at the end we must decide whether such an entity, relationship or attribute will appear or will not appear in the implementation. The second level is useful too, but it is important to consider different degree meanings (membership degree, importance degree, fulfillment degree...). A list of authors using different meanings may be found in [20]. The third level is useful, and it is similar to writing the data type of some attributes, because fuzzy values belong to fuzzy data types.

3 Proposal of Yazici et al.

In [21] propose an extension of the IFO model, shown in Figure 2 a), for the processing of imprecise data, and special treatment of data where similarity exists in a label. They call this extension ExIFO, and by means of examples they explain the implementation and validation of the representation of a fuzzy conceptual scheme by looking at a representation of uncertain attributes. In the model three new constructors are added and using these new constructors it is possible to represent explicitly attributes that have uncertain values.

The ExIFO conceptual model [9] allows imprecision and uncertainty in database models, based on the IFO conceptual model [9,21]. They use fuzzy-valued attributes, incomplete-valued attributes and null-valued attributes. In the first case, the true data may belong to a specific set or subset of values, for example the domain of this attribute may be a set of colors {red, orange, yellow, blue} or a subset {orange, yellow} where there is a similarity relation between the colors. In the second case, the true data value is not known, for example, the domain of this attribute may be a set of years between 1990 and 1992. In the third case, the true data value is available, but it is not expressed precisely, for example the domain of this attribute may be the existence or not of a telephone number. For each of these attribute types, there is a formal definition and a graphical representation. In this study, the authors introduce a high-level primitives to model fuzzy entity type whose semantics are related to each other with logic operators OR, XOR or AND. An example involving an Employee-Vehicle scheme is used in Figure 2 b) to illustrate the aggregation and composition of fuzzy entity types. The main contribution of this approach is the use of an extended NF^2 relation (Non First Normal Form) to transform a conceptual design into a logical design. Consequently, the strategy is to analyze the attributes that compose the conceptual model in order to establish an NF^2 model.

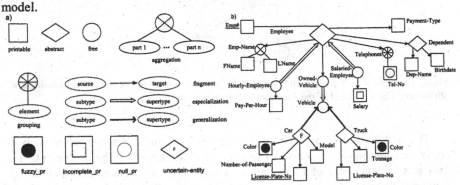

Fig. 2. Fuzzy ExIFO Model proposed by Yazici and Merdan [21]. a) Notation. b) Example Employee-Vehicle.

The study in [22] is, mainly, a conceptual modeling approach for the representation of complex-uncertain information [21] using object-oriented paradigm and an algorithm for transforming a conceptual schema specification of the model introduced here (ExIFO) into a logical schema of the fuzzy object-oriented databases model (FOOD) is proposed. ExIFO attempts to preserve the acquired strengths of semantic approaches, while integrating concepts from the object paradigm and fuzziness by adding new constructors.

4   The Chen and Kerre Approach

In [7,8,11] these authors introduced the fuzzy extension of several major EER concepts (superclass, subclass, generalization, specialization, category and shared subclass) without including graphical representations. The basic idea is that if E1 is a superclass of E2 and $e \in E2$, then $E1(e) \leq E2(e)$, where $E1(e)$ and $E2(e)$ are the membership functions of e to E1 and E2, respectively. They discussed three kinds of constraints with respect to fuzzy relationships but they do not study fuzzy constraints: a) The inheritance constraint means that, a subclass instance inherits all relationship instances in which it has participated as a superclass entity. b) The total participation constraint for entity E is defined when for any instance in E, $\exists\ \alpha_i$ such that $\alpha_i > 0$, where α_i is one membership degree in the fuzzy relationship. c) The cardinality constraints 1:1, 1:N and N:M are also studied with fuzzy relationships.

The fuzzy ER model, Chen [7] proposes a model generated by $M = (E, R, A)$ expressed by E as entity type, R as interrelation type, and A as attributes, also including label types which generate, at the first level, $L1(M) = (E, R, A_E, A_R)$, and proposes four set types, with notation shown in Figure 3 (see an Example in Figure 1), and where μ_X is the membership function to the set X (one Entity, one Relationship or one Attribute) and D_E is the domain of E composed of all possible entity types concerned:

- $E = \{\mu_E (E)/E : E \in D_E \text{ and } \mu_E (E) \in [0,1]\}$.
- $R = \{\mu_R (R)/R : R \text{ is a relationship type involving entity types in } D_E \text{ and } \mu_R (E) \in [0,1]\}$.
- $A_E = \{\mu_{AE} (A)/A : A \text{ is an attribute type of entity type E and } \mu_{AE} (A) \in [0,1]\}$.
- $A_R = \{\mu_{AR} (B)/B : B \text{ is an attribute type of relationship type R and } \mu_{AR} (B) \in [0,1]\}$.

The participation constraint (Figure 3) is modeled setting that an entity E λ-participates in R if for every e of E, there exists a f in F such that $\mu_R(e,f) >= \lambda$. The cardinality constraint is shown at the end of Figure 3, where N and M are fuzzy sets. The concept of fuzzy quantifier is not used in this approach.

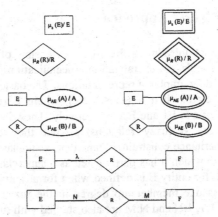

Fig. 3. ER Fuzzy notation proposed by Chen [7].

At the second level, for each entity type E and relationship type R, the sets of their values can be fuzzy sets, reflecting possible partial belonging of the corresponding values to their types. The third level of fuzzy extensions concerns with attributes and their values. For each attribute type A, any of its values can be a fuzzy set.

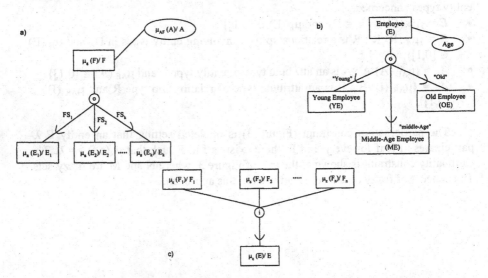

Fig. 4. Notation proposed by Chen [7]: a) An attribute-defined overlapping specialization whit FS$_i$, ∈ F(Dom(A)) at the first level, b) Employee in an overlapping specialization with the fuzzy attribute Age, c) Shared subclass intersection .

Later on, in another section, an attribute-defined specialization is defined with $FS_i \in F(Dom(A))$, where all the FS_i are fuzzy sets on $Dom(A)$, the domain of the attribute A. Graphically, this kind of attribute-defined specialization can be represented as shown in Figure 4 a). Figure 4 b) shows the entity Employee, and the fuzzy attribute Age with the labels "Young Employee", "Middle-Aged Employee", and "Old Employee". He also includes the fuzzy definition for categories and shared subclass, i.e. union and intersection (see Figure 4 c)). This proposal, makes always reference to linguistic labels, and to the trapezoidal function over an attribute or specific entity, not to a set of different attributes or different entities. This author, just like [21], establishes his data models from the attributes, and creates the object class or entity by using generalization and specialization tools.

In [7] defines that a linguistic variable X is composed of the tuple (T, U, G, M) where: T is the set of linguistic terms of X, U is the universe of discourse, G is the set of syntactic rules that generate the element T, and M is the set of semantic rules translated from T that correspond to the fuzzy subset of U. With this, he defines a conceptual model and its mathematical representation. For example, let us X = Age in Figure 5, T is generated via G by the set {Young, Middle-Aged, Old}. Each term of T is specifically handled by M by fuzzy sets. The type of correspondence between an entity and a fuzzy entity is also established, as well as the set of values that a membership degree obtains from a fuzzy set: 1:1, 1:N, N:M, incorporating fuzziness to the ER model.

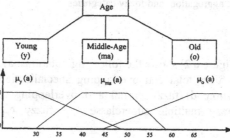

Fig 5. Linguistic variable "Age" with its corresponding values and conceptual model, according to Chen [7].

5. Proposal of Ma et al.

In [13] work with three levels of [15] incorporate in the Fuzzy Extended Entity-Relationship model (FEER model) a way of managing complex objects in the real world at a conceptual level, associating an importance degree of each of the components (attributes, entities, etc.) to the scheme. However, their definitions (of generalization, specialization, category, and aggregation) impose very restrictive conditions. They also provide an approach to mapping a FEER model to a Fuzzy Object-Oriented Database scheme (FOODB).

Figure 6 1) shows the following: a) single-valued attribute type, b) multivalued attribute type, c) disjunctive fuzzy attribute type, d) conjunctive fuzzy attribute type, e) null attribute type, f) open or null attribute type, g) disjunctive imprecise attribute type, h) conjunctive imprecise attribute type, i) entity with grade of membership, j) relationship with grade of membership, and k) attribute with grade of membership.

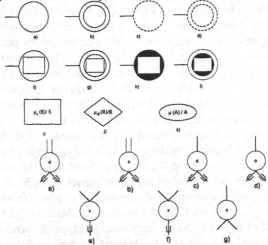

Fig. 6. FEER Notation by Ma et al. [13]: 1) Fuzzy attributes, entities, and interrelations, 2) Specialization, aggregation, and fuzzy categories

In addition, Figure 6 2) shows the following notations: a) fuzzy total and disjoint specialization, b) fuzzy total and overlapping specialization, c) fuzzy partial and disjoint specialization, d) fuzzy partial and overlapping specialization, e) fuzzy subclass with fuzzy multiple superclasses, f) fuzzy category, and g) fuzzy aggregation.

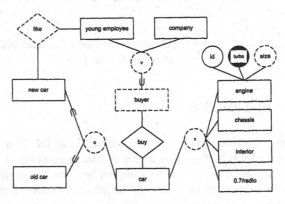

Fig. 7. Example of Ma et al. [13] notation for a car assembly company case.

Figure 7 shows an example of the EER Fuzzy model utilizing some of the notions proposed by Ma et al [13]. Thus, the "car" entity is a superclass with two fuzzy subclasses "new car" and "old car" in a overlapping specialization. Besides, the "young employee" fuzzy entity, having fuzzy instances from the "company" entity, consists of the "union" category from the fuzzy entity "buyer". Also, "young employee" has a fuzzy relationship "like". Finally, the "car" entity is an aggregation of some entities: "engine", "chassis", "interior" and "radio" (with an associated fuzzy degree of 0.7). Note that "engine" has some fuzzy attributes like *size* and *turbo*.

Ma et al. [23] introduce an extended object-oriented database model to handle imperfect as well as complex objects. They extend some major notions in object-oriented databases such as objects, classes, objects-classes relationships, subclass/superclass, and multiple inheritances.

6. Proposal of Urrutia et al.

The notation of the FuzzyEER model. It defines fuzzy attributes Type 1, Type 2 and Type 3 (Type 4 it is not shown here), and Fuzzy Relationship, Fuzzy degree associated to an attribute shown to Example 1 [24-29]. This fuzzy entity, attributes and relationship it is very common to be seeking someone with particular features for representing a specific character, which must have particular physical characteristics.

Example 1: For a real estate agency, the entity District can have the attributes (District_Id, Name, Quality). The attributes District_Id and Name are crisp. The attribute Quality of the district is defined as a fuzzy attribute Type 3, with the following labels: {Low, Regular, Good, Excellent}.

The relationship of proximity of the neighborhoods can be represented as the fuzzy relationship Close_to, which appears in Figure 8. This expresses that a proximity degree exists between any two districts.

Furthermore, the entity Landed_Property is modeled with some attributes, which can also be seen in Figure 8. Each landed property can be situated in such a place that it belongs to several districts, or that it belongs to one district but it is relatively close to another or other districts. For example, for a property, it can be indicated that its neighbourhood has the following possibility distribution (0.5/North, 1/East, 0.2/Plaza_España), indicating that it is situated in the eastern district closer to the northern district than to the España square district.

If District were an attribute of Landed_ Property it would be sufficient to define it as Type 3, to define each district as a label and establish a similarity relationship (or proximity in this case) for every two districts. But this is a special case, because District is an entity with some attributes and it is related to the Landed_Property entity, so that a property may be related to several districts (3 at most). At the same time, a district for a certain landed property may have a membership degree that measures to what extent that property belongs to that district. In our model it is represented by the degree $G^{Membership}$.

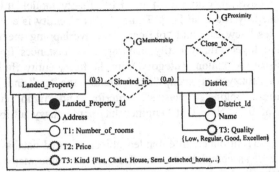

Fig. 8. Example 1, Fuzzy relationships whit Fuzzy degree associated to an attribute and Fuzzy attribute Type 1, 2 y 3.

Therefore, the fuzzy relationship Close_to in fact generates a similar structure to a Type 3 fuzzy attribute. On the other hand, the fuzzy relationship Situated_in generates a similar structure in the Landed_Property entity, as if that entity had a Type 3 fuzzy attribute called District. The model reflects that the entities Landed_Property and District are related in such a way that each landed property may be situated in a maximum of 3 districts and each one of those associations gives the degree at which that landed property belongs to the district. Due to the fact that District has several attributes it can not be used as a fuzzy attribute Type 3 of Landed_Property.

A more detailed example of this case is found in [26,28]. other types of treatment of uncertainty: Fuzzy degree to the model, fuzzy degree with its own meaning, fuzzy aggregation of entities, fuzzy aggregation of attribute are treated in [25,26,29]. In the example 2 the Fuzzy entity is shown, other entities: weak entity (existence and identification) are treated in [26, 27].

Example 2: We may consider a fuzzy entity Employee, with an attribute which stores the total number of hours worked per week. For each employee, a membership degree to the entity can be defined, in such a way that the employees will belong to the Employee type of entity with a certain degree, according to the number of weekly hours. This degree will be calculated by dividing the total number of hours worked by the minimum number of hours, so that the belonging is total. Note that this is a derived fuzzy attribute in order to obtain the membership degree to the entity.

Figure 9 models this example, where $Q(h)$ is the calculus of the degree and h is the number of hours worked per week. We can see that, $Q(h) = \min\{1, h/m\}$, where m is the minimum number of hours for the total membership.

Therefore, if $m = 35$, an employee who works in the company for 15 hours, will be considered an employee with a degree of 0.43 (the result of the division 15/35), so that this degree can be maintained in diverse calculations (selections with different aims, gratifications...).

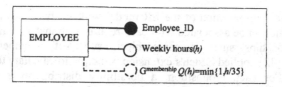

Fig. 9. Example 2, Fuzzy entity with a membership degree for each instance, which depends on the number *h* of hours worked per week.

Example 3: Let us consider an entity for Special Employees with its own attributes (extra payment, number of awards, motive...). A member of this shared subclass must be an engineer, a chief (boss) and a permanent employee. Figure 10 depicts this model with the following participation constraint: Almost all the chiefs and permanent employees must be special employees. It is interesting to note how this constraint means that almost all the chiefs and permanent employees must also be engineers (because all special employees belong to the engineer superclass).

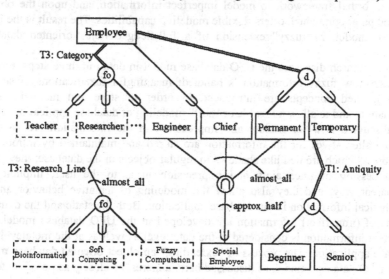

Fig. 10. Examples 3, Three Fuzzy Attribute-Defined Specializations and Fuzzy Constraints in a Shared Subclass.

On the other hand, the fuzzy completeness constraint establishes that approximately half of the employees who are engineers, chiefs and permanent employees must be special employees [24,30,31]. At the present time one has to disposition a tool CASE that it allows to model part of FuzzyEER.

7. Approaches by Other Authors

In [14] proposes an extension of the ER model with fuzzy values in the attributes, and a truth value can be associated with each relationship instance. In addition, some special relationships such as same-object, subset-of, member-of... are also introduced. In [32] applied Zadeh's extension principle to calculate the truth value of propositions. For each proposition, a possibility distribution is defined on the doubleton true, false of the classical truth values. In this way, the concepts such as entity, relationship and attribute as well as subclass, superclass, category, generalization and specialization... have been extended.

In [33] discussed of two types of imperfect information, appearing in database applications: fuzzy information representing information with inherent gradations, for which it is impossible to define sharp or precise borders, and uncertain or imprecise information, representing information which is (temporarily) incomplete due to a lack of sufficient or more precise knowledge. Dealing with this kind of imperfect information within the formal and crisp environment of a computer, is based in this paper upon the fuzzy set theory and its related possibility theory, which offers a formal framework to model imperfect information, and upon the object-oriented paradigm, which offers flexible modeling capabilities. The result is the UFO database model, a "fuzzy" extension of a full-fledged object-oriented database model.

This research discusses the UFO database model in detail in three steps. First, it is shown how fuzzy information is handled: meaningful fuzzifications of several object-oriented concepts are introduced in order to store and maintain fuzzy information, and to allow a flexible or "soft" modeling of database application. Then, it is discussed how uncertainty and imprecision in the information are handled: possible alternatives for the information are stored and maintained by introducing role object, which are tied like shadows to regular objects in the database; they allow the processing of uncertainty and imprecision in a, to the user, implicit and transparent way, and they also allow the modeling of tentative behavior and of hypothetical information in the database application. Both the static and the dynamic aspects of (imperfect) information are developed in the UFO database model, and imperfect information is considered at the data level as well as at the metalevel of a database application. The process of "extending" an object-oriented database model to the UFO database model, as discussed here, adheres, as closely as possible, to the original principles of the object-oriented paradigm, to allow a flexible and transparent, but semantically sound modeling of imprecise information. The object-oriented database model, which the extension process starts off from, adheres to the standard proposal ODMG-93, to allow for practical implementations of the UFO database model. For the same purpose, this paper also discusses an interface of the UFO database model to an extended relation database model, capable of handling some imperfect information, and for which some prototypes are already available.

In [5] propose a method for designing Fuzzy Relational Databases (FRDB) following the extension of the ER model of [15] taking special interest in converting crisp databases into fuzzy ones. The way to do so is to define n linguistic labels as n fuzzy sets over the universe of an attribute. After, each tuple in the crisp entity is transformed to up to n fuzzy tuples in a new entity (or n values in the same tuple).

Each fuzzy tuple (or value) does not store the crisp value but a linguistic label and a grade of membership giving the degree to which the corresponding crisp entity belongs to the new entity. Finally, the crisp entity and the new fuzzy entity are mapped to separate tables.

Their ER model includes fuzzy relationships as relationships with at least one attribute, namely, the membership grade. They propose FERM, a design methodology for mapping a Fuzzy ER data model to an crisp relational database in four steps (constructing a Fuzzy ER data model, transforming it to relational tables, normalization and ensuring correct interpretation of the fuzzy relational operators). They also presented the application of FERM to build a prototype of a fuzzy database for a discreet control system for a semiconductor manufacturing process.

In [5] expand the model presented in [10], focusing on their proposal for the *control processes* example. In each process imprecise values are observed, associated to linguistic labels, and every value involves a process called "DBFuzzifier construct".

8   Fuzzy Comparison of Some Fuzzy Models

In other section we discussed some conceptual models proposed by other authors. None of these investigations uses a CASE support tool proposed to help in a system design that involves uncertainty.

Table 1. Comparison of some fuzzy models: FEER, ExIFO, Fuzzy ER and FuzzyEER

Fuzzy Models/ Components	ExIFO Yazici y Merdan (1996)	Fuzzy ER Chen (1998)	FEER Ma et al. (2001)	FuzzyEER Urrutia et·al. (2003)
1. Fuzzy values in fuzzy attributes	Yes*	Yes*	Yes*	Yes
Type 1	Yes*	Yes*	Yes*	Yes Yes
Type 2	Yes*		Yes*	Yes
Type 3				Yes
Type 4				Yes
2. Fuzzy degree associated to an attribute	Yes*	Yes*	Yes*	Yes
3. Fuzzy degree assoc. to some attributes				Yes
4. Fuzzy degree with its own meaning				Yes
5. Fuzzy degree to the model	Yes*	Yes	Yes*	Yes
6. Fuzzy entities	Yes*	Yes*	Yes*	Yes
7. Fuzzy weak entity (existence)				Yes
8. Fuzzy weak entity (identification)				Yes
9. Fuzzy relationship	Yes*	Yes*	Yes*	Yes

10. Fuzzy aggregation of entities	Yes*	Yes*	Yes*	Yes
11. Fuzzy aggregation of attributes	Yes	Yes	Yes	Yes
12. Fuzzy degree in the specialization	Yes*	Yes	Yes	Yes
13. Fuzzy degree in the subclasses		Yes	Yes	Yes
14. Fuzzy constraints		Yes*		Yes
15. Graphic and CASE Tool				Yes
16. Fuzzy oriented object	Yes		Yes	

Our proposal has a tool called FuzzyCASE, which allows us to model using EER and FuzzyEER tools. It incorporates all the notations shown in this work and in other works related to the FuzzyEER model (like the fuzzy constraints which are not detailed in Table 1, but which have not been dealt with by any author in his publications).

Some of the most important models are those proposed by [13, 21]. Table 1 shows a comparison of the FuzzyEER model with those models. Each cell shows a "Yes" if the model has that component or modeling tool (even if it has another notation). In the opposite case the cell is empty. On the other hand, if the cell has a "Yes*" this means that the component has been confined in that model but with different characteristics than those of the FuzzyEER model, or, its characteristics are limited and more reduced than those of the FuzzyEER model proposed here. In general this difference is caused by the use of different types of domains and treatment of imprecision, or, by a type of degree.

The filling of the Table 1 was based in two real experiences. First of all, in [26,28] we explore the role played by a client in a Real Estate Agency located in Malaga (Spain), where the issues was the degree measures the importance with which a client is "seeking for" or "offering" a property, without taking into account the "similarity" between the two roles. In this requirement we use the four models: FEER, ExIFO, Fuzzy ER and FuzzyEER, but the only that allow representing Type 3 and 4 was last one. Second of all, the Fuzzy Autopoietic Knowledge Management (FAKM) model develop in [15][1], uses a FuzzyEER model to represent Knowledge attribute Type 1, Type 2, and Type 3 related at the quality control process of the

---

[1] The aim of the model is to integrate the system theory of living systems, the cybernetic theory of viable systems, and the autopoiesis theory of the autopoietic systems, with the hope of going beyond the knowledge management models that are based, among other things, on Cartesian dualism cognition/action (i.e., on a model of symbolic cognition as the processing of representational information in a knowledge management system). Instead, the FAKM model uses a dualism organization/structure to define an autopoietic system in a socio-technical approach [15].

paper in a manufacturing company located within the Maule Region south of Santiago in Chile, studied in [26].

9 Conclusions and Future Lines

Fuzzy databases have been widely studied with the aim of allowing the storage of imprecise or fuzzy data and the imprecise queries about the existing data [34,35].

However, the application of fuzzy logic to databases has traditionally paid little attention to the problem of the conceptual model. Few investigations study a complete and exhaustive notation of the many characteristics, which may be improved using fuzzy logic. The FuzzyEER model intends to do so and in this study we have focused on the following: types of fuzzy attributes (T1, T2, T3 and T4), fuzzy degrees associated or not with different items and with different meanings, degrees with respect to the model, fuzzy aggregations, fuzzy entities and relationships, fuzzy weak entities and degrees in a specialization.

All these concepts allow to extend the EER model to a fuzzy FuzzyEER model [26]. Therefore it may be stated that a data model which contemplates fuzzy data, allows us to represent a type of data in an information system, which the traditional systems do not deal with and so, this information is lost in such systems. This reduces the risk of obtaining empty answers from queries in the database, since fuzzy logic allows us to use a finer scale of discrimination, as it considers the interval [0,1] instead of the set {0,1}. In other words, it allows us to recover instances that would not be obtained using a precise method, as they only partially meet the imposed conditions. Furthermore, the set of instances can be ordered according to the level at which it satisfies the conditions. This leads the way for creating queries and operations, which would be non-viable in a traditional system

Some of the FuzzyEER notations may be used in a FSQL (Fuzzy SQL) server, which is an extension of SQL for permitting fuzzy queries and operations [34].

In the Table 1 it has been shown that the model FuzzyEER proposed by the authors of this paper, allows to model using the components of EER a treatment of uncertainty: degree and attributes that generate outlines that model in good part the uncertainty using fuzzy logic.

Finally, we think that this paper gives an interesting overview of the subject, first step to establish a formal approach to deal with uncertainty in fuzzy relational databases. As a future line we hope to get this formal approach, nevertheless, for the moment we have in [15, 26,28] two serious works related.

References

1. M. Umano and S. Fukami. Fuzzy Relational Algebra for Possibility-Distribution-Fuzzy-Relational Model of Fuzzy Data. Journal of Intelligent Information System, 3, pp. 7-28. (1994)

2. A. Motro. Management of Uncertainty in Database System, Modern Database System the Object Model, Interoperability and Beyond, Won Kim, editor, Addison-wesley publishing Company (1995).

3. A. Zvieli and P. Chen. ER Modeling and Fuzzy Databases. 2nd International Conference on Data Engineering, pp. 320-327. (1986).

4. N. Marín, Pons O., Vila M.A.. Fuzzy Types: "A New Concept of Type for Managing Vague Structures". International Journal of Intelligent Systems, 15, pp. 1061-1085 (2000).

5. N.Chaudhry, J. Moyne J., and E.A. Rundensteiner; An Extended Database Design Methodology for Uncertain Data Management. Information Sciences, 121, pp. 83-112. (1999).

6. B.P. Buckles and F.E. Petry. Uncertainty Models in Information and Database Systems. Information Sciences, 11, pp. 77-87. (1985).

7. G. Chen. Fuzzy Logic in Data Modelling, Semantics Constraints, and Databases Design. The Kluwer International Series on Advances in Database Systems. Series Editor A.K. Elmagarmid, U.S.A (1998).

8. E.E. Kerre and G.Q. Chen. An Overview of Fuzzy Data Models. In Studies in Fuzziness: Fuzziness in Database Management Systems, pp. 23-41. Eds. P. Bosc and J. Kacprzyk. Physica-Verlag (1995).

9. A. Yazici and R. George. Fuzzy Database Modeling. Physica-Verlag (Studies in Fuzziness and Soft Computing), New York (1999).

10. N. Chaudhry, J. Moyne, and E.A. Rundensteiner. A Design Methodology for Databases with Uncertain Data. 7th International Working Conference on Scientific and Statistical Database Management, pp. 32-41, Charlottesville, VA (1994).

11. G.Q. Chen, E.E. Kerre. Extending ER/EER Concepts Towards Fuzzy Conceptual Data Modeling. IEEE International Conference on Fuzzy Systems, 2, pp. 1320-1325 (1998).

12. E.E. Kerre and G. Chen. Fuzzy Data Modeling at a Conceptual Level: Extending ER/EER Concepts. In "Knowledge Management in Fuzzy Databases", pp. 3-11. Eds. O. Pons, M.A. Vila and J. Kacprzyk. Ed. Physica-Verlag (2000).

13. Z.M. Ma, W.J. Zhang, W.Y. Ma, and Q. Chen. Conceptual Design of Fuzzy Object-Oriented Databases Using Extended Entity-Relationship Model. International Journal of Intelligent System, 16(6). pp. 697-711 (2001).

14. E. Ruspini. Imprecision and Uncertainty in the Entity-Relationship Model, In Fuzzy Logic in Knowledge Engineering, Eds. H. Prade and C.V. Negoita. Verlag TUV Rhein-land, pp.18-22. (1986)

15. L. Jiménez. Gestion des connaissances imparfaites dans les organisations industrielles : cas d'une industrie manufacturière en Amérique Latine. Ph. Doctoral Thesis, Institut National Polytechnique de Toulouse, Toulouse, France. http://ethesis.inp-toulouse.fr/archive/00000140/ (2005)

16. C. Batini, S. Ceri, S. Navathe. Diseño Conceptual de Bases de Datos. Addison_Wesley/Díaz de Santos. (1994).

17. T. Connolly, C. Begg. Database System, a Practical Approach to Design, Implementation and Management. Third edition, Addison Wesley (2001).

18. A. De Miguel, M. Piattini, E. Marcos. Diseño de Bases de Datos Relacionales. Rama (1999).

19. R. Elmasri and S.B. Navathe. Fundamentals of Database Systems. Addison-Wesley, Third Edition (2000).

20. J. Galindo, A. Urrutia, R. Carrasco, and M. Piattini. Fuzzy Constraints Using the Enhanced Entity-Relationship Model. Proceedings published by IEEE-CS Press of XXI International Conference of the Chilean Computer Science Society (SCCC 2001),   pp.   86-94.   Punta   Arenas   (Chile). http://computer.org/proceedings/sccc/1396/13960086abs.htm (2001).

21. A. Yazici and O. Merdan. Extending IFO Data Model for Uncertain Information. 4th International Conference on Information Processing and Management of Uncertainty, IPMU'96, pp. 1283-1282 (vol. III). Granada (Spain) (1996).

22. A. Yazici and A. Cinar. Conceptual Modeling for the Design of Fuzzy Object Oriented Database. In Knowledge Management in Fuzzy Databases, Eds. O. Pons, M.A.Vila and J. Kacprzyk. Ed. Physica-Verlag, pp. 12-35 (2000).

23. Z.M. Ma, W.J. Zhang, and W.Y. Ma. Extending Object-Oriented Databases for Fuzzy Information Modeling. Information Systems, 29, pp. 421-435 (2004).

24. J. Galindo, A. Urrutia, and M. Piattini. Fuzzy Databases: Modeling, Design and Implementation. Idea Group Publishing Hershey, USA (2005).

25. A. Urrutia, J. Galindo, and L. Jiménez. "Extensión del Modelo Conceptual EER para Representar Tipos de Datos Difusos". I+D Computación, Noviembre de 2002, Volumen 1, número 2, ISSN:1665-238X. http://www.sd-cenidet.com.mx/Revista, (México) (2002).

26. A. Urrutia. Definición de un Modelo Conceptual para Bases de Datos Difusas. Ph. Doctoral Thesis, University of Castilla-La Mancha (Spain) (2003).

27. A. Urrutia, J. Galindo, and M. Piattini. *Propuesta de un Modelo Conceptual Difuso.* Libro de Ingeniería de Software, Ediciones Cyted Ritos2, ISBN;84-9602307-9, pp 51-76 (2003).

28. A. Urrutia and J. Galindo. Algunos Aspectos del Modelo Conceptual EER Difuso: Aplicación al Caso de una Agencia Inmobiliaria, XI Congreso Español sobre Tecnologías y Lógica Fuzzy (ESTYLF'2002), pp. 359-364. León (Spain) (2002).

29. A. Urrutia, J. Galindo, and M. Piattini. Modeling Data Using Fuzzy Attributes. IEEE Computer Society Press, XXII International Conference of the Chilean Computer Science Society (SCCC 2002), pp. 117-123. Copiapó (Chile). ISBN: O-7695-1867-2 ISSN: 1522-4902 (2002).

30. J. Galindo, A. Urrutia, M. Piattini: "Fuzzy Aggregations and Fuzzy Specializations in Fuzzy EER Model". Chapter VI in "Advanced Topics in Database Research", Vol. 3, pp. 105-126. Ed. Keng Siau. Idea Group, Inc.. (2004) http://www.idea-group.com

31. Galindo J., Urrutia A., Carrasco R., Piattini M.: "Relaxing Constraints in Enhanced Entity-Relationship Models using Fuzzy Quantifiers". IEEE Trans. on Fuzzy Systems. pp. 780-796 (2004).

32. R. M. Vandenberghe. An Extended Entity-Relationship Model for Fuzzy Databases Based on Fuzzy Truth Values, Proceeding of 4th International Fuzzy Systems Association World Congress, IFSA'91, Brussels, pp. 280-283 (1991).

33. N. Van Gyseghem and R. De Caluwe. Overview of the UFO Database Model, Proceeding of EUFIT96, September 2-5, Aachen, Germany, pp.858-862 (1996).

34. J. Galindo. Tratamiento de la Imprecisión en Bases de Datos Relacionales: Extensión del Modelo y Adaptación de los SGBD Actuales. Ph. Doctoral Thesis, University of Granada (Spain). (www.lcc.uma.es) (1999).

35. F.E. Petry. Fuzzy Databases: Principles and Applications (with chapter contribution by Patrick Bosc). International Series in Intelligent Technologies. Ed. H.J. Zimmermann. Kluwer Academic Publ. (KAP) (1996).

Reinventing the Future: A Study of the Organizational Mind

Isabel Ramos, João Álvaro Carvalho

Information Systems Department, University of Minho, Campus de
Azurém, 4800-058 Guimarães, Portugal {iramos, jac}@dsi.uminho.pt

Abstract. This paper describes the concept of the self- and meta-representation capabilities of the organization, a constituent of what we call the organizational mind. Our claim is that these capabilities are responsible for the emergence of a collective self that is of central importance in the formation of the organizational identity. These capabilities are relevant to the information systems field, as Information Technology applications play a central role in the support of those representational capabilities. The paper presents a summary of a theoretical perspective that supports a research project aimed at developing a framework to guide managers diagnosing identity dysfunctions resulting from impaired representational capabilities of the organization.

1 Introduction

This paper focuses on the self- and meta-representation capabilities of organizations, a constituent of what we call the organizational mind. Our claim is that these capabilities are responsible for the emergence of a collective self that is of central importance in the formation of organizational identity. These capabilities are relevant to the information systems field as Information Technology (IT) applications play a central role on the support of those representational capabilities.

The idea that an organization forms and uses representations of itself and of relevant external entities with which it interacts as well as meta-representations derived from self-representations, is based on an analogous phenomenon occurring in the human mind. Human representational capabilities are herein taken as a metaphor to explain the organization's ability to think and act as a coherent whole – a collective and distributed self.

Please use the following format when citing this chapter:

Ramos, I., Carvalho, J.Á., 2006, in IFIP International Federation for Information Processing, Volume 214, The Past and Future of Information Systems: 1976–2006 and Beyond, eds. Avison, D., Elliot, S., Krogstie, J., Pries-Heje, J., (Boston: Springer), pp. 219–230.

Although the exploration of this metaphor might demand empirical work, we believe that it constitutes a plausible and promising foundation to be applied in organizations for diagnosing the origins of performance problems arising from identity dysfunctions and for defining structural requirements for successful performance.

Section 2 provides the context for the representational capabilities of the organization – the organizational mind framework. It is not the purpose of this paper to present the details of current knowledge about the human mind developed in Neurosciences due to the limited space of a paper. Thus, in section 2.1, we provide only an overview of the main concepts supporting the metaphor from which we will develop the organizational mind framework. Section 2.2, we identify specific capabilities of the human mind that will be used to locate and study equivalent capabilities of the organization. These organizational capabilities will be approached as complex collective constructs that will be incrementally developed and validated in multilevel research and theory development [1].

Section 3 details the concept of self- and meta- representation capabilities and states its relevance for organizations, the first multilevel construct to be studied. In Section 3, we briefly describe how current and emerging IT may be used to leverage the representational capabilities of the organization.

2   Representational Capabilities and the Organizational Mind

The representational capabilities of organizations are only one aspect of a comprehensive framework we designate as the organizational mind that we aim to develop further and whose usefulness we expect to demonstrate in a broader and interdisciplinary research program. The organizational mind concept will be developed and operationalized by defining the organizational equivalent to human perception, cognition, emotion, and consciousness. This concept will relate organizational aspects such as structure, human resources management, power, culture, strategy, change management, leadership, innovation, learning, and IT applications. The interconnection of all these aspects may lead to an integrated view of distributed perception, cognition, emotion, and consciousness in organizations.

Our approach does not imply reifying the organizational mind but to use those human-mind-centered concepts metaphorically to establish the basis for an explanation of how the organization's members collectively gather information from the environment and from its interior, interpret it, build an image of the organization as a whole, recognize the organization's problems and needs, project its action and construct its future.

2.1 Human Mind

According to scientific knowledge produced in the neurosciences (e.g., [2-5]), the human mind emerges from the brain devices that support the mental processes of:

Perception. This mental process enables human beings to know external objects and events, events happening inside the body, mental objects such as thoughts and modes of thinking, and of the self in relation to perceived physical or mental objects.

Cognition. This mental process includes aspects such as vigil, production of thoughts, attention, memory, language, and reason.

Emotion. This mental process is built from simple and automatic responses to competent stimuli. Emotions are specific repertoires of action that help an individual to achieve the circumstances conducive to survival and well-being.

Consciousness. This mental process enables the knowing of an object or action that can be ascribed to the self. The nuclear consciousness provides the individual with a sense of the self, the now, and the here. The extended consciousness provides a complex sense of self, corresponding to an individual's identity. Consciousness permits also the knowledge of an individual's history, and his or her past and anticipated future, and enables him or her to stay alert to the surrounding world.

In conjunction, these mental processes give rise to mental phenomena such as:

Feelings. Mental images that assist in making choices regarding self-preservation. They are the expression of emotions at the mind level. Feelings help us to solve non-standard problems involving creativity, judgment, and decision-making, requiring the display and manipulation of vast amounts of knowledge. Feelings can help or impede learning and recall.

Learning. The construction of new knowledge about the world that surrounds an individual and her or his role in that world, and about the self and its own potential for action and interaction. It is intimately related with life experience. Learning changes the way the individual perceives, thinks, and behaves in order to accommodate new experiences.

Intelligence. The capacity to manipulate knowledge for the planning and execution of new answers to any problem perceived as endangering survival or well-being.

Creativity. The capacity to produce new ideas and new things. It is rooted in the cognitive functions of memory, reason, and language and is informed by the revelations of consciousness.

The above processes and phenomena support human action and its adaptive characteristics They demand the existence of representations that enable humans to exercise self-control in social situations and to use the "I" in a fluent and correct way, know the current body configuration and status, engage in self-imagery, identify feelings such as happiness, and show sympathy with the distress of others [2].

Such representations include (i) the internal milieu and viscera via chemical and neural pathways, (ii) musculoskeletal structures, (iii) autobiographical events, (iv) causal and simulation models of the relevant aspects of a body's movable parts, the relations between them, the relations to its sensory input, and its goals, (v) causal and simulation models of the social world in which it finds itself, and (vi) where one is in space-time and the social order.

Disturbances in the self- and meta- representation capabilities of humans may result in inability to acquire new knowledge, loss of autobiographical information; inability to recognize thoughts as one's own thoughts, inability to recognize body parts as one's own, inability to inhibit unwise impulses, personality changes, reckless in decision-making, and social insensitivity.

Representational damages impair identity [6]. Identity enables the integration of body-state signals, the evaluation of options, and the choice-making. Thus, humans are able to act as a coherent whole, not as a group of independent sub-systems with competing interests. Identity also permits the self/non-self distinction, and enables to distinguish between inner-world representations and outer-world representations and to build a meta-representational model of the relation between the outer and the inner identities.

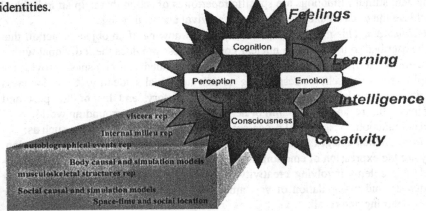

Fig. 1: Mental processes and supporting self- and meta- representations

2.2 Organizational Mind: An Evolving Concept

Terms such as knowledge management, organizational memory and identity, business intelligence, and organizational learning are becoming usual in the discourse of the social and organizational sciences. Each presupposes a parallel between the human mind and the organizational capability of intelligent manipulation of knowledge to support the planning and execution of new and better solutions to problems concerning survival and well-being. However, when the literature in the fields conveyed by those terms is analyzed, this parallel is lost in favor of sociological, economic, and technological views, often explored separately.

One of the earliest references to the term "organizational mind" is provided by Ian Mitroff, in his book "Stakeholders of the Organizational Mind" [7]. The organizational mind is equated with the collective thinking of organizational managers and the consequential management and organizing practices. In his book, Mitroff relates the organizational types with the personality types and ego states of top managers.

Other authors have brought the concept of organizational mind into relation with a shared understanding of strategic problems, competitive conditions, and the internal and external environments they face [8].

In general, this initial view presents the organizational mind as the global information processing system of the organization, which includes human and technological processors. This global system permits the access, transformation and delivery of information from a variety of perspectives.

This view has evolved by integrating important insights from Psychology and Social Constructionism. Weick and Roberts [6] state that the heedful interactions between its members generate the collective mind of an organization. In order to be effective, newcomers must be socialized into the collective mind. The collective mind emerges from the joint production of thoughts (cognition) in the process of heedful action and interaction. This view brought to consideration organizational mindfulness, considered important to organizational learning ([9,10]). Organizational mindfulness is local and situated, involves thinking in "real time" and is simultaneous with the execution of action. Thus, it involves both action and cognition. Organizational mindfulness enables the organization, as a whole, to reveal new opportunities in the ongoing activity and keep its action close to the defined plans and expectations.

Another view of the organizational mind emerged from the claims of complex systems theory [11]. The organization is seen as a self-organizing, adaptive, nonlinear, and complex system showing the following properties [12]:

Connectivity: resources, human and non-human, are interconnected; managers should think global and act locally.

Indeterminacy: although reality abides the law of causation, knowledge of the effect of any particular cause is an approximation and never a fact that can be known in advance; the how of change must be constructed as the change unfolds.

Dissipation: reality is the product and the framework of thinking, action and interaction. It is in permanent motion.

Emergence: Thinking, action, and interaction are continuously changing and producing emergent phenomena; managers should let go of command and control.

Consciousness: it is an emergent phenomenon in organizations and comprises the collective consciousness of every individual within the bounds of the organization.

The above properties support the emergence of organizational mind. The organizational mind is ever in motion. It is an emergent, distributed and transactional phenomenon conceiving shared thoughts and feelings, shaping desires, assembling plans, evaluating experience, interpreting perceptions, and initiating actions. Leadership is a discretionary role open for every employee rather than a fixed privilege of a particular hierarchical position in the organization.

The chaordic view of the organizational mind is often criticized for its lack of empirical research and by not providing an useful operationalization of the theoretical claims. Another critic is that there is a tendency to reify the organizational mind, seeking the social mechanisms responsible for the emergence of a new being or a meta-consciousness independent from the individual consciousnesses that give rise to it.

The above theoretical views of the organizational mind advance some important explanations for collective and distributed cognition and action in organizations, but they have not been successful in providing methodological tools to study the working of organizational mind or to improve its intelligence, learning ability or creativity. We consider that recent knowledge on human mind developed in Neurosciences may provide those methodological tools.

The next paragraphs of this section offer a first glance at the concepts that can be used to develop the organizational mind concept. This concept can then be used to develop the necessary tools to diagnose possible dysfunctions in the organizational mind and to improve its intelligence. Some of the ideas here expressed are already being explored separately by some authors ([13-15]).

The organizational mind comprises processes and phenomena corresponding to those found in the human mind. It is our expectation that the organizational mind constitutes an interesting and useful framework to assist the study of how collective experience is understood and memorized, highlighting the events and objects that organizations choose to pay attention to. It has also the potential to assist in understanding the language elements upon which the organizational experience is constructed and what processes enable organizations to reason about that experience. By constructing representations about itself and its environment, an organization, as a collective self, creates a sense of meaning about the world and its action in that same world. The organizational mind framework can be used to improve an organization's capabilities for survival and also to guide its members' search for their collective well-being.

Using the organizational mind framework, researchers and managers will be able to evaluate an organization's mental capabilities of:

- *Intelligence* – how its members use the available knowledge to plan and implement solutions to problems and environmental challenges, ensuring the organization's survival and well-being;
- *Learning ability* – how their members collectively accommodate new experience by changing the way they perceive, think and behave;
- *Creativity* – the organizations' capability to produce new ideas and new things to ensure a dynamic adaptation to the internal and environmental challenges and opportunities.

To consider the organizational mind concept presupposes to view an organization as a whole capable of coherent behavior and of holding some sense of a collective self.

2.3 Representational Capabilities of Organizations: A Collective Construct

Research constructs can be thought of as "conceptual notions whose existence must be inferred from more observable actions or features of an entity" [1]. Constructs that describe phenomena observed at the level of any interdependent and goal-directed combination of individuals, groups, organizational units, organizations or industries are collective constructs.

Collective constructs may be measured at various levels of analysis. The most elementary unit of analysis of any collective construct is the individual behavioural act. Individual action is influenced by a multitude of situational and contextual factors. Within a social system, the action of individuals meets each other in space and time, resulting in interpersonal interaction. "As interaction occurs within larger groups of individuals, a structure of collective action emerges that transcends the individuals who constitute the collective" [1]. In organizations, human interaction is mediated or made possible by IT applications. Therefore, IT applications are a key element of the structure of collective action.

A collective construct may manifest itself at several levels of analysis, presenting similarity of function but not of structure. The function of a construct refers to its causal outputs or effects. Functional analysis is the assessment of a construct's outputs in the organizational system.

The self- and meta- representation capability of organizations is a collective construct describing a phenomenon that can be observed at several levels of analysis. Individuals create representations of themselves as members of the organization they work for, their work interactions, their job history, [mental and material] models of the organization's social systems in which they are integrated, and their place in space-time and social order.

The actions of individuals are constrained and guided by the above representations. In the process of acting, individuals also create and transform representations. At the group level, collective action emerges that transcends the individuals who constitute the collective. Collective action that becomes recurrent, materially bounded and situated may be called practice [16]. This practice is mediated or enacted by IT applications.

As groups try to make sense of their actions within the context of the organization, they create and transform shared representations of themselves as social systems working within a larger social system, the organization. These are collective self- and meta-representations mediating the perceptions of group members and the understanding of their reality [16].

The organization is the highest level of analysis considered in our research. The structure of the construct is similar to the structure of the construct at the level of organizational groups. The only difference is that we have to consider groups and inter-groups practices and representations as well as representations of relevant entities outside the organization and of organizational interactions with those entities.

Self- and meta-representation capabilities at all levels in the organization enable the acquisition of new knowledge, production and retention of autobiographical information, recognition of thoughts as one's own thoughts, define boundaries and recognize the constituent of one's social body, inhibit unwise impulses, create a sense of personality continuity, produce coherent decision making and create social sensitivity. The representational capabilities are the main holders of identity.

One last point that must be considered in our research is that, at all levels of analysis, the process of self- representing is shaped by contextual dimensions such as structural, political and symbolic characteristics of the larger social system within which the object of analysis operates.

The organizational self- and meta- representation capabilities imply that the organization is capable of forming and using representations of itself and of the interactions with relevant external entities (self-representations), and representations built upon self-representations (meta-representations). Self- and meta-representations address (i) what is "perceived", moment-by-moment, as happening in its internal and external environments; (ii) its envisaged future; (iii) past experience; (iv) its structure, causal, and process models of its internal workings; (v) structure, causal and process models of its social and economic environment; (vi) presumed image held by relevant stakeholders about the organization.

Accordingly, disturbances in the representational capabilities of an organization may result in inability to acquire new knowledge, loss of autobiographical information, inability to define shared insights, concepts, and motivations, inability to recognize organizational units as integrating parts of a whole, inability to agree to sanctioned action, inability to set up consistent patterns of decision and action, and environmental and social insensitivity.

Organizational identity may also be impaired by representational damages ([6,17]). Although there are obvious and fundamental differences between how identity and representations are implemented in humans and organizations [18], there are also important conceptual similarities that can be explored, contributing to a more precise conceptualization of the organizational identity [19].

3   Why Monitoring the Representational Capabilities of the Organization is Important

In humans, the representational capabilities are essential to intelligent behavior since they are the foundation of human identity. Likewise, we can assume these capabilities are essential to organizational intelligent behavior because they are the foundation of organizational identity.

An organization's representational capabilities are distributed by different organizational actors, both human and automatic. Furthermore, as these representations have multiple usages they are relevant to very different organizational activities and phenomena. Finally, the different nature of these representations imply different ways of creating, storing and retrieving them..

All these aspects of organizations' representational capabilities justify that they are cared for in organizations. This is actually already happening. However, the organizational activities/processes that deal with representational capabilities are independent from each other, therefore concealing the common aspects and object of these different activities.

3.1 Organizational Identity

Organizational identity has been the focus of much work in organizational sciences, psychology, and management sciences. Organizational identity is particularly relevant since our research addresses a key component of identity formation, the self- and meta- representations required for the emergence of a collective and distributed sense of self. While this is a reasonably unexplored organizational phenomenon, some efforts have already been developed ([18-22]).

- *Self-categorization theory* focus on the self-categorization of individuals as members of groups;
- *Symbolic interactionism* focuses the construction of the self from the representations individuals and groups hold about the perceptions of others.
- *Studies of communities of practice, role playing theory, structuration theory, and communication theory* focus the construction of self-representations through interaction inside and with the outside environment of the organization.
- *Narrative and discourse analysis* focus the elicitation of self-representations and their reformulation through organizational dialogues.
- *Institutional theory* focuses stable self-representations.

- *Boundary phenomenology* addresses the concept of autopoietic unity as a metaphor to explore issues of organizational identity and integrity.
- *Theories of shared mental models and transactive memories* focus how self-representations are held in organizations.
- *Information Systems theories* have been highlighting the requirements for systems and technological architectures that effectively support representations and meta-representations of the collective self.

3.2   Information Technology Support to Organizational Representation Capabilities

IT applications constitute one of the key components of the representational capabilities of an organization. This section provides a first approach to the IT's role in leveraging an organization's ability to create, preserve, and transform representations. Table 1 presents some types of IT applications and the representations that they deal with. For the purposes of this presentation, we regrouped self- and meta- representations in 5 types.

Moment-by-moment organizational experience: the transactions, operations, measurements, and communication happening in all levels of the organization which are mediated or enacted by the system. *Envisaged future:* goals, strategies, forecasts, and objectives stored or defined with the help of the system. *Past experience:* patterns of behavior, decision or interaction with stakeholders elicited by the system. *Structural, process, and causal models:* models of the organization itself, models of the organization's business and market, and models of the economic, social or political environments. These models include the relevant parts of each of those domains, the relations between the parts, the relations of the parts with the inputs of the domain, and the domain's goals. These models may be produced by information systems and used to simulate and predict behavior as well as to define the appropriate action to avoid or solve problems and to take advantage of opportunities. *Organizational image:* the image that organizational members believe relevant stakeholders, business partners or competitors have of their organization and that information systems help shaping.

Table 1. Representations created or handle by information systems used in organizations

	Moment-by-moment experience	Envisaged future	Past experience	Models	Perceived organizational image
Just-in-time inventory systems	X			X	
Value Chain Mng Systems	X			X	X
E-business Systems	X		X		X
Decision Support Systems		X		X	
Business Intelligence Systems			X	X	
Human Capital Systems		X	X	X	
Systems to Support Communication	X				X
Collaborative Systems	X	X	X		

Just in time inventory systems hold representations of the innards of an organization, the stored items and their quantities as well as the needs for new items or their arrival. At the heart of these systems is a certain model of supplier behavior and of the organization's interaction with suppliers.

Value chain management systems hold representations of the internal workings of the organization and its interactions with suppliers and customers. They can also elicit patterns of behavior and of interaction with suppliers and clients, and simulate their reactions to different organizational initiatives. Finally, these systems help organizational members, either intentionally or unintentionally, projecting an image of their organization.

E-business systems register transactions and communication. They also serve as gateways to the internal workings of the organization, thus helping to define its boundaries. They help form a view of the past experience of the organization by linking different kinds of stored representations. E-business systems also help shaping the organizational image.

Decision support systems, by allowing the simulation of decisions, help organizational members envisage possible futures for the organization or of an organizational unit. They are rooted in causal models of the organization or relevant domains of its environment. More sophisticated systems of this kind generate these models.

Business Intelligence Systems, with their typical data mining tools, support the elicitation of the past experience of an organization and generate causal models.

Systems that support communication register and deliver representations of the thinking and action, both of organizational members and external entities that communicate with them.

Collaborative systems support the moment-by-moment thinking and action of work groups, helping them to form views of the organizational past and decide for the future.

The categories of systems included in the table were chosen for their widespread use, facilitating the understanding of their role in the creation and transformation of organizational self- representations. In our future work, we intend to develop a systematic mapping of the information systems categories together with the representations they handle. The table also emphasizes the possibility of an organization having several, possibly conflicting, representations of the same object, either physical or conceptual.

Our research will present new ways of using present IT to leverage the representational capabilities of an organization, therefore improving the collective capabilities of problem solving, decision making, adaptation to changing conditions, and construction of a common future.

4   Conclusion

This paper focuses on one of the aspects of what we called the organizational mind: the self- and meta- representation capabilities of the organization. We described the concept as defined for the human mind and tried to build a bridge to what may be similar capabilities in organizations. In doing this we are assuming that such organizational capabilities are responsible for the emergence of a collective self which is of key importance for the ability of the organization to act coherently and intelligently in response to internal or external threats to its survival and well-being.

In future research, we intend to verify the propositions we are assuming in this paper, namely, that it is possible to define the requirements of healthy representational capabilities for the organization and that disturbance in these capabilities may lead to identity dysfunctions that negatively affect the organization's performance.

At the Information Systems Department of the University of Minho (Portugal), we are starting a research project within the lines of thought described in this paper. The objectives of the project are:

1. To define the concepts of "organizational self-representation capability" and "organizational meta-representation capability", using the human capability for self-representation and meta-representation as the supporting metaphor.
2. To define the structural, socio-cultural, and technological components of the above concepts in organizations.
3. To design an architecture for the organizational key components of the concept.
4. To develop key performance indicators to measure the maturity of the self- and meta- representation capabilities of the organization.
5. To define a model linking the organizational representational capabilities to the emergence of organizational identity.
6. To create a method and a prototype of a supporting computer based tool to assist (a) the diagnosis of potential identity dysfunctions related with problems in representational capabilities of the organization, and (b) the planning of effective interventions to reduce the diagnosed dysfunctions.

References

1. F. P. Morgeson and D. A. Hofmann. The structure and function of collective constructs: implications for multilevel research and theory development. Academy of Management Review 24(2): 249-265. (1999).

2. P.S. Churchland. Self-representation in nervous systems. Science 296: 308-310. (2002).

3. A. Damásio. The feeling of what happens: body and emotion in the making of consciousness. New York, Harcourt Brace. (1999).

4. A. Damásio. Looking for Spinoza: joy, sorrow, and the feeling brain. London, William Heinemann. (2003).

5. S. Greenfield. The Private Life of the Brain: emotions, consciousness, and the secret of the self. New York, John Wiley & Sons, Inc. (2000).

6. K.E. Weick and K.H. Roberts. Collective mind in organizations: heedful interrelating on flight decks. Administrative Science Quarterly 38(3): 357-381. (1993).

7. I. Mitroff. Stakeholders of the Organizational Mind. San Francisco, Jossey-Bass. (1983).

8. C.R. Schwenk. Strategic Decision Making. Journal of Management 21(3): 471-493. (1995).

9. D.A. Levinthal and C. Rerup. Bridging Mindful and Less Mindful Perspectives on Organizational Learning. (2004).

10. P. Pawlowsky. Management science and organizational learning. Handbook of Organisational Learning and Knowledge. M. Dierkes, A. Berthoin-Antal, J. Child and I. Nonaka, Oxford University Press. (2001).

11. E.C. Hoogerwerf and A.-M. Poorthuis. The network multilogue: A Chaos approach to organizational design. Journal of Organizational Change Management 15(4): 382-390. (2002).

12. F.M.V. Eijnatten and L. W. L. Simonse. Organizing for Creativity, Quality and Speed in Product Creation Processes. Quality And Reliability Engineering International 15: 411-416. (1999).

13. B. Sen. Organisational mind: Response to a paradigm shift in the Indian business environment. International Journal of Human Resources Development and Management. 3(1). (2003).

14. T. Ambler and C. Styles. Connecting Firm-level Learning with Performance, Center for Marketing, London Business School. (2002).

15. C.B. Gibson. From Knowledge Accumulation to Accommodation: cicles of collective cognition in work groups. Journal of Organizational Behavior 22: 121-134. (2001).

16. E. Vaast and G. Walsham. Representations and actions: the transformation of work practices with IT use. Information and Organization 15: 65-89. (2005).

17. Hatch, M. J. and M. Schultz "The dynamics of organizational identity." Human relations 55(8): 989-1018. (2002).

18. R.J. Boland, R. V. Tenkasi, et al. Designing Information Technology to Support Distributed Cognition. Organization Science 5(3): 456-475. (1994).

19. D. Ravasi and J. v. Rekom. Key issues in organizational identity and identification theory. Corporate Reputation Review 6(2): 118-132. (2003).

20. V, Anand, C. C. Manz, et al. An organizational memory approach to information management. The academy of management review 23(4): 797-809. (1998).

21. H.R. Nemati, D. M. Steiger, et al. Knowledge warehouse: an architectural integration of knowledge management, decision support, artificial intelligence and data warehousing. Decision Support Systems 33: 143-161. (2002).

22. Y. Merali. The role of boundaries in knowledge processes. European Journal of Information Systems 11(1). (2002).

Semiotic Engineering – A New Paradigm for Designing Interactive Systems

Clarisse Sieckenius de Souza

SERG – Semiotic Engineering Research Group
Departamento de Informática, PUC-Rio
Rua Marquês de São Vicente, 225
22453-901 Rio de Janeiro, RJ – Brazil
clarisse@inf.puc-rio.br
http://www.inf.puc-rio.br/~clarisse

Abstract. This paper presents semiotic engineering – a semiotic theory of HCI. The theory has the advantage to integrate *back end* and *front end* design and development perspectives into a single metacommunication process that affects the user's experience and, ultimately, the success of any system. By means of illustrative examples, we show the kinds of effects that can be achieved with the theory, and discuss why a semiotic perspective is relevant for the future of information systems.

1 Introduction

This paper presents the gist of semiotic engineering, a semiotic theory of human-computer interaction (HCI) 0. Back in 1980, Ives et al. proposed a model to organize Information Systems (IS) research 0. They structured the world of IS in three layers: the external environment, the organizational environment, and the IS environment. In their view, as a discipline, IS should investigate three embedded environments within the IS environment, namely: the user environment, the IS development environment, and the IS operation environment. Although at the time HCI did not exist as a discipline, in retrospect we see that in the last two decades, the contribution of HCI to IS research comes from complementary perspectives. From *inside* the IS environment, HCI sets out to discover, organize and instrumentalize knowledge about the user environment. From the *outside*, HCI sets out to provide knowledge about how the whole IS environment interacts with the organizational environment and the external environment.

The specific contribution of semiotic engineering to IS design and evaluation is twofold. First, it has the ability to integrate the perspectives of back end and front

Please use the following format when citing this chapter:

de Souza, C.S., 2006, in IFIP International Federation for Information Processing, Volume 214, The Past and Future of Information Systems: 1976–2006 and Beyond, eds. Avison, D., Elliot, S., Krogstie, J., Pries-Heje, J., (Boston: Springer), pp. 231–242.

end development activities, and to let the users know and enjoy the benefits of all the intellectual efforts that eventually crystallize into *software artifacts*. Second, it has the ability to frame the users' experience within increasingly broader contexts of communication – from basic *user-system* dialogue, to contemporary *user-in-cyberspace* activity. Bearing on key concepts drawn from the work of such semioticians as Peirce 0 and Eco 0, this theory views all instances of HCI as involving a particular case of computer-mediated communication (CMC). In it, the producers of interactive technology talk to users through the interfaces of the artifacts they build. Although this CMC perspective is the hallmark of all semiotic approaches to HCI and IS [5-8], semiotic engineering is different because it is a theory, not a semiotic analysis, of HCI. Hence, it has its *own* ontology, from which specific models and methods to support design and evaluation can be derived [1,9].

One of the difficulties for practical collaboration between HCI and IS researchers is that mainstream HCI is heavily influenced by cognitive theories, like Norman's cognitive engineering and user-centered design (UCD) 0. A study of about research in Computer Science (CS) found that HCI publications are *outliers* compared to others. For example, they do not have Mathematics as a reference discipline, they do not use mathematical methods of analysis, and don't aim to formulate processes or algorithms 0. Because these three features are predominant throughout CS, there is a gap between disciplines, which makes it difficult to turn HCI contributions into a scientific and practical asset for both CS and IS. Semiotic engineering, however, may constitute an important step for bridging this gap.

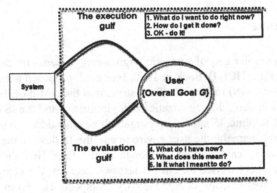

Fig. 1. Norman's execution and evaluation gulfs

A brief illustration of the kinds of contrast between semiotic engineering and Norman's influential cognitive engineering 0, for example, helps to show why IS design and evaluation can benefit from what we propose. Cognitive engineering views human-computer interaction as the traversal of two gulfs (see Figure 1). All interaction is dominated by the user's overall goal. Given this goal, interaction starts by *the user* establishing her immediate intent (*e.g.* playing back her favorite CD in her new laptop), then planning how to achieve it as result of various software functions, and finally executing the plan by activating interface controls. These three steps help the user traverse the execution gulf that spans between user and system. Next, *the user* must perceive the signal corresponding to the system's reaction (*e.g.* the button ▶ turns from grey to black), interpret what it means (she can press it to start the playback), and evaluate her success. These three steps help the user traverse the evaluation gulf. *User-centeredness* springs from the fact that all relevant activity for HCI is enacted by *the user*, even if as a response to what the system suggests. Norman's original theory does not include *the system* as a partner in HCI, which represents a radical shift from the once traditional view that user and system play equal (or, more often than not, *unequal*) parts in interaction. By the same token, his theory makes it difficult for IS researchers and developers to connect to HCI.

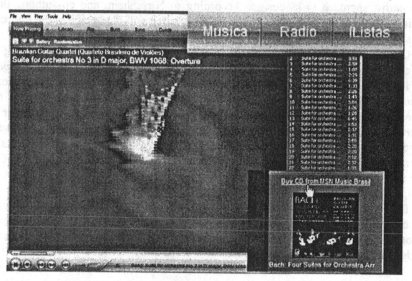

Fig. 2. A screen shot of Windows® Media Player®

The kinds of design concerns that the theoretical foundations of UCD help address are eminently cognitive: How difficult is it for the user to know what to do or expect? How difficult is it to learn something new? How difficult is it to retain and recall it? Which analogies and metaphors can be used to accelerate the appropriate framing of concepts to be learned? As a result, voluminous research and valuable techniques based on cognitive theories helped designers *make interaction easier* for users, and account for most that is meant by *usability*. Nevertheless, usable technologies have to exhibit qualities other than cognitive. For example, what other sorts of theories will explain (or support) design choices and decisions in the Windows Media Player® interface (see Figure 2)? How does a designer integrate *being connected* (and takes full advantage of it) into the user's experience while she is listening to her CD? Which theories and techniques support choices about what information to display on screen, what links to offer (for further details about artists and music), what related activities to enable (buying other CD's or chatting with other fans)? And how should all these things be expressed – through words, images, sounds, movement? The best answers to each of these and other related questions determine the success of technology, and they are not always easy to find. Notice, for example, that in Figure 2, although the preferred interface language is *English*, an effect of automatic customization (based on the user's IP being located in Brazil) incorrectly introduces linguistic miscellanea in the user's experience (the three rightmost tabs magnified in Figure 2 contain words in Portuguese), but correctly directs the user to "MSN Music Brasil".

Various HCI approaches have helped address the above questions and issues. Some examples are: activity theory 0, the language-action perspective (LAP) 0, social computing 0 and online communities 0. Language and communication-centered approaches like LAP, in particular, have been praised as a relevant *alternative* approach to IS design. According to Hirschheim and co-authors, they "point the direction which some important IS research will likely take in the future to strengthen the interpretive and critical traditions [...] within the field" 0.

Compared to both cognitive approaches and LAP, semiotic engineering is different because it emphasizes the communicative role of *designers and developers* in HCI, and brings them up into *the user environment* of IS research. It promotes *intent* (users' and designers') to first-class citizen in HCI, and centers around the necessary communicative settings that will bring designers and users together *at interaction time* 0, to negotiate the scope and evolution of shared meanings encoded in software. Cognitive approaches, for instance, deny the presence of designers at interaction time. And LAP, in spite of its explicit account of IS as communication systems, typically focuses on IS-enabled *communication among users*, and not on designer-user communication.

In the remainder of this paper we will: briefly outline the profile of semiotic engineering; present an example of the kinds of account and epistemic tools that the theory can provide; and discuss the advantages of semiotic engineering as a means to bridge the gap between HCI and IS.

2   Semiotic Engineering

Our theory centers around two fundamental concepts: metacommunication and meaning. Metacommunication is "communication *about* communication". It is the main process taking place in user interfaces and, ultimately, in HCI: interfaces and interaction enable designer-to-user communication$_{(i)}$ about all designed types of system-user communications$_{(ii)}$ and their corresponding effects. Top-level communication$_{(i)}$ is a one-shot comprehensive message that can be paraphrased as:

> *Here is my understanding of who you are, what I've learned you want or need to do, in which preferred ways, and why. This is the system that I have therefore designed for you, and this is the way you can or should use it in order to fulfill a range of purposes that fall within this vision.*

The addresser "I" in the message is the artifact's designer (or a spokesperson for the design team), and the addressee "you" is the user (or the users). The content of the message is strongly referenced to the context of design (where the design vision is elaborated and imprinted in the design product). It is unfolded through the process of interaction, just like the content of a book is unfolded through reading. Hence, ontologically, designers and users belong to the same category – they are interlocutors at interaction time. This is one of the major differences between semiotic engineering and prevailing HCI theories. It underlines the fact that the legitimacy and consistency of the message ("this is the systems that I have build for you") depend on the design intent being shared and restated at every single stage of the software development cycle. In other words, all developers must understand the metacommunication message, agree with it, and contribute to making it clear and useful to the end user. Another difference, related to the second central concept in the theory, is taking meaning to be a culturally-determined constantly evolving process, rather than a fixed target to be captured, encoded and met. Most implicit or explicit theories of meaning supporting computation and software engineering postulate that, just like computer (program) symbols each have their established (enumerable) meaning(s), human meanings occurring in various domains of activity are also fully determined *a priori*. However, human meanings like human life evolve in both predictable and unpredictable ways. In other words, "the user's meaning" is a moving target, and we as developers or designers can never claim to have fully captured it. But we can and do capture relevant parts of it, which are encoded in programs that inexorably compute and predict their occurrence according to well-specified semantic rules. They encode our interpretation of users' meanings in a finite range of possible contexts. The better the job we do at the initial stages of design (through user studies), the greater our chances to communicate and share our understanding with users. When the unavoidable step to outside the boundaries of encoded meanings is made, and the user begins to mean things that are "knowable" but not "known", user's satisfaction will be more dependent on "communicability" than on "usability" 0. Here is a plausible e-commerce scenario to illustrate this.

Scott has been using E-Store for a number of years and different purposes: buying books and computer supplies; buying music CDs, DVDs and cooking books; buying gifts for friends and family of all ages. E-Store uses sophisticated recommendation systems and powerful customization techniques. So, Scott has "his" E-Store, that is nothing like his wife's. Hers looks a different locale – a department store, whereas Scott's feels like a huge music and entertainment warehouse. Based on his purchasing habits over the years, Scott's E-Store puts together recommendations for HCI books back to back with others for children books. Likewise, the organization of store sections gives the same priority access to computer supplies as to flowers (which he often sends to his Mom). He understands this, but he really doesn't like it that much – he'd rather not get the flowers in the way when he visits E-Store for professional purposes, not get recommendations for Dr. Seuss books when trying to check the latest design guidelines for cell phone browsing.

He then decides to use his email strategy to get around the annoyance. Just like he has 5 different emails accounts for different purposes, he chooses to create specialized *personas* for E-Store. He clicks on the 'If you are not Scott click here' link to create "Skip", his "professional clone". All works fine till "Skip" decides to purchase his first lot of professional books. As he provides his credit card and billing address information, a red light flashes online: "The information you provided is apparently that of another user. Our Customer Service Department will get in touch with you, both electronically and through regular mail. If you want to save the data you have provided so far, click on 'Save information for future use'. We are sorry for the inconvenience."

A number of meaning-related aspects are illustrated by this scenario. First, Scott is happy that *E-Store* provides recommendations and customized shopping experiences. Second, Scott understands how recommendations and customization work. The only annoyance is that over time the mixed types of purchases he makes online mess up *Scott's E-Store*. But, third, no problem: he thinks he knows how to get around the issue, using knowledge from his online culture. Fourth, *E-Store* supports his strategy for a while, but breaks down when it comes to finishing Skip's first purchase online. Why? Because parts of information provided by customers as they conclude purchasing processes online are used as identity keys. As it is usually the case in social life, identity is a *unique* image of you. No two people can share the same *identity*. But online we can have multiple identities, often confused with multiple roles by both users *and* designers.

So what about *evolving meanings* as opposed to fixed meanings? When *E-Store* was developed, all agreed that identifying the users was a key need if security and trust were expected to qualify the users' experience. They decided to identify users by means of a particular tuple of data extracted from the most reliable and valuable piece of information they provide – their credit card information and their personal name and address. Nothing wrong with that. But nobody could predict (not even Scott, if you asked him) that *E-Store* customers would ever wish or need to create clones online. So, designers and developers feel justified with respect to their original choices, Scott feels justified with respect to his current needs. And an interactive problem is in place.

The issues involved in the above scenario are not only strictly pertinent to *the user environment* and how it interacts with the E-Store organizational environment, but also to how the *user environment* relates to the *external environment*, helping users engage in existing social and cultural practices. Lyytinen 0 remarks that sociotechnical approaches to IS bring together "features of the information system, user, and organizational environment". However, he says, because they focus on the *technical* aspects of IS, they may miss important factor lying beyond these (*e.g.* factors that belong to the external, socio-cultural, environment). Semiotic approaches are promising because Semiotics can be viewed as *the logic of culture* 0.

Taking into account cultural signs and practices, and the way they are communicated, semiotic engineering can explain why Scott is right and angry, even if *E-Store* designers and developers are also right and justified. It can also call the designers' and developers' attention to the fact that the systems they produce will necessarily be used in *different* scenarios than the ones they thought of. Therefore, the more efficiently and effectively designers and developers communicate the key concepts of design rationale to users, the more efficiently and effectively users will work around the demands of context evolution and situational change. In this particular case, although the creators of E-store may be excused for not anticipating Scott's specific problems and preferences, merely signaling at the interface that the user's name, address and credit card info combine and constitute his identity should have put Scott's imagination on a more productive path. He would probably realize that his email strategy would not work for E-Store.

Semiotic engineering also explores the design and development consequences of the fact that *computer* meanings have *human* origin and destination. In spite of all formal verification procedures that can prove symbols to be consistently computed one after the other through all layers of software programming, semantic adequacy and relevance actually depends fully on human judgment. It takes a human mind to ascertain that any particular computation is, for all practical purposes, *semantically adequate*, and ultimately *useful* **Feil! Fant ikke referansekilden.**. Hence, although HCI research does not use Mathematics as a foundational discipline or mathematical analysis as a method, knowledge about human meanings should contribute to both CS and IS.

Semiotic engineering proposes to connect both ends by postulating that designers/developers, systems, and users, *all* belong to the same ontological category: they are all interlocutors whose conversations are inter-related. Designers are brought onto the stage of human computer interaction, where *they* communicate what they have done, how, and why, to the users of the artifact they have designed. The system's interface *speaks for designers* at interaction time. The interface conveys all communication that designers must and wish to exchange with users, effect all the expected results, exhibit all the expected behavior, and make all the possible sense of the conversation with the users. They are the legitimate representatives of the designer's *mind*. To design a system thus amounts to designing a rational mechanic spokesperson that will tell users what sense (predicted or not) to make of the artifact 0. Most importantly, it also amounts to designing the remedial sense-making and meaning-negotiating dialogues, which will give users resourceful signs to reason upon and recover from communicative breakdowns and misunderstandings.

Implicit in the above is the fact that the system, as the *designers' deputy*, must be able to explain itself to end users, to disclose the essence of its logic and rationale, in case of interactive breakdowns and/or system repurposing. This can only be achieved with sound underlying models that are comprehensible and satisfactory for all members of the development team. If the semantics of the design rationale, as intended by the designer, is tweaked or misinterpreted by developers, the users will suffer the consequence of nonsensical interface discourse.

3   Communication and Metacommunication with an Online Store

Like many other online stores, Amazon.com® makes extensive use of recommendation and customization techniques. Figure 3 shows a piece of the page *Clarisse* gets as she goes to http://www.amazon.com.

Notice the explicit conversational style of interaction ("Hello, Clarisse"), reinforced in numerous dialogues as, for example, in the "Frequently Asked Questions" about recommendations (see Figure 4). FAQ techniques introduce a "user's deputy" in the conversation, one that speaks for the user (*e.g.* "Are my recommendations saved so I can look at them again later?"). The use of "I", "you", "we" establishes a speaker/listener structure, and even signs of persuasive rhetoric are present in the dialogue (*e.g.* "We wouldn't want you to miss something you might enjoy!"). However, this natural conversation feeling is shaken when the user's deputy asks: "How do I turn off recommendations?" The advice is: "Simply click the link on our home page that says 'If you're not (your name), click here.' Then, leave the e-mail and password spaces blank and click the 'Amazon.com' tab. This will remove our recommendations for you until you sign in again."

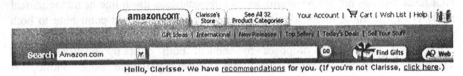

Hello, Clarisse. We have recommendations for you. (If you're not Clarisse, click here.)

Fig. 3. A detail of Clarisse's customized entry page at Amazon.com

How Recommendations Work

Are my recommendations saved so I can look at them again later?

No. Your recommendations will change when you purchase or rate a new item. Changes in the interests of other customers may also affect your own recommendations. Because your recommendations will fluctuate, we suggest you add items that interest you to your Wish List or Shopping Cart. We wouldn't want you to miss something you might enjoy!

Why was a particular item recommended for me?

You'll notice "Why?" and "Why was I recommended this?" links next to recommended items on most product home pages. Click these links for a chance to rate or exclude the specific purchases and ratings we used to make a recommendation and therefore influence future recommendations that we make.

How do I turn off recommendations?

Simply click the link on our home page that says "If you're not (your name), click here." Then, leave the e-mail and password spaces blank and click the "Amazon.com" tab. This will remove our recommendations for you until you sign in again.

Fig. 4. A detail of Amazon.com explanations about how recommendations work

By framing HCI as metacommunication and shifting the traditional user-system interaction to a user-designers' deputy conversation, semiotic engineering provides conversational models and methods for designing critical parts of such metacommunication. For example, it calls the designer's attention to the importance of observing factors like topical structure in conversation. Notice that the user (through his deputy) is asking about "turning off recommendations". But the designer's deputy responds with apparent *non sequitur* discourse: "Click on the link that says 'If you're not (your name), click here'". Why raise a question of identity for turning off recommendations? Even worse: Why advise the user to belie her own identity? What other kinds of convenient side effects may this socially serious misbehavior cause? Why not simply have a link saying "Turn recommendations off", or another saying "Visit the store anonymously"?

Following Schön's reflection-in-action design paradigm 0, semiotic engineering bets on epistemic tools, which fire the designer's semiosis along certain structured paths for reflection. Thus, when the interaction style is explicitly and prominently conversational as with Amazon.com, the designer is led to ask himself questions about fundamental issues for productive verbal interchange: the consistent identification of interlocutors, topic and purpose of each message, turn-taking and rhetorical structure, and so on. More than that, in the spirit of semiosis, the designer is prompted to ask further questions, and explore the design space, taking semiotic engineering on board as an *epistemic* resource theory.

In order to highlight the relevance of such issues for both front end and back end design and development activities, note that semiotic engineering has the power to raise issues of *reuse* in the Amazon.com example. Epistemic tools for designing communication in multi-user applications like groupware, online communities and others capture the design rationale and use it extensively for building the designer's deputy discourse 0. Thus, in the process, a designer is not likely to explain and justify a change of identity as a rational solution for turning off recommendations. This would be in obvious contradiction with one of Grice's famous maxims for a *logic of conversation* 0, which we integrate to our tools.

Although the same range of effects caused by a given *program* may be interpreted in a number of different ways and serve many different purposes (*e.g.* allow for anonymous visits to an e-store and momentarily clear the recommendation list of long-time customers), there must be a differentiation of expression and representation when humans are engaged in interpretive processes for which such differences matter. This is the case not only of end users, but also of maintenance programmers and technical documentation writers. They must all know what the system can and cannot do, no matter how extensively reuse techniques have been applied to accelerate its development cycle or optimize its size and performance.

Just for illustration, one of our tools walks the designer through the communication design space, asking questions like: Who is speaking? To whom? What is the speaker saying? Using which code and medium? Are code and medium appropriate for the situation? Are there alternatives? Is(are) the listener(s) receiving the message? What if not? How can the listener(s) respond to the speaker? Is there recourse if the speaker realizes the listener(s) misunderstood the message? What is it?

A walkthrough of FAQ-style interaction reveals some interest facets. Is "the user" really speaking? Are the words in the questions phrasing really hers? And if they aren't, should "you" and "yours" be used instead of "the customer"?

One last aspect that is somewhat related to identity, but more precisely to legitimate agency, can be seen on the snapshot in Figure 5, on the FAQ about "the page you made". Curiously, the designer's deputy is telling the user that she is (unknowingly and perhaps unwillingly) *making* an HTML page as she navigates through the store. But *she* isn't. The *system* is automatically assembling this page on the user's behalf, which raises issues of control and legitimacy in the whole cycle of interaction. Users may end up asking themselves what *they* are doing, and even who they *are,* given that the system is apparently taking the user's identity and doing unsolicited things along the way. Some may be pretty nice, some may not. Can the user always trust this system then? The ethical implications of such choices are all very likely to emerge in the designer's semiosis along the design process.

What Is the Page You Made?

The Page You Made is meant to help you keep track of some of the items you've recently viewed, searches you've recently made, and product categories you've recently visited, and help you find related items that might be of interest. As you browse through the store, we will bring to your attention items similar to those you are looking at. The Page You Made continually updates as you browse. We try to offer purchase suggestions that are most relevant to your recent shopping sessions. Our record of your activity on our site expires after a few hours.

Fig. 5. A detail of Amazon.com explanations about the page you made

4 Concluding Remarks

Although semiotic engineering is firmly established in the HCI camp, it sheds light on universal semiotic processes that occur throughout the development cycle, and on the kinds of commitments and consequences that one is expected to assume when it comes to producing useful, pleasurable, high-quality information technology.

Among the points we've raised in this paper, we want to highlight the following. First, we reject the view that meaning is a fixed ideal value that designers can elicit from users and hopefully encode into a system. The expectation that well done user studies will capture *the* user's meaning and *entail* satisfaction denies the intrinsic creative and evolutionary character of human nature. In terms of the future of IS research, this point suggests that abductive reasoning systems 0 and even evolutionary computing 0 may provide radically different conceptions of computation, and consequently broaden the spectrum of meanings that can be exchanged between the internal components of the IS environment, and between the IS environment and the socio-cultural environment (not only the sociotechnical environment).

Second, semiotic engineering favors model-based design and development, although for a somewhat different purpose than is usually the case in literature 0. Instead of using models to generate implementations of specifications automatically, we propose to use them to generate explanations about design and implementation. These explanations should be primarily used to elicit and negotiate interpretations and meanings throughout the development cycle, with a positive effect on the user's experience at the very end of the process chain. That these models can be used for program generation or transformation is the object of formal methods investigation. The semiotic engineering point is that the semantic adequacy of representations used for specifications and programming is the object of *human* judgment, and not of automatic syntactic manipulations of symbols.

Third, because the fundamental process in HCI is metacommunication of design rationale, it is of prime importance that this rationale be not undermined by programming practices (like the case of reuse, in our example) that cannot guarantee the consistency of the designer's deputy's *discourse at interaction time*, and hence make sense to users.   The role of contingency and context in intelligible communication 0 challenges the idea that design and implementation components can be *reused* without problems in communicative situations other than the ones they have been originally used for. The reuse ideal is fundamentally dependent on fixed and universal meanings. In terms of the future of IS research, this point suggests that software and design components, objects or patterns should include representations of the metacommunicative meanings with which they are thought to be associated. This *integrative* view of back end and front end issues is one of the strengths of semiotic engineering.

Fourth and finally, because meanings evolve in unpredictable ways, allowing users to customize and extend applications (broadly covered by the term *end user development* 0) deserves high-priority among development techniques that are in line with our theory. Users should be able to incorporate contingent meanings to the technology, achieving *evolutionary computing* in a very particular way. Viewed from the perspective of the *external environment*, the *IS environment* would evolve on demand.

Other theories and approaches to HCI usually don't bring all the above issues together. They tend to focus on one or another aspect only, contributing to the feeling that IS and HCI belong to worlds apart. The separation creates tension and favors independent initiatives that try to take care of the user environment within IS based on ontologies and models that exclude some of the most fundamental aspects of the users' experience. Because of its semiotic foundations, whereas other theories seek to provide tools and methods that generate *answers* to design problems, semiotic engineering's tools and methods are meant to generate *questions*. As *epistemic* tools, they are not intended to replace other tools, neither is the theory intended to replace other theories. This may frustrate IS developers and researchers, who would like to get answers for long-standing questions in the field. But, as Hirschheim and co-authors say 0, alternative IS development approaches, including those based on language and communication, are important because they represent useful scientific counterparts of orthodox views. Altogether, we strongly believe that semiotic engineering is a useful bridging theory for bringing together IS and HCI.

Acknowledgment

The author thanks CNPq, the Brazilian Council for Scientific and Technological Development, for giving continued financial support for her research.

References

1. C.S. de Souza. *The semiotic engineering of human computer interaction.* Cambridge, MA. The MIT Press (2005).

2. R. Hirschheim, J. Iivari, and H.K. Klein. A Comparison of Five Alternative Approaches to Information Systems Development. *Australian Journal of Information Systems*, Volume 5(1). (1997).

3. C.S. Peirce. *Collected papers of Charles Sanders Peirce, Vols. 1-8*, C. Hartshorne and P. Weiss. Cambridge, MA. Harvard University Press (1931-1958).

4. U. Eco. *A theory of semiotics*. Bloomington, IN. Indiana University Press (1976).

5. P.B. Andersen, B. Holmqvist, and J.F. Jensen *The computer as medium*. Cambridge. Cambridge University Press (1993).

6. J. Kammersgaard. Four Different Perspectives on Human-Computer Interaction. *International Journal of Man-Machine Studies* 28(4) pp. 343-362. (1988).

7. K. Liu. *Semiotics in Information Systems Engineering*. Cambridge. Cambridge University Press. (2000).

8. M. Nadin. Interface design and evaluation. In R. Hartson, D. Hix (Eds.) *Advances in Human-Computer Interaction, Vol. 2*. Norwood, NJ. Ablex Publishing Co. (1988).

9. C.S. de Souza. Semiotic engineering: bringing designers and users together at interaction time. *Interacting with Computers*, 17 (3) pp. 317-341. (2005)

10. D.A. Norman and S.W. Draper. *User-centered system design*. Hillsdale, NJ. Laurence Erlbaum (1986).

11. V. Ramesh, R.L. Glass, and I. Vessey. Research in computer science: an empirical study. The Journal of Systems and Software 70 (2004) pp. 165-176

12. B.A. Nardi. *Context and consciousness*. Cambridge, MA. The MIT Press. (1996).

13. T. Winograd and F. Flores. *Understanding computers and cognition*. New York, NY. Addison-Wesley (1986).

14. P. Dourish. *Where the action is*. Cambridge, MA. The MIT Press (2001).

15. J. Preece. *Online Communities: Designing Usability and Supporting Sociability*. New York, NY. John Wiley & Sons, Inc (2000).

16. K. Lyytinen. Different Perspectives on Information Systems: Problems and Solutions. *ACM Computing Surveys*, Vol. 19, No. 1, March 1987. pp. 5-46 (1987).

17. D. A. Schön. *The Reflective Practitioner*. New York, NY. Basic Books (1983).

18. H.P. Grice. Logic and Conversation. In: P. Cole & Morgan (eds.), *Syntax and Semantics 3: Speech Acts*. New York, NY. Academic Press (1975).

19. J.R. Josephson and S.G. Josephson. *Abductive inference: computation, philosophy, technology*. Cambridge. Cambridge University Press (1994).

20. D.B. Fogel. *Evolutionary Computation: Toward a New Philosophy of Machine Intelligence*. Piscathaway, NJ. IEEE Press (1995).

21. F. Paternò. *Model-Based Design and Evaluation of Interactive Applications*. Heidelberg. Springer (1999).

22. L.A. Suchman. *Plans and Situated Action*. Cambridge. Cambridge University Press (1987).

23. Lieberman, H.; Paternò, F.; Wulf, V. *End-User Development*. Human-Computer Interaction Series, Vol. 9. Heidelberg. Springer. (2006).

The Benefit of Enterprise Ontology in Identifying Business Components

Antonia Albani, Jan L.G. Dietz
Delft University of Technology
Chair of Information Systems
PO Box 5031, 2600 GA Delft, The Netherlands
{a.albani|j.l.g.dietz}@tudelft.nl

Abstract. Companies are more than ever participating in so-called value networks while being confronted with an increasing need for *collaboration* with their business partners. In order to better perform in such value networks information systems supporting not only the intra- but also the inter-enterprise business processes are necessary in order to enable and ease collaboration between business partners. Therefore, they need to be *interoperable*. As the basis for building these information systems the concepts of *enterprise ontology* and *business components* are very promising. The notion of enterprise ontology, as presented in this paper, is a powerful revelation of the essence of an enterprise or an enterprise network. Reusable and self-contained business components with well-defined interaction points facilitate the accessing and execution of coherent packages of business functionality. The *identification of business components*, however, is still a crucial factor. The reported research seeks to improve the identification of business components based on the *ontological model* of an enterprise, satisfying well-defined quality criteria.

1 Introduction

Due to drastic changes in the competitive landscape, enterprises are more and more focusing on their core competencies, outsourcing supporting tasks to their business partners. Companies are therefore becoming part of so-called *value networks* [1-3] with the increasing need to identify, improve, and automate as much as possible their core business processes. In order to enhance the competitive advantage of value networks an effective *collaboration* between enterprises is of great relevance. Technological innovations such as global, web-based infrastructures, communication

Please use the following format when citing this chapter:

Albani, A., Dietz, J.L.G., 2006, in IFIP International Federation for Information Processing, Volume 214, The Past and Future of Information Systems: 1976–2006 and Beyond, eds. Avison, D., Elliot, S., Krogstie, J., Pries-Heje, J., (Boston: Springer), pp. 243–254.

standards and distributed systems, enable the implementation of business processes in and the integration of business processes between companies, thus increasing the flexibility of the business system and enabling the *interoperability* of their information systems. However, the deployment of the information and communication technologies does not always meet expectations. While developing inter- and intra-enterprise information systems, it is necessary to use a suitable *methodology* for modeling the business domain. Additionally, information systems need to be modeled on a high-level of abstraction that is understood also by business people, who are defining the requirements and using the respective systems. The use of *business components* for the development of a high-level information system is valuable since they 'directly model and implement the business logic, rules and constraints that are typical, recurrent and comprehensive notions characterizing a domain or business area' [4] (all other components are considered either to deliver services to these business components or to offer some general functionality). The identification of business components thus is the first step in the development of an information system according to current standards. It is a very crucial one and, therefore, it should be performed at the highest possible level of quality. In the field of identifying reusable and marketable business components there is still little research initiative to date (e.g., [5-7]). As recognized by [8], 'more formal methodologies are needed to make the component based software development paradigm into an effective development tool'.

The starting point is the set of requirements that have been elicited from the business domain, preferably on the basis of an abstract model of the organizational activities. In [9] some quality criteria are proposed regarding such a model, which we adopted for our current research: it should be *consistent* (i.e., there are no contradictions or irregularities), *comprehensive* (i.e., all relevant issues are dealt with), *concise* (i.e. the model does not contain superfluous matters), and *essential* (i.e., it shows only the deep structure, independent of the realization and the implementation of the enterprise). We call a model of the organizational activities of an enterprise that satisfies these requirements enterprise *ontology*. Most of the current process modeling techniques, like the Petri Net [10, 11], Event Driven Process Chains (EPC) [12], and Activity Diagrams [13], next to the traditional flow charts, do not satisfy all of the quality criteria mentioned. The notion of business process is not well defined and there exists no distinction between business and informational actions. Consequently, the difference between business processes and some other types of process remains unclear. This leads to the conclusion that they do not specifically address business processes but can be used for any discrete event process. Other approaches, as e.g. from the Language/Action Perspective (LAP), claim to offer a solution for the mismatch between social perspectives and technical perspectives by explicitly focusing on business specific communication patterns, where social beings achieve changes in the (object) world by means of communication acts [14]. The *enterprise ontology* [15] methodology is an approach that incorporates LAP and that additionally distinguishes between essential (business), informational and documental actions. Because of these advantages, we chose the methodology referred to, also known as DEMO (Design and Engineering Methodology for Organizations), for producing the ontological model of an enterprise, providing the basis for identifying business components.

Based on the enterprise ontology, this article introduces a new method for the identification of business components. It is structured as follows: To exemplify the usability of the approach, the domain of *strategic supply network development (SSND)* and its ontological model is introduced in section 2. SSND is used throughout the paper as an example domain for inter-enterprise collaboration. In section 3, the method for identifying business components is applied to the SSND case. Discussions of the results as well as the conclusions that can be drawn are provided in section 4.

2 Enterprise Ontology and its Application to the SSND Case

The example domain of *strategic supply network development* comes from the domain of strategic purchasing [16-19]. The most evident differences regard the functions with cross-enterprise focus. Purchasing has become a core function in enterprises in the 90s. Current empiric research shows a significant correlation between the establishment of a strategic purchasing function and the financial success of an enterprise, independent from the industry surveyed [17]. One of the most important factors in this connection is the buyer-supplier-relationship. At many of the surveyed companies, a close cooperation between buyer and supplier in areas such as long-term planning, product development, and coordination of production processes led to process improvements and resulting cost reductions that were shared between buyer and suppliers [17]. In practice, supplier development is widely limited to direct suppliers (suppliers in tier-1), without taking into consideration the suppliers in subsequent tiers. Because of the increasing importance of supplier development we postulated the extension of the traditional frame of reference in strategic sourcing from a supplier-centric to a supply-network-centric scope [20]. This refocuses the object of reference in the field of strategic sourcing by analyzing and selecting supplier networks instead of single suppliers. The details of the domain are described while introducing the enterprise ontology of the SSND case.

As motivated in the introduction, we use the enterprise ontology for modeling the business domain according to DEMO [14, 15, 21, 22]. As is explained in [15, 21, 22] a distinction is made between production acts and facts and coordination acts and facts. Consequently, two worlds are distinguished: the production world (P-world) and the coordination world (C-world). The transaction axiom aggregates these acts/facts into the standard pattern of the (business) transaction. The complete ontological model of an organization consists of four aspect models. The Construction Model (CM) specifies the composition, the environment and the structure of the organization. It contains identified *transaction types*, which are executed by associated *actor roles* and describes the *links* to relevant information stored in *production* or *coordination banks*. The Process Model (PM) details each single transaction type of the CM by means of *transaction patterns*. Next to these patterns, it contains the *causal* and *conditional relationships* between transactions. The PM is based on business process patterns [22] and shows how the distinct transaction types are related. The Action Model (AM) specifies the *action rules* that serve as guidelines for the actors in dealing with their agenda. The State Model (SM) specifies the *object classes*, *fact types* and ontological *coexistence rules* in the production world.

Based on this method, the ontology for the SSND case has been constructed. Space limitations prohibit us to provide a more extensive account of how the models in the figures hereafter are developed. Also, we will not present and discuss the Action Model. The basic idea of the SSND example is the identification of suppliers, located not only in tier-1 but also in the subsequent tiers, which are able to deliver specific components to the original equipment manufacturer (OEM) for constructing a specific product. This is established in sending out an offering request for a specific product to the tier-1 suppliers, which execute a bill-of-material explosion in order to decide which products need to be requested from their suppliers. This repeats until the request has reached the last tier. The information is then aggregated and split-lot transferred to the initial tier. Fig. 1 exhibits the Construction Model of the SSND case. The corresponding Transaction Result Table is shown in Table 1.

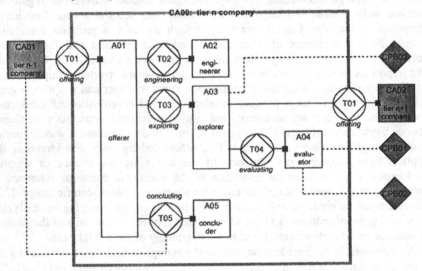

Fig. 1 Construction Model of the SSND case

Table 1. Transaction Result Table of the SSND case

transaction type	resulting P-event type
T01 offering	PE01 supply contract C is offered
T02 engineering	PE02 the BoM of assembly A is determined
T03 exploring	PE03 supply contract C is a potential contract
T04 evaluating	PE04 supply contract C is evaluated
T05 concluding	PE05 supply contract C is concluded

The top or starting transaction type is the offering transaction T01. Instances of T01 are initiated by the environmental actor role CA01, which is a company in tier n-1 and executed by actor role A01. This company asks the direct supplier (company in tier n) for an offer regarding the supply of a particular product P. In order to make such an offer, A01 first initiates an engineering transaction T02, in order to get the bill of material of the requested product P. This is a list of (first-level) components of P, produced by A02. Next, A01 asks A03 for every such component to get offers from companies that are able to supply the component. So, a number of exploring transactions T03 may be carried out within one T01, namely as many as there are components of P which are not produced by the tier n company. In order to execute each of these transactions, A03 has to ask companies for an offer regarding the supply of a component of P. Since this is identical to a starting transaction T01, we model this also as initiating a T01. Now however, the executor of the T01 is a company in tier n+1. Consequently, the model that is shown in Fig. 1 must be understood as to be repeated recursively for every tier until the products to be supplied are elementary, i.e. non-decomposable. Note that, because of the being recursive, an offer (the result of a T01) comprises the complete bill of material of the concerned component of P.

Every offer from the companies in tier n+1 is evaluated in a T04 transaction. So, there is a T04 for every 'output' T01, whereby each company can have its own evaluation rules. The result of a T04 is a graded offer for some component of P. So, what A03 delivers back to A01 is a set of graded offers for every component of P. Next, A01 asks A05, for every component of P, to select the best offer. The result is a set of concluded offers, one for every component of P. This set is delivered to A01. Lastly, A01 delivers a contract offer to CA01 for supplying P, together with the set of concluded offers for delivering the components of P. Because of the recursive character of the whole model, this offer includes the complete bill of material of P, regardless its depth.

The CM in Fig. 1 contains three external production banks. Bank CPB01 contains the data about a company that are relevant for the evaluation of offers. Bank CPB02 contains the different evaluation methods that can be applied. In every instance of T04, one of these methods is applied. CPB03 contains identifiers of all companies that may be addressed for an offer. The dashed lines represent access links to these banks. Lastly, in the transaction result table (see Table 1), the supply of a product by a (supplying) company to a (customer) company is called a contract.

Fig. 2 exhibits the Process Model of the SSDN case. A coordination step is represented by a (white) disk in a (white) box; it is identified by the transaction number (see Table 1) and a two-letter extension: rq (request), pm (promise), st (state), or ac (accept). A production step is represented by a (gray) diamond in a (gray) box; it is identified by the transaction number. For modeling the SSND example case the so-called basic pattern (*request, promise, execute, state, accept*) has been used.

From the state T01/pm (promised) a number of transactions T03 (possibly none) and a number of transactions T05 (possibly none) are initiated, namely for every first-level component of a product. This is expressed by the cardinality range 0..k. Likewise, from the state T03/pm, a number of transactions T01 and a number of transactions T04 are initiated, namely for every offer or contract regarding a first-level component of a product. The dashed arrows, from an accept state (e.g. T02/ac) to some other transaction state, represent waiting conditions. So, for example, the performance of a T03/rq has to wait for the being performed of the corresponding T02/ac.

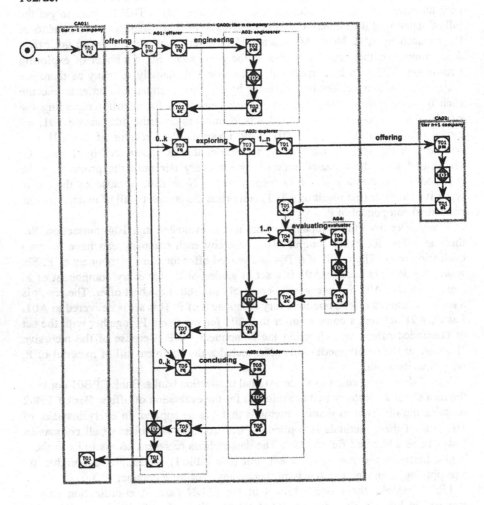

Fig. 2 Process Step Diagram of the SSND case

Fig. 3 exhibits the object fact diagram (OFD) and Table 2 the object property table (OPT). Together they constitute the State Model of the example case. The OFD is a variant of the ORM model [23]. Diamonds represent the (unary) fact types that are the result of transactions, also called production fact types. They correspond with the transaction results in Table 1. A roundangle around a fact type or a role defines a concept in an extensional way, i.e. by specifying the object class that is its extension. For example, the roundangle around the production fact type "C is evaluated" defines the concept of evaluated contract. Properties are binary fact types that happen to be pure mathematical functions, of which the range is set of, usually ordered, values, called a scale. Instead of including them in an OFD they can be more conveniently represented in an Object Property Table (Table 2). The information items as defined in the SM, including the derived fact types, constitute all information that is needed to develop a supply network for a particular product.

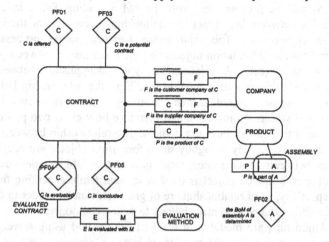

Fig. 3 Object Fact Diagram of the SSND case

Table 2. Object Property Table of the SSND case

property type	object class	Scale
< company information >	COMPANY	< aggregated data >
< contract terms >	CONTRACT	< aggregated data >
evaluation_mark	CONTRACT	NUMBER

3   Identification of Business Components in the SSND Case

Having introduced the main models of the ontology of an enterprise, the information gained in the models is used for the identification of business components. The principle of modular design, on which business components are based, demands reusable, marketable, self-contained, reliable and manageable business components. They need to provide services at the right level of granularity and to have a formal and complete specification of its external view. The enterprise ontology, as introduced in section 1, provides the necessary basis for the realization of business components. With the enterprise ontology for the SSND case, the complete information related to that business domain is available. The *three dimensional method for business components identification (BCI-3D)*, applied in this section, aims at grouping business tasks and their corresponding information objects into business components satisfying defined metrics. The metrics used − being minimal communication between and maximum compactness of business components − are the basic metrics for the component-based development of inter-enterprise applications.

Since the identification of business components is strongly dependent on the underlying business model, the BCI-3D method uses the object classes and fact types from the SM and the process steps from the PM, including their relationships. One can distinguish between three types of relationships necessary for the identification of business components. The relationship between single process steps, the relationship between information objects and the relationship between process steps and information objects. A relationship type distinguishes between subtypes expressing the significance of a relationship. E.g., the relationship between single process steps expresses – based on their cardinality constraints – how often a process step is executed within a transaction and therefore how close two process steps are related to each other in that business domain. The relationship between information objects defines how loosely or tightly the information objects are coupled, and the relationship between process steps and information objects defines whether a corresponding information object is used or created while executing the respective process step. All types of relationship are of great relevance in order to define which information object and process steps belong to which component.

The relationships are modeled in the BCI-3D method using a weighted graph. The nodes represent either information objects or process steps and the edges characterize the relationships between the nodes. Weights are used to define the different types and subtypes of relationships and build the basis for assigning nodes and information objects to components. Due to display reasons the graph is visualized in a three-dimensional representation having the process steps and information objects arranged in circles, and without showing the corresponding weights (see Fig. 4).

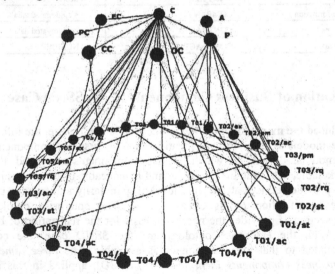

Fig. 4 Relevant relationships for the business component identification method (BCI-3D)

The graph shows all process steps and information objects with the relevant relationships of the SSND case. The shortcut names for the information objects are:

P (Product), A (Assembly), C (Contract), CC (Concluded Contract), EC (Evaluated Contract), OC (Offered Contract), and PC (Potential Contract). All information needed is gained from the enterprise ontology models introduced in section 0.

The relationship between the process steps is provided through the sequence in which the single process steps are executed (visualized by a *link* between two process steps). For the identification of business components we distinguish between *standard*, *optional* and *main* relationships, defining the significance of the relations between two process steps. This is expressed in Fig. 2 by the cardinality constraints assigned to the links. If a link has the cardinality range 0..k we call it an *optional* link, since the following process step does not need to be executed. If the cardinality range is set to 1..n then we call it a *main* link, indicating that the following process step is executed at least once. If no cardinality range is assigned, we call it a *standard* link, having the following process step executed exactly once. For the different types of links different weights are assigned in the weighted graph.

Let us have a closer look at the information objects. Fig. 3 and Table 2 introduce different types of potential information objects, namely, the object classes, fact types, and property types. Since property types define specific data belonging to an object class we do not consider that information in the BCI-3D method. Object classes, which are provided by external information systems – that concern the data, which is provided by the external production banks (see Fig. 1) – are traded in a special way in the BCI-3D method.

In addition to the relationships already introduced, the relationships between information objects and process steps play an important role in the business component identification method. The information to define those relationships can be gained from a Create/Use Table, showing which objects and facts are used or created in which process steps. For the SSND case, the relationships between information objects and process steps and their weights are visualized in Fig. 5.

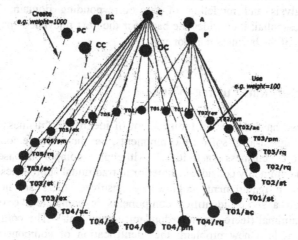

Fig. 5 Relationship between business services and information objects

In order to provide optimal grouping while minimizing communication and to ensure compactness of components, an optimization problem needs to be solved for which a genetic algorithm has been developed. A detailed description of the algorithm would go beyond the scope of this paper. Applying the BCI-3D method to the graph introduced in Fig. 4 (including the different types of relationships with the corresponding weights as shown e.g., in Fig. 5) results in the following graph partition (see Fig. 6). Two business components can be identified immediately: one containing the business tasks related to *product management* and one containing the business tasks related to *contract management*.

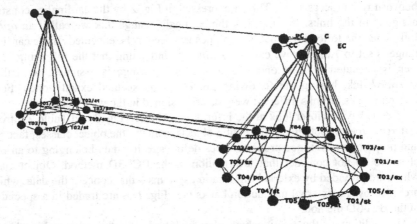

Fig. 6 Identified business component

Although in this small example only two business components were found, we have demonstrated a systematic identification of business components, considering all relevant information of the domain, which would not have been possible without a detailed analysis and modeling of the corresponding domain. The domain information is essential; it provides the basis for the next relevant steps, namely, the implementation of the business components.

4   Conclusions and Future Work

In this paper, we have addressed the problem of identifying business components, defined as the highest-level software components, i.e. the software components that directly support business activities. Although component-based software development is commonly considered superior to traditional approaches, it leaves the basic problems in requirements engineering unsolved: there are no criteria for determining that a set of identified components is complete (no component is missing) and minimal (there are no redundant components). The component-based approach also adds a new problem: the identification of components. We have addressed both problems by starting from the ontological model of the enterprise at hand. The methodology, as presented and demonstrated in this paper, does solve these problems in a satisfactory way.

First, the enterprise ontology constructed by means of DEMO is an appropriate model of the business domain. It satisfies the quality criteria as proposed in the introduction. As a consequence, the identified business components do really and directly support the business activities in which original new facts are created. Moreover, since the process steps (cf. Fig. 2) are atomic from the business point of view, one can be sure to have found the finest level of granularity that needs to be taken into account. Also, one can be sure that this set of process steps is complete and minimal.

Second, the BCI-3D method, based on the resulting models and tables of the enterprise ontology, provides an automated approach for the identification of business components. In using the BCI-3D method, different business component models could be generated for several business domains, e.g., for the domain of strategic supply network development (as presented in this paper), of educational administration, of automotive industry and of network operators. Its predecessor, the BCI method (Business Components Identification) [24], focused only on relationships between information objects and process steps, without taking into account the other types of relationships (between different information objects, and between different process steps). With this 'old' BCI method, however, we also generated component models for several domains. Worth mentioning is the one in the area of Customer Relationship Management (CRM) and Supply Chain Management (SCM) with more then 500 information objects and 1000 business functions [25]. But since the BCI method did not take into account all information available from the business domain, and was not implemented as a weighted graph, the optimization algorithms did not generate optimal solutions. We used all experiences with the old BCI method in order to develop a superior method for the identification of business components, the BCI-3D method. We demonstrated the suitability of the presented methodology by means of the SSND case. Because of its recursive nature, this case is not at all trivial. Yet, as we have shown, the process of identifying the business components is transparent and systematic.

Further investigations for the BCI-3D method are needed in evaluating reliability and stability of the resulting component models. Also, the types of relationships used and the corresponding weights assigned to the relationships need to be verified in additional example cases.

References

1. D. Tapscott, Ticoll, D., and Lowy, A., *Digital Capital: Harnessing the Power of Business Webs*. 2000, Boston.
2. T.W. Malone and Lautbacher, R.J., *The Dawn of the E-Lance Economy*. Harvard Business Review, 1998(September-October): p. 145 - 152.
3. B.J. Pine, Victor, B., and Boynton, A.C., *Making Mass Customization Work*. Havard Business Review, 1993. 36(5): p. 108-119.
4. F. Barbier and C. Atkinson. *Business Components*, in *Business Component-Based Software Engineering*, F. Barbier, Editor. 2003, Kluwer Academic Publishers Group. p. 1-26.
5. A. Réquilé-Romanczuk et al. *Towards a Knowledge-Based Framework for COTS Component Identification*. In *International Conference on Software Engineering (ICSE'05)*. 2005. St. Louis, Missouri, USA: ACM Press.

6. Y.-J. Jang, E.-Y. Kim and K.-W. Lee. *Object-Oriented Component Identification Method Using the Affinity Analysis Technique.* In *9th International Conference on Object-Oriented Information Systems (OOIS).* 2003. Geneva, Switzerland: Springer-Verlag.

7. K. Levi and A. Arsanjani. *A Goal-driven Approach to Enterprise Component Identification and Specification.* Communications of the ACM, 2002. 45(10).

8. P. Vitharana, F. Zahedi, and H. Jain. *Design, Retrieval, and Assembly in Component-based Software Development.* Communications of the ACM, 2003. 46(11).

9. J.L.G. Dietz. *Deriving Use Cases from Business Process Models.* In *Conceptual Modeling - ER 2003, LNCS 2813.* 2003: Springer Verlag.

10. W.M.P. van der Aalst and K.M. van Hee. *Workflow Management: Models, Methods and Tools.* MIT Press, MA, 2001.

11. K. Jensen. *Coloured Petri Nets. Basic Concepts, Analysis Methods and Practical Use.* Monographs in Theoretical Computer Science. Vol. 1, Basic Concepts. 1997: Springer Verlag.

12. A.-W. Scheer. *ARIS - Business Process Modeling.* 2 ed. 1999, Berlin: Springer.

13. OMG, *OMG Unified Modelling Language, Version 2.0*, in *Secondary OMG Unified Modelling Language, Version 2.0*, Secondary OMG, Editor. 2003: Place Published. p. Pages.http://www.omg.org/technology/documents/modeling_spec_catalog.htm#UML.

14. V.E. van Reijswoud, J.B.V. Mulder, and J.L.G. Dietz. *Speech Act Based Business Process and Information Modeling with DEMO.* Information Systems Journal, 1999.

15. J.L.G. Dietz. *Enterprise Ontology - Theory and Methodology.* 2006: Springer Verlag.

16. L. Kaufmann. *Purchasing and Supply Management - A Conceptual Framework*, in *Handbuch Industrielles Beschaffungsmanagement.* 2002, Hahn, D, Kaufmann, L. (Hrsg.): Wiesbaden. p. 3 - 33.

17. A.S. Carr and J.N. Pearson. *Strategically managed buyer - supplier relationships and performance outcomes.* Journal of Operations Management, 1999. 17: p. 497 - 519.

18. R. McIvor, P. Humphreys, and E. McAleer. *The Evolution of the Purchasing Function.* Journal of Strategic Change, 1997. Vol. 6(3): p. 165 - 179.

19. L.M. Ellram and A.S. Carr. *Strategic purchasing: a history and review of the literature.* International Journal of Physical Distribution and Materials Management, 1994. 30(2): p. 10 - 18.

20. A. Albani et al. *Dynamic Modelling of Strategic Supply Chains.* In *E-Commerce and Web Technologies: 4th International Conference, EC-Web 2003 Prague, Czech Republic, September 2003, LNCS 2738.* 2003. Prague, Czech Republic: Springer-Verlag.

21. J.L.G. Dietz. *The Atoms, Molecules and Fibers of Organizations.* Data and Knowledge Engineering, 2003. 47: p. 301-325.

22. J.L.G. Dietz. *Generic recurrent patterns in business processes.* In *Business Process Management, LNCS 2687.* 2003: Springer Verlag.

23. T.A. Halpin. *Information Modeling and Relational Databases.* 2001, San Francisco: Morgan Kaufmann.

24. A. Albani, J.L.G. Dietz, and J.M. Zaha. *Identifying Business Components on the basis of an Enterprise Ontology.* In *Interop-Esa 2005 - First International Conference on Interoperability of Enterprise Software and Applications.* 2005. Geneva, Switzerland.

25. B. Selk et al. *Experience Report: Appropriateness of the BCI-Method for Identifying Business Components in large-scale Information Systems.* In *Conference on Component-Oriented Enterprise Applications (COEA 2005) in cunjunction with the Net.Objectdays.* 2005. Erfurt, Germany.